From Optimal Tax Theory to Tax Policy

Munich Lectures in Economics
edited by Hans-Werner Sinn

The Making of Economic Policy: A Transaction Cost Politics Perspective, by Avinash K. Dixit (1996)

The Economic Consequences of Rolling Back the Welfare State, by A. B. Atkinson (1999)

Competition in Telecommunications, by Jean-Jacques Laffont and Jean Tirole (2000)

Taxation, Incomplete Markets, and Social Security, by Peter A. Diamond (2003)

The Economic Effects of Constitutions, by Torsten Persson and Guido Tabellini (2003)

Growth and Empowerment: Making Development Happen, by Nicholas Stern, Jean-Jacques Dethier and F. Halsey Rogers (2005)

Happiness: A Revolution in Economics, by Bruno S. Frey (2008)

From Optimal Tax Theory to Tax Policy: Retrospective and Prospective Views, by Robin Boadway

In cooperation with the council of the Center for Economic Studies of the University of Munich

From Optimal Tax Theory to Tax Policy

Retrospective and Prospective Views

Robin Boadway

CES

The MIT Press
Cambridge, Massachusetts
London, England

MIT Press books may be purchased at special quantity discounts for business or sales promotional use. For information, please email special_sales@mitpress.mit.edu or write to Special Sales Department, The MIT Press, 55 Hayward Street, Cambridge, MA 02142.

This book was set in Palatino by Toppan Best-set Premedia Limited. Printed and bound in the United States of America.

Library of Congress Cataloging-in-Publication Data

Boadway, Robin W., 1943–
From optimal tax theory to tax policy : retrospective and prospective views / Robin Boadway.
    p.   cm. — (Munich lectures in economics)
Includes bibliographical references and index.
ISBN 978-0-262-01711-4 (hardcover : alk. paper)
1. Taxation. 2. Fiscal policy. I. Title.
HJ2305.B63   2012
336.2001—dc23
2011028993

10 9 8 7 6 5 4 3 2 1

Contents

Series Foreword

Every year the CES council awards a prize to an internationally renowned and innovative economist for outstanding contributions to economic research. The scholar is honored with the title "Distinguished CES Fellow" and is invited to give the "Munich Lectures in Economics."

The lectures are held at the Center for Economic Studies of the University of Munich. They introduce areas of recent or potential interest to a wide audience in a nontechnical way and combine theoretical depth with policy relevance.

Hans-Werner Sinn
Professor of Economics and Public Finance
Director of CES
University of Munich

Acknowledgments

This work draws liberally on joint work with many authors including Neil Bruce, Emma Chamberlain, Katherine Cuff, Carl Emmerson, Firouz Gahvari, Richard Harris, Laurence Jacquet, Michael Keen, Nicolas Marceau, Steeve Mongrain, Maria Racionero, Motohiro Sato, Jean-François Tremblay, Marianne Vigneault, and David Wildasin. I am especially indebted to Pierre Pestieau for ongoing discussions, collaboration, and stimulation on the ideas in this study, and to the late Maurice Marchand from whom I learned many lessons about both economic and normative analysis. I am very grateful for the assistance and advice from Alex Armstrong, Jean-Denis Garon, Adnan Khan, and Louis Perrault, each of whom contributed to parts of the study. Nicholas Chesterley provided helpful detailed comments on an earlier draft, and made many well-taken suggestions for improvement in the content and coverage. To all these contributors, I am enormously grateful. I am also indebted to the Center for Economic Studies at the University of Munich and its members, especially Hans-Werner Sinn, for giving me the opportunity to prepare this book and the lectures on which it is based. Of course, the shortcomings of the current project are my responsibility.

1   Introduction

Mirrlees' lecture was on optimal taxation, a branch of public finance that had conquered the academic world and, so far, has been largely ignored by the real world. Enormous intellectual resources have gone into it and, literally, thousands of papers have been written analyzing all possible ramifications of the theory. The problem is that no tax reform that I know of has ever applied it. The statistical or informational requirements are just beyond what countries can produce and the political requirements are beyond what governments want to live with. Thus, in terms of concrete results, optimal taxation theory must be considered a highly unproductive activity. Its recommendations often conflict with what governments want to do or what taxpayers expect them to do.

—Tanzi (2008), pp. 116–17, speaking about a plenary lecture given by the Nobel Laureate James Mirrlees at the 1997 Congress of the International Institute of Public Finance in Kyoto, Japan.

The choice of a tax (and transfer) system is one of the most important economic decisions governments take. In OECD countries, total tax revenues absorb in the order of half of national income. In developing countries, the proportions are somewhat smaller, but that is mainly due to the lesser importance of transfers as a source of government expenditures to be financed. The proportion of goods and services diverted by taxation from the private sector in developing economies is substantial.

Many things inform the choice of a tax system, including politics, public opinion, bureaucratic influence, administrative complexities, information technology, and ideas drawn from theoretical considerations. These lectures focus mainly on the role of scientific ideas as means of informing and influencing tax policy design. Those of us who are public economics scholars study the effect that the tax system has on economic outcomes, and formulate models of optimal tax-transfer systems based on normative principles that reflect efficiency and equity considerations. We use that analysis to form views about the optimal design or reform of actual tax systems in economies that are much more complicated than our models. We hope that our views will have some influence on real-world policy choices. These lectures review what normative analysis has taught us about optimal tax policy, how tax policy choices reflect those views, and what outstanding issues exist that optimal tax analysis must address in the future.

Despite the judgment about the relevance of optimal taxation expressed above by Tanzi (2008), and despite his considerable and important contribution to tax policy around the world, one can make a strong case that there is an important symbiosis between ideas drawn from normative tax analysis and tax policies actually enacted. Tax policy must necessarily be informed by *some* ideas and principles, and it is inconceivable that normative optimal tax analysis does not play an important role. The connection is not a direct one. Instead, it is rather subtle. Ideas germinated by normative tax analysis have always informed policy prescription by tax policy specialists and tax commissions. Some of these ideas challenge the way in which tax-transfer systems are designed and propose alternatives. Recent examples include the near-universal worldwide adoption of the value-added tax, the use of refundable tax credits, and various reforms of business tax systems. Other ideas provide normative rationales for features that already exist in tax systems and seem worth keeping, an example being the tax treatment of retirement savings and human capital investment. Even where specific proposals do not emerge from the theory, the latter provides a manner of looking at the policy problem that informs policy makers. A prime example of this is the lesson from optimal income tax theory that asymmetric information is an important constraint on policy. Many policy proposals are conditioned on alleviating information constraints, such as monitoring transfer recipients, addressing tax compliance and basing taxes on what can be observed.

The ideas of normative analysis are disseminated in many ways: through scholarly articles, informed debate, university curricula, the bureaucracy, and the media. Over time decision makers are subject to all these influences and take them on. In turn they persuade the public and tax reforms are enacted. Although much of my discussion will be devoted to exploring what we have learned from normative tax-transfer policy analysis, I will indicate several key areas where, contrary to Tanzi's views, practice has been heavily influenced by optimal tax principles. While there is undoubtedly some truth in Tanzi's allegation that policy makers cannot directly use the results of optimal tax analysis, that misinterprets the role of such analysis. Given that it is based on abstract and often unrealistic models, normative analysis cannot be expected to yield implementable results. Rather, normative analysis serves to inform policy analysis at a different level. It uncovers some basic ideas that inform the policy process, and it provides a way of thinking about normative policy issues that allow policy advisors and policy makers to frame complicated issues in meaningful ways. No doubt, Tanzi's remark was intended to be provocative and cautionary. My guess is that he might underestimate the extent to which even his own ideas have been affected by ideas that originated in the optimal taxation literature, even simple ones like the role of demand elasticities as considerations in tax design. Part of the intent of this book is to take stock of the most important of these ideas.

Optimal tax analysis has been evolving for the past half century, although the seminal works appeared some three decades earlier.[1] Over that period the analysis has grown exponentially, with some significant innovations along the way, especially those by Diamond and Mirrlees (1971), Mirrlees (1971), Atkinson and Stiglitz (1976), Stern (1982), and Stiglitz (1982).[2] The analysis has gone through a long period of refinement of the seminal approach, and in recent years has begun to be confronted with new theoretical challenges as a result of the findings in diverse areas such as behavioral and experimental economics, political economy, social choice, happiness economics, and dynamic macroeconomic analysis. Part of my purpose here will be to review the evolution of optimal tax analysis and how it might adopt to these new paradigms.

Tax systems around the world have also evolved over the past half century, with many broad trends spreading from country to country. Similarities have come to outweigh differences. There has been widespread adoption of value-added tax (VAT) systems, in many cases

---

1. Modern optimal tax analysis can be thought of as originating with Samuelson's 1951 memorandum to the US Treasury, reprinted as Samuelson (1986). It was essentially a restatement of Ramsey's (1927) seminal paper on optimal commodity taxation. See, however, also Dupuit (1844), Boiteux (1956, 1971), and Hotelling (1932).

2. There are various surveys available, all focusing on specific aspects of the theory. See, for example, Atkinson and Stiglitz (1980), Stiglitz (1987), Myles (1995), Boadway and Keen (2000), Auerbach and Hines (2002), Salanié (2003), Golosov, Tsyvinski, and Werning (2007), and Kaplow (2008). A recent paper by Sørensen (2002) has surveyed some of the main policy lessons from optimal tax theory.

replacing highly differentiated systems of sales, excise, and trade taxes. VATs tend to be broad-based, including almost all goods and services, and with one main tax rate, albeit with some exceptions. Besides the VAT, two other broad-based taxes are commonly used: income and payroll taxation. Income taxes and transfers are the main vehicle for addressing redistributive objectives, and do so through progressive rate structures. However, rate structures have become flatter over time. There has been experimentation in some countries with virtually fully flat rate structures, and in others with schedular rate structures with different structures applying to different sources of income. The common model is the dual income tax originating in the Nordic countries, in which a progressive rate structure is applied to earnings and transfers, and a flat rate to capital income. Some important forms of asset income are sheltered from income tax, either for policy reasons or for reasons of administrative convenience, and this is so even in dual income tax systems. Particularly important in this regard are savings for retirement, owner-occupied housing and human capital investments. These provisions have likely served to reduce progressivity even more, as has the gradual demise of wealth and wealth transfer (inheritance/bequest) taxation (Cremer and Pestieau 2006b).

This tendency for the income tax system to become less progressive has been countered at the bottom end of the income distribution by various forms of refundable tax credits, which are relatively recent innovations. These may apply, for example, to low-income families, especially those with children, and to low-income working persons. Transfers to those who are not employed for whatever reason tend to be done by stand-alone systems that are proactively administered rather than being based on self-reporting as in income tax systems. As well, much, or even most, redistribution to low-income persons is achieved by in-kind transfers and social insurance. Other tendencies in tax policy have included some interesting experiments in business taxation (e.g., rent tax systems, like the so-called Allowance for Corporate Equity [ACE], which allows firms to deduct as costs not only interest and depreciation but also costs of equity finance), some enhancement of environmental taxation, and greater use of user fees.

Major policy reforms have sometimes drawn on commissions or panels established by governments or independent policy research institutes. Some examples of these in the Anglo-Saxon world include the Royal Commission on the Taxation of Profits and Income of 1955 in the United Kingdom, the Royal Commission on Taxation of 1966 in Canada, the US Treasury's Blueprints for Basic Tax Reform in 1977, the Meade Report of 1978 in the United Kingdom, the Technical Committee on Business Taxation (1997) in Canada, the President's Advisory Panel on Federal Tax Reform in 2005 in the United States, the Henry Review of 2010 on Australia's Future Tax System, and the 2011 Mirrlees Committee Report in the United Kingdom on Reforming the Tax System for the 21st Century. These various reports typically involved public economics scholars, and served the indispensable purpose of drawing on state-of-the-art thinking about tax policy to make policy recommendations.

The study of public economics has always been a heterogeneous endeavor involving many methodological approaches. These have included normative theoretical analysis, empirical analysis, computable general equilibrium analysis, and other forms of quantitative modeling, public choice, and historical or institutional approaches. In recent years there has been a shift in focus, and some new challenges have arisen. Empirical analysis has taken a more prominent role, owing partly to advances in computational technology and data availability. Political economy has become prominent and has evolved considerably in both theoretical advances and empirical implementation. Implications of game theory have driven many innovations in public economic analysis, such as the understanding of the implications of the inability of governments to commit. Dynamic public economic approaches pursued especially by macroeconomists have led to new insights and challenges.

There are two areas that pose particularly difficult challenges for normative public economics since they go to the heart of some of the most basic principles. One of these involves the implications of recent findings in behavioral economics. Standard assumptions about the rationality of individual decision-making have been called into question by experimental, neurological, and field evidence. Some decisions are simply too complicated to be made without spending excessive time becoming informed. Even if well informed, decisions may be made irrationally because of too much weight being put on immediate payoffs to the neglect of longer term ones. Moreover decisions may be based on motives other than self-interest. All these problems call into question the individualistic basis of standard normative analysis, and invite considerations of whether government is justified in interfering with decisions voluntarily made by individuals.

The other area involves the normative basis for interpersonal comparisons, which are necessary for virtually all normative policy recommendations. The standard methodological approach is to base normative decisions on the welfare levels attained by members of society and to propose some social welfare function as a vehicle for aggregating those welfare levels. This aggregation becomes troublesome in principle when persons have different preferences, and when interdependent utility functions apply. The literature on social choice has offered some possible ways out of this problem, but much work remains to be done to make these suggestions implementable for policy purposes. These challenges are ones that must be dealt with by future normative analysis.

Given these developments in the theory and practice of tax policy, and especially the recent emphasis of new ideas in public economic theory, it is an opportune time to take stock of the role that optimal tax theory has played in establishing the principles underlying tax reform in the past and in assessing the challenges that lie ahead. In the following chapter I begin with an overview of the evolution of optimal tax theory, the main lessons we have learned for tax policy, and the challenges that lie ahead. I then turn in subsequent chapters to a more detailed discussion of the policy lessons from optimal tax theory, and then to the issues that must be resolved.

2 From Tax Theory to Policy: An Overview

Our focus in this chapter is on the relevance of optimal tax theory for tax policy. To put this into context, it is useful to begin with a brief overview of the development of optimal tax theory, and the parallel evolution of tax systems in practice. And, to pave the way for subsequent discussion, I review some of the key challenges that optimal tax theory faces. All of these issues will be taken up in more detail in subsequent chapters.

2.1 Landmarks of Optimal Tax Theory

A characterizing feature of optimal tax theory is its second-best nature. The question it addresses is how best to raise revenues in a distorted economy. To the extent that distortions are immutable, the optimal outcome is "second-best," that is, inferior to what can be achieved in a nondistorted, or first-best, setting. While there are no doubt many precursors to this key policy question, the seminal paper from a conceptual point of view is by Ramsey (1927), who characterized how to raise a given amount of revenue from a representative person using only commodity taxes (i.e., with lump-sum taxes arbitrarily ruled out).[1] As his analysis made apparent, optimal policy analysis in a second-best setting is inherently complicated since there is no one-to-one identification of prices with shadow values, an implication that has pre-occupied applied welfare analysis more generally, and cost–benefit analysis in particular, as well. In a first-best world, prices equal the shadow value of commodities, that is, the value of an additional increment of the

---

1. Ramsey showed that raising an infinitesimal amount of revenue from a representative consumer in an optimal way involves a proportionate reduction in all demands. This also applied for finite amounts of revenue if utility is quadratic.

commodity to the society, and this is reflected in both producer and consumer prices. In a distorted economy, where producer and consumer prices diverge, the value of an increment of a commodity to the society, its shadow price, generally differs from market prices.

Ramsey's contribution remained dormant for many years, until its restatement by Samuelson in his famous memorandum to the US Treasury in 1951, subsequently published as Samuelson (1986).[2] It basically restated Ramsey's optimal commodity tax problem in more modern terms using the principles of duality theory and the envelope theorem, an approach that has come to epitomize optimal tax analysis as a form of principal-agent problem with the government as the principal and the taxpayers as agents.

The same form of principal-agent problem has also been applied to public enterprises. Boiteux (1956) analyzed the case of a multi-product public enterprise choosing prices for its products subject to a profit constraint. The relevance of the profit constraint in this context arises from the fact that public enterprises are often characterized by increasing returns to scale, so that first-best marginal cost pricing involves the enterprise making a loss. If lump-sum financing is not available for the public enterprise, imposing a profit constraint is a natural approach. Boiteux showed that the optimal-pricing regime bore a striking similarity to Ramsey optimal taxation, a result noted and further exploited by Baumol and Bradford (1970) and Feldstein (1972).[3] Indeed much of the early theory of second best (Lipsey and Lancaster 1956–57) was inspired by the inability of public enterprises to use first-best pricing.

The Ramsey problem and much of the optimal tax theory that it spawned was concerned with the design of an optimal tax system. In a parallel literature, typically associated with the theory of the second best per se, the analysis involved optimal incremental or piecemeal policy reforms in a second-best setting: so-called tax reform analysis. The highly influential paper by Corlett and Hague (1953) studied a tax reform analogue of the Ramsey problem for the special case of three commodities: two goods and leisure. In a celebrated result that was subsequently absorbed into optimal tax analysis, they showed that starting from proportional taxes on the two goods, a revenue-neutral reform that increased the tax on one good and reduced it on the other

2. Actually, in a little-cited piece, Hotelling (1932) extended the optimal commodity tax problem to a many-person setting with endogenous producer prices.
3. Reviews of optimal public sector pricing can be found in Rees (1984) and Bös (1985).

would be welfare-improving if the higher tax was applied to the good that was more complementary with leisure. The equally important converse was that uniform taxation is optimal if the two goods are equally complementary with leisure.

Corlett and Hague's approach to incremental policy reform formed the basis for the second-best policy analysis pursued by Meade (1955) and Lipsey and Lancaster (1956–57), and was ultimately generalized into a workable policy approach to applied welfare analysis by Harberger (1971), albeit based on efficiency considerations alone. Notably it was Harberger (1964) who essentially converted the Corlett–Hague three-commodity tax reform analysis into an optimal tax analysis. He came up with the clearest and most intuitive interpretation of the optimal commodity tax rules to date, emphasizing as in Corlett and Hague the role of substitute–complement relations of the taxed goods with untaxed leisure. I return to this in more detail in the next chapter.

The Ramsey–Corlett–Hague–Harberger–Lipsey–Lancaster model of optimal commodity taxation, tax reform and second-best policy analysis has had a profound and lasting impact on the intuition behind many policy issues. Harberger's (1971) scheme for applied welfare economics, which is based on a generalized version of a static second-best economy with given distortions, forms the basis for much policy analysis. An intertemporal version of the Corlett–Hague model has been influential in debates over consumption versus income taxation (Atkinson and Sandmo 1980; King 1980). It was also the setting for the seminal work on the time-inconsistency of second-best optimal policy by Fischer (1980). And it has featured in the literature on corrective taxes on pollution and other externalities in a second-best setting, starting with Sandmo (1975) and culminating in the double-dividend debates of recent years (Bovenberg and de Mooij 1994; Cremer, Gahvari, and Ladoux 1998).

The full general equilibrium treatment of optimal commodity taxation with heterogeneous persons was provided by Diamond and Mirrlees (1971). It ushered in the modern era of optimal tax analysis and its applicability to tax policy. Besides providing a generalization of optimal commodity tax analysis, this paper contained important results on production efficiency in the private sector and between the private and public sectors, which have had profound implications for both tax policy and cost–benefit analysis. For example, the Little and Mirrlees (1974) manual drew on the production efficiency results to generate

practical rules for cost–benefit analysis, especially in developing economies, as did Ray (1984).

The multi-person optimal tax analysis introduced by Diamond and
Mirrlees introduced an equity dimension into the problem. Naturally,
distributive weights would generally influence the structure of tax
rates, but the relationship to the Corlett and Hague result was also
interesting. In this context the natural analogue to uniform taxation,
which translates into a proportional income tax, is uniform commodity
taxation combined with an equal lump-sum transfer to generate some
redistribution. This is equivalent to a linear progressive income tax.
One set of sufficient conditions was provided by Deaton (1979), who
showed that if preferences were weakly separable in goods and leisure,
and generated Engel curves that were linear and of the same slope for
all persons, the optimal commodity tax cum lump-sum transfer system
would involve uniform taxes.[4] An example of this is the linear expenditure system obtained from Stone–Geary preferences, as shown by
Atkinson (1977).

An important feature of this characterization is that such preferences
do not rule out the fact that some goods are luxuries and others necessities. A common argument for differential commodity tax rates is that
imposing a higher tax on luxuries than necessities contributes to redistributive equity, so should be a good thing. Deaton's result shows that
this argument is misleading. Weak separability and linear, parallel
Engel curves do not rule out the fact that some goods can be luxuries
and other necessities. Apparently satisfactory equity outcomes can be
achieved solely by the linear progressive income tax without relying
on differential goods taxes.

This should not be too surprising on reflection. Goods with high
income elasticities of demand (luxuries) tend also to be more price
elastic, and vice versa. This follows from the Slutsky equation, which
for good x_i, price q_i and income m is

$$\frac{\partial x_i}{\partial q_i} = \left.\frac{\partial x_i}{\partial q_i}\right|_u - x_i \frac{\partial x_i}{\partial m}$$

or, converting to elasticities,

$$\frac{q_i}{x_i}\frac{\partial x_i}{\partial q_i} = \left.\frac{q_i}{x_i}\frac{\partial x_i}{\partial q_i}\right|_u - \frac{q_i x_i}{m}\frac{m}{x_i}\frac{\partial x_i}{\partial m}.$$

---

4. With weakly separable preferences, the utility function can be written $u(f(x_1, \ldots, x_n), \ell)$,
where x_i denotes good i and ℓ denotes labor (or equivalently, leisure). Preferences over
goods $(x_1, \ldots, x_n)$ are independent of leisure.

While equity tends to favor taxing goods with high income elasticities of demand, efficiency favors those with low price elasticities and therefore income elasticities. Apparently these effects just offset given the preferences posited by Deaton. It is not desirable in these circumstances to treat necessities preferentially for redistributive purposes: optimal redistribution can be achieved through the linear progressive income tax.

One of the limiting features of the Ramsey–Samuelson–Diamond–Mirrlees optimal commodity tax analysis is the presumption that only distortionary commodity taxes, and in the multi-consumer case a uniform poll tax, are available to the government. Lump-sum redistributive taxes are simply ruled out, although interestingly profits are presumed to be taxed at 100 percent. This arbitrary presumption is relaxed when optimal tax theory is extended to nonlinear direct taxes, where distortionary taxes become the result of choice rather than assumption. In particular, distortionary taxes are useful to relax an information constraint that prevents the government from implementing first-best optimal tax policies that involve lump-sum person-specific taxes. Vickrey (1945) and de Van Graaff (1957) were among the first to note the relevance of such information constraints. The latter discussed explicitly how high-income persons would have an incentive to mimic low-income persons if the tax system became too redistributive,[5] while Vickrey formally set up a version of the optimal nonlinear tax without solving it explicitly.

Stern (1982) and Stiglitz (1982) showed this argument most clearly for the case of two skill-types. If the government could observe each person's type, it could levy person-specific lump-sum taxes, that is, taxes with a zero marginal income tax rate for the two types. If the objective function of the government has nonnegative aversion to inequality, it would want to redistribute from the high- to the low-skilled persons at least to the point where their marginal utility of incomes are equalized. However, if the government cannot observe types, but only the incomes they earn, it cannot redistribute as much as it would like using nondistorting income taxes. High-skilled persons

---

5. As de Van Graaff put it: "If we tax able men more than dunderheads, we open the door to all forms of falsification: we make stupidity seem profitable—and any able man can make himself seem stupid. Unless we really do have an omniscient observing economist to judge men's capabilities, or a slave-market where prices they fetch reflect expert appraisals of their capacities, any taxing authority is bound to be guided by elementary visible criteria like age, marital status, and—above all—ability to pay. We are back with an income tax" (de Van Graaff 1957, p. 78).

would have an incentive to mimic the income and consumption of
low-skilled persons, which they can do by supplying less labor and still
being better off than the low-skilled. The way in which more redistribution can be achieved is to distort the labor supply choice of the low-
skilled so as to deter the high-skilled from pretending to be the
low-skilled by earning less income. The reason is that the rate at which
the low-skilled are willing to forgo consumption to compensate them
for earning less income when the tax rate is increased is greater than
that of the high-skilled. Imposing a positive marginal tax on income
causes low-skilled persons to reduce their consumption more than their
income, and this is more costly for the high-skilled than the low-
skilled.[6] We return to the details of this and other optimal tax analyses
in the next chapter.

It remained to Mirrlees (1971) to fully and formally characterize
optimal nonlinear taxes in a model that has since become standard. The
model consisted of a continuum of persons who differed only in their
fixed wage rates, and who had identical utility functions in consumption and leisure. The government observed income, but not labor supplied or wage rates, and chose a nonlinear income tax function to
maximize an additive and symmetric social welfare function. The
income tax system that emerged was distorted as a way to cope with
the information-induced incentive constraints faced by the government. Marginal tax rates were nonnegative, being zero at the top only
if the skill distribution was truncated and at the bottom only if there
was no bunching there. Marginal tax rates generally followed an

---

6. More formally, the problem of the government can be posed as one of choosing
consumption-income bundles for the high- and low-skilled types, (c_1, y_1, c_2, y_2), to maximize the utility of the low-skilled (type 1's), $u(c_1, y_1/w_1)$, for a given level of utility of the
high-skilled (type 2's),

$$u\left(c_2, \frac{y_2}{w_2}\right) \geq \bar{u}$$

subject to a revenue constraint, $n_1(y_1 - c_1) + n_2(y_2 - c_2) = R$, and incentive constraints,

$$u\left(c_1, \frac{y_1}{w_1}\right) \geq u\left(c_2, \frac{y_2}{w_1}\right), \qquad u\left(c_2, \frac{y_2}{w_2}\right) \geq u\left(c_1, \frac{y_1}{w_2}\right).$$

As long as the extent of redistribution from either type to the other is not too great, the
incentive constraints will be nonbinding and the outcome will be nondistorting. However,
such nondistorting outcomes leave the high-skilled better off than the low-skilled. An
egalitarian government will want to redistribute more, which will imply a violation of
the second incentive constraint, and a distortion on the low-skilled labor supply.

inverted U-shape unless the wage distribution was unbounded at the top.[7]

The qualitative results emerging from the Mirrlees model seem sparse, and should not be overemphasized. The model itself was fairly parsimonious and served as a platform for launching more detailed analyses by many subsequent scholars. However, the true measure of the Mirrlees analysis lay elsewhere. Much more important was the manner in which the approach influenced our way of thinking about normative analysis. The emphasis on information constraints became the standard way of approaching normative second-best analysis, and continues to be the method of choice.

The Mirrlees model was extended in a number of interesting and relevant ways. Some of the more prominent ones were as follows. Perhaps the most important was the generalization to a multi-good context. In the Mirrlees model, emphasis was on the labor supply as the only margin of choice for individuals. Atkinson and Stiglitz (1976, 1980) analyzed the case parallel to Corlett and Hague (1953) of many consumption goods and leisure. Assuming that the government could not observe individuals' consumption purchases, its policy instruments were restricted to a nonlinear income tax and indirect linear commodity taxes. The result that emerged was startling. As long as goods were weakly separable from leisure in the utility function, an income tax alone was sufficient for optimal second-best tax policy: the *Atkinson–Stiglitz theorem*. As in the linear progressive tax case discussed above, the fact that some goods were luxuries did not imply that they should bear a higher commodity tax. Indeed weak separability is consistent with very differing income elasticities of demand across commodities.

In the absence of separability, the analogue of the Corlett–Hague theorem applied. A higher tax ought to be imposed on goods that are more complementary with leisure. Higher taxed goods need not be those with higher income elasticities of demand and thus a higher proportion of consumer spending for high-income persons. The intuition behind this result was clearly established in Edwards, Keen, and Tuomala (1984) and Nava, Schroyen, and Marchand (1996): Imposing higher taxes on goods more complementary with leisure relaxes the information constraint facing government by making it more costly for

---

7. The details of the kinds of qualitative results one can obtain in the Mirrlees model are carefully analyzed and illustrated in Tuomala (1990).

high-wage persons to pretend to be low-wage persons by taking more leisure.

The Atkinson–Stiglitz theorem establishes a prime facie case for uniform commodity taxation. The optimal tax structure can be achieved by a nonlinear income tax or, equivalently, by combining a nonlinear income tax with a uniform sales tax such as a broad-based VAT with a single tax rate. The Atkinson–Stiglitz theorem is consistent with various tax mixes of income and sales taxes: only the overall tax structure is pinned down. An increase in the rate of VAT can be accompanied by a uniform reduction in income tax rates without changing the tax structure. Of course, the case for uniformity relies on preferences being separable and an optimal nonlinear tax being deployed. If we knew which goods were relatively more complementary with leisure, we would know which goods should bear higher rates. However, complementarity with leisure is not a transparent observable property of goods, especially goods that must be aggregated into a manageable number of groups. Given that we cannot reliably say which goods should bear a higher rate, the case for uniformity prevails.

A second extension was by Stern (1982), Stiglitz (1982), and Guesnerie and Seade (1982) who applied the analysis to the case of a discrete distribution of skills, as mentioned briefly above. In this setting the problem resembles a standard principal-agent screening problem whose solution involves using the revelation principle. Now, the marginal tax rate at the bottom becomes strictly positive, the difference being technically attributable to the fact that in the Mirrlees continuum formulation the number of persons at the bottom is atomistically small.[8]

In another important extension, Diamond (1980) considered the case where the labor supply decision involves a discrete choice as to whether to participate in the labor market and obtain a given income or to remain idle and collect transfers from the government. Saez (2002b) extended this discrete choice case to allow also for a form of occupational choice whereby workers could choose to work at the wage rate of those less productive. When the only choice is participation, a negative marginal tax rate at the bottom is optimal (except when the social welfare function exhibits high aversion to inequality, as in the maximin case), while the standard results continue to apply if the discrete choice involves choosing an occupation. When both participation and

8. A positive marginal tax rate at the bottom also emerges when the government uses a maximin social welfare function. See Seade (1977) and Boadway and Jacquet (2008).

occupational choice are possible, negative marginal tax rates at the bottom emerge if the elasticity of participation is high enough relative to the elasticity of occupational choice.

Nichols and Zeckhauser (1982) initiated a separate literature by showing that in a world of second-best optimal taxation, it might be desirable to supplement the income tax with other nonstandard policy instruments, such as in-kind transfers or price controls. This idea was also discovered in Guesnerie and Roberts (1984) for the general case of optimal linear commodity taxation and nonlinear income taxation.[9] It forms the basis for an extensive literature on in-kind transfers, workfare, minimum wages, and rent controls. The basic idea is that these complementary policy instruments can serve to weaken the incentive constraint that restricts redistribution to low-skilled persons. They rely on the fact that the relative benefit of, say, in-kind transfers may be higher for the low-skilled than the high-skilled who mimic the low-skilled.

Finally, a paper that was not written in the context of optimal income taxation but has had a significant impact on the literature was Akerlof (1978). This paper drew attention to the consequences of the government acquiring information that might help relax the incentive constraint. Akerlof studied the case of tagging, where the government can make use of a signal that is correlated with persons' types to separate the population into subgroups. A separate tax schedule can be offered to each tagged subgroup, and with lump-sum intergroup transfers, social welfare can generally be improved. The analogue would be statistical discrimination in insurance. This is one example of the government being able to acquire information that allows it to be more effective in redistribution. Another example involves monitoring of individuals to learn more about their type, as is done in stand-alone transfer programs like welfare, disability pensions, or unemployment insurance.

The extension of optimal tax analysis to an intertemporal setting raises a number of additional interesting issues. An early focus was on the taxation of capital income. Judd (1985) and Chamley (1986) showed that in an infinitely lived representative individual setting reminiscent of Ramsey (1928), it is efficient to tax capital at a zero rate in the long run.[10] However, this result is sensitive to a number of assumptions.

---

9. Some of this literature is surveyed in Boadway and Keen (2000).
10. For a full discussion of this result and its intuition, see Bernheim (2002); see also Banks and Diamond (2010).

Erosa and Gervais (2001, 2002) show, for one, that the result no longer generally applies in an overlapping-generations model of identical persons. For another, it applies only if the government's utility discount rate is the same as the representative agent's, as Banks and Diamond (2010) point out. Perhaps most important, the result requires that the government be able to commit forever to the tax system that is optimal at the beginning of the planning period. In the absence of commitment, capital income taxes will generally be positive and perhaps very high, as shown by the simple analysis of Fischer (1980).

The Judd–Chamley–Fischer analyses assumed linear taxes. Recently dynamic optimal nonlinear tax analysis has been pursued in the more complicated world of heterogeneous households. A different form of the commitment problem emerges here. In the standard optimal non-linear income tax problem, persons reveal their types by their observed choice of income. The government is assumed not to use that information once it is revealed. Even in a static context, this is not an innocuous assumption, and it is even more suspect in a multiple period setting. Much of the literature simply assumes full commitment and succeeds in generating useful dynamic generalizations to the standard results that emphasize the importance both of capital income and of uninsured wage or productivity risk. Golosov, Tsyvinski, and Werning (2007) provide a useful summary of the results that can be obtained in an intertemporal setting, notably illuminating the role of capital income taxation. Banks and Diamond (2010) provide a useful review of the results of dynamic optimal income tax analysis and their lessons for policy. We return in the next chapter to the details of this dynamic optimal tax literature. It is to the lessons of optimal taxation for policy that we now turn.

2.2   The Evolution of Policy and Advice

The conventional wisdom among tax policy specialists about tax policy has evolved a great deal in the past half century. The norm in earlier times was the comprehensive income tax associated with the distinguished names of Shanz (1898), Haig (1921), Simons (1938), and Musgrave (1967), who saw income as a reasonable measure of a taxpayer's ability to pay. Tax policy practice was very much informed by comprehensive income taxation, following the prescription of tax policy commissions such as the Royal Commission on the Taxation of Profits and Income (1955) in the UK and the Royal Commission on

Taxation (1966) in Canada (the Carter Commission). Capital income was taxed on a par with other sources of income and using the same rate structure, following the dictum of the Carter Report that "a dollar is a dollar" no matter what its source. The business income tax system was seen essentially as a necessary complement to the personal income tax. Its main function was to withhold taxes against equity income earned by corporations on behalf of shareholders. In the absence of such withholding, shareholders could postpone taxation of capital gains on corporate shares by retaining and reinvesting equity income within the corporation. Samuelson (1964) showed how the taxation of business investment could be designed such that it taxed capital income in a uniform way.

There were, however, always equally distinguished detractors, including John Stuart Mill (1848), Pigou (1917), and Alfred Marshall (1917) in the United Kingdom and Irving Fisher (1937, 1939) in the United States, whose preferred alternative was taxation based on consumption.[11] It remained for Kaldor (1955) to put the case for consumption taxation, or as he put it expenditure taxation, in a timely and persuasive way as an outgrowth of his dissenting views from the majority in his Memorandum of Dissent to the UK Royal Commission on the Taxation of Profits and Income.[12] As mentioned earlier, the case for personal consumption taxation was taken up by the US Treasury Blueprints for Basic Tax Reform (1977) and the Meade Report (1978) in the United Kingdom, as well as similar advocacy documents in other countries.

The proponents of consumption taxation were more in tune with the growing welfarist tradition of optimal taxation than those who maintained loyalty to comprehensive income taxation, whose appeal was seemingly only vaguely related to an index of personal welfare or utility. Nonetheless, there remained an uneasy case for at least some taxation of capital income, partly supported by optimal tax principles, but partly also reflecting elements of both political reality and inevitability based on time-consistency arguments. Taken over a taxpayer's lifetime, inequality is apparently due more to earnings differentials than capital income. Nonetheless, taxation of capital income could still be supported on social welfare grounds. The arguments are recounted

---

11. See the recent summary of Irving Fisher's "spendings tax" proposal in Shoven and Whalley (2005).
12. Kaldor's views on taxation and other issues are carefully documented in Targetti (1992).

in detail in the next chapter, but they include the following. Capital income might be correlated with individual skills to the extent that high-skilled persons save at a higher rate than the low-skilled. Capital income might reflect in part inheritances that have otherwise gone untaxed. Capital income taxation might also serve as an insurance device in a world of uncertain incomes. Last, the inability to make income taxation age-specific can lead to arguments for capital income taxation.

To satisfy these arguments, while at the same time recognizing that capital income should not, and probably could not, be taxed at the same rate as labor income, dual income tax systems offered a seemingly ideal compromise between comprehensive income and pure consumption taxation, especially if accompanied by wealth transfer taxes that assuage worries that those whose well-being relies primarily on inherited wealth do not escape their fair share of taxation. Dual income taxation taxes earnings and capital income using different rate structures. The standard dual income tax system, such as adopted in some Scandinavian countries, uses a progressive rate structure for earnings (and transfers), while taxing capital income at a flat and relatively low rate. The acceptance of the dual income tax with concessionary tax rates on capital income as a serious policy proposal has been reinforced by its advocacy by the President's Advisory Panel on Federal Tax Reform (2005) in the United States and the Henry Review (2010) in Australia. It is increasingly the direct tax system of choice in European countries.

The dual income tax was clearly an option being considered by the Mirrlees Review (2011) in the United Kingdom, but it opted for a Meade-Report-style expenditure tax instead. The Meade Report (1978), along with the Treasury Blueprints (1977), had recommended a progressive expenditure tax system to be achieved by sheltering savings in either of two forms. One form was tax prepayment, whereby saving was not deductible and future capital income was not taxable. This was referred to by the Mirrlees Review as TEE treatment (savings not tax exempt, interest exempt as it accumulated, and drawing down the asset exempt), which is equivalent to noncapital income being the tax base. The other form was registered asset treatment that allowed a deduction for saving, did not tax capital income as it accumulated, but taxed accumulated the asset value when the asset was sold. This was called EET treatment, and corresponded to using consumption as the tax base. Assets like housing would be suitable for TEE treatment, while saving for retirement, human capital investment and personal business investment could most readily be afforded EET treatment. The most important difference between the two is that under EET, nonnormal asset returns, such as those on risky assets, would be included in the tax base. The Mirrlees review opted for a variant of the TEE-EET combination of the Meade Report. Some assets that might normally be treated as EET would instead be treated by what they referred to as TtE. Savings would be exempt, but instead of all subsequent capital income being exempt, only normal (risk-free) returns would be tax exempt. Thus, the small "t" referred to taxing supernormal capital income. This would be essentially equivalent to EET, except taxation would not be deferred until assets were sold. The Mirrlees Review suggested that TtE treatment was suitable for saving in company shares, while EET would still be used for pension savings. Overall, the system was equivalent to the progressive expenditure tax system advocated by the Meade Report rather than the dual income tax system that would tax all capital income, albeit at a low rate. Notably the Mirrlees Review recommended a lifetime inheritance tax alongside the progressive expenditure tax, arguing that inheritances were a source of income that would otherwise go untaxed. What is especially relevant for our purposes is the extent to which the Mirrlees Review drew on optimal tax analysis, as carefully summarized in their background study (Mirrlees et al. 2010) to inform their proposals.

The preferential treatment of capital income is further emphasized by the substantial share of tax revenue now raised by payroll taxes and VATs. In effect, a tax system consisting of a mix of income tax, payroll tax, and a VAT is effectively a schedular tax system, since capital income is taxed under the income tax but not under the other two. However, the progressivity of the non–capital-income part of the tax system is compromised by the fact that payroll taxes and VATs are far from progressive, and the progressivity of the income tax is constrained to the extent that the same tax schedule applies to both capital income and earnings. Payroll taxes are often used as means of financing employment-related social insurance schemes such as public pensions, unemployment insurance, and accident and disability insurance, and so they are typically nonprogressive or even regressive in nature. Under a dual tax system, payroll taxes would be a key element of the personal tax-transfer system and would constitute the main tax policy instrument for redistribution. VATs on the other hand are primarily revenue raisers. The flourishing of them worldwide has been one of the most widespread tax policy innovations in modern times. They offer an opportunity to raise substantial amounts of revenue in an efficient way, given their broad base and built-in self-reporting and auditing capabilities.[13]

Nonetheless, there are controversial aspects to the heavy reliance on the VAT. Its apparent regressivity poses acceptability problems, although these can be overcome by accompanying measures elsewhere in the tax system, such as refundable tax credits, that protect the progressivity of the tax system as a whole. Still, few countries are able to take full advantage of an efficient broad-based VAT, since most offer preferential treatment to at least some necessity items like food and shelter. The fact that the tax applies on virtually all domestic transactions leads to some problems of compliance and collection. Small traders are typically exempt from the tax on administrative cost grounds. Some aspects of the VAT lend themselves to tax evasion behavior, especially the tax on services and on cross-border transactions in the European Union and elsewhere. Moreover, in some countries, tax morale—the willingness to voluntarily pay one's proper tax liabilities—has been eroded by the VAT and its broad applicability. And, in countries with large informal sectors, the avoidance of VAT can lead to substantial inefficiencies. This has been particularly controversial in developing countries where some authors have argued that it is more efficient to continue to rely on trade taxes that are harder for the informal sector to evade than the VAT.[14]

Other forms of taxation are emerging or being reinvented. Excise taxes for corrective reasons are taking on a new life for a couple of reasons. The first one is their usefulness in dealing with pollution, most notably in the form of carbon taxes (or analogous pricing schemes, e.g., cap-and-trade schemes for restricting emissions) to deal with global warming. Another is their potential, but controversial, role in affecting taxpayer behavior. So-called sin taxes on tobacco and alcohol products,

---

13. More precisely, the VAT is collected on the sale of goods and services by businesses. It applies to sales both to consumers and to other businesses. In the standard "invoice-credit" approach, businesses remit only the net amount due to the government, deducting the amount of tax charged on their own purchases against the liability on their sales. If the tax is levied on a destination basis, exporters obtain a tax credit on their input taxes, and the VAT is levied on imports. In the end, no net revenue is collected from the sales of intermediate goods, and the resulting tax base is final domestic consumption.

14. Emran and Stiglitz (2005) have made such an argument, although it has been vigorously countered by Keen (2008). Boadway and Sato (2009) argue using optimal tax techniques that, in principle, either trade taxes or a VAT with differentiated rates may be more efficient in a developing country context, depending on the extent to which profits earned in the economy go untaxed (trade taxes being a way of indirectly taxing profits).

and potentially on products deemed to be unhealthy or addictive, have taken on added credibility with the growth of behavioral economics.[15]

Business taxation policy has also undergone some rethinking. Two reform directions are notable. One is related to the withering away of the full taxation of capital income at the personal level. This compromises the role of corporate taxation as a backstop to the personal tax system, and leads to a rethinking of its role as an efficient revenue raiser. It has been known for a long time, at least since Brown (1948), that a cash-flow tax on business income is a neutral tax that captures rents generated by firms. The Meade Report (1978) took the idea fully on board and developed various versions of cash-flow business taxation to complement its preferred system of personal consumption taxation. The two main ones were the R-based tax, which included only real cash flows in the base (i.e., those involving purchases and sales of inputs and outputs), and the S-based tax, which included both real and financial cash flows. The latter includes all financial transactions that firms make on behalf of their shareholders, such as the issue and repayment of debt including interest payments and new equity issues, as a way of getting at the economic profits of financial intermediation.

Despite the parsimonious information requirements of cash-flow taxation, its application has always been held back by the need for refundability of losses, which typically occur early on in a firm's development. However, as the tax literature has taught us, there are alternatives to cash-flow taxation that are equivalent in present value terms and almost as easy to implement.[16] The above-mentioned ACE (Allowance for Corporate Equity) system advocated by the Institute for Fiscal Studies (1991) and more recently by the Organisation for Economic Cooperation and Development (2007) is one such example.[17] It has been used in various countries in recent years, including

---

15. A useful and wide-ranging summary of the issues can be found in Diamond and Vartiainen (2007).

16. See, for example, Boadway and Bruce (1984) for a general characterization of cash-flow equivalent business taxes, and the extension to a setting of uncertainty by Bond and Devereux (1995).

17. The ACE is a variant of the cash-flow tax, and exists in two different versions. In one, mimicking Boadway and Bruce (1984), the firm is allowed to deduct each year a proportion of its book value of capital equal to a depreciation rate and a risk-free nominal interest rate. The book value of the capital stock increases with new investment and falls by the depreciation rate used. The other version allows interest to be deducted, but introduces a separate allowance for the cost of equity financing. In both versions the tax is neutral and the rate of relief required for neutrality is the risk-free rate.

Austria, Belgium, Brazil, Croatia, and Italy (as summarized in Klemm 2007).

Second, and related to this, is the growing policy interest in the taxation of natural resources, especially in developing countries that rely on them for much of their revenues. Here again, taxes on economic rents offer an efficient way to divert a share of rents on natural resources to the public sector, a cause supported by the notion that natural resource endowments are an important element of public property in most countries.

Cash-flow equivalent taxes like the ACE would be one possible way to stake a public claim on natural resource rents, and has been recommended for Australia by the Henry Report (2010). But they are not the only way to tax resource rents. An alternative is the so-called resource rent tax (RRT) proposed by Garnaut and Clunies Ross (1975), first implemented in Papua New Guinea and since then followed by many other countries. The RRT taxes cash flows once cumulative cash flows discounted at the normal rate of return have become nonnegative. Essentially, the RRT gets around the requirement of standard cash-flow taxes to provide refunds when cash flows are negative, although it does so by giving no relief to projects that never become profitable, and so can discourage risk-taking. (For a detailed analysis of the RRT and its relation to cash-flow taxes, see Boadway and Keen 2010.) Another alternative is to sell resource property rights to private firms at competitive market prices, for example, by auction. These various devices, if designed attentively, are equivalent to rent taxes. They differ mainly in the timing of revenues.[18]

Natural resource-owning countries in fact often use revenue-raising devices that are not neutral except under special circumstances. A common example is a royalty or severance tax, which is essentially a tax on output or revenues. Royalties have the advantage that they are relatively easier to implement than cash-flow taxes since output is more readily observable than costs. Moreover royalties might be useful as a way of discouraging too rapid extraction when the right to extract is

---

18. The recent survey of the taxation on nonrenewable natural resources by Boadway and Keen (2010) discusses in detail the issues involved in taxing natural resources and their implications for policy choice. For example, the pros and cons of various taxes depend on such things as asymmetric information between the government and the resource firm, the treatment of uncertainty and the inevitability of loss firms, differences between resource firms' discount rates and that of the government, and especially problems of commitment given the extent of sunk costs in resource projects.

restricted to a period of time that is less than the life of the deposit (Conrad, Shalizi, and Syme 1990; Boadway and Keen 2010).

Natural resource taxation raises a number of important policy issues because of some features of natural resource exploration, extraction and development. Three properties in particular make natural resource taxation challenging, although similar issues arise to a lesser extent in other tax areas. The first is the high level of uncertainty involved in finding, developing, and selling natural resources. The proportion of exploration investments that prove to be successful is small, and for those that are successful, there may be considerable uncertainty about resource prices. The second is the longevity of the resource exploitation process. It can be decades before resource properties become profitable, long after heavy investments are sunk. Third, there is likely to be a significant asymmetry of information between resource producers and the government. Together, these problems give rise to a number of policy concerns. One is that there is an enormous time-consistency problem. It is very tempting for the government to impose high taxes on profitable ventures that have already sunk their investment costs. Naturally this can reduce investment in the first place. Governments may recognize this and design their tax system to reduce temptation, such as by setting progressive rent tax structures ex ante. Issues of risk-sharing are also important. If the government is less risk-averse than resource producers (e.g., because the latter face political risk arising about uncertainty about future tax changes or expropriation), it might want to skew its revenue collections into the future, tending to favor royalties at the expense of auctions. Finally, asymmetric information problems will also influence tax design, perhaps favoring auctions, which are suitable for extracting information about resource values if designed properly.

The tax policy initiatives discussed thus far have focused on the choice of tax bases. It should be apparent that many of these initiatives have drawn on the theoretical tax literature to formulate and evaluate alternatives. This is a main theme that we will return to in more detail below. Tax policy measures have also affected the progressivity built into tax systems, and here the contribution of optimal tax theory has been less apparent, if only because the optimal extent of progressivity is nowhere close to resolution. Optimal income tax analysis is relatively agnostic about the extent of redistribution, even in the tightly struc-tured models that have been used. As we discuss in more detail later, most models derive schedules of marginal tax rates based on skills rather than marginal and average tax rates based on incomes, and even then, relatively few unambiguous results apply to inform policy makers.

In standard Mirrlees-type optimal income tax models, the optimal schedule of marginal tax rates tends to be relatively flat throughout most of the range of skills. Simulations of Mirrlees (1971) and Tuomala (1990) tended to show modestly rising marginal tax rates over the interior of the skill distribution, although more recent work using the maximin social welfare function finds declining marginal tax rates throughout the skill distribution (Boadway and Jacquet 2008). Notably the marginal tax rate is typically positive at the bottom (assuming the lowest-skill persons do not work and that the social welfare function is not maximin) and increases quite rapidly. At the top, the marginal tax rate falls off rapidly to zero if the skill distribution is truncated; otherwise, it continues to rise mildly in the interior of the skill distribution, depending on the specific assumptions made.[19] However, different assumptions can give rise to very different patterns. At the bottom end, as we have noted, the marginal tax rate can become negative to the extent that the participation decision is dominant (Saez 2002b). If the temptation to evade income taxation is prevalent, the degree of progressivity can be dampened considerably, and can even become regressive (Chander and Wilde 1998). Still, to the extent that incomes are heavily influenced by luck rather than effort, so that incomes are uncertain for a given effort level, higher progressivity will be favored. The income tax system then serves both as an effective redistribution system and as an income insurance scheme. But, the relationship between risk and progressivity is a subtle one. As Eaton and Rosen (1980) argued, uncertainty can increase labor supply to increase precautionary income. While progressivity improves income insurance, it also reduces self-insurance, and the balance between the two can be ambiguous. More generally, progressivity may encourage socially beneficial risk-taking, as suggested by Sinn (1996).

Tax policies have reflected the ambivalence about progressivity. The form and extent of progressivity have varied both over time and over countries. The general tendency in recent years is for tax systems to become less progressive at the top, but somewhat more progressive at

---

19. Thus Diamond (1998) concocted an example involving quasi-linear–in-consumption preferences in which the marginal tax rate is U-shaped in skills at the upper end when the skill distribution is unbounded.

the bottom. Thus income tax rate structures, while remaining progressive, have flattened, and the share of tax revenues coming from nonprogressive taxes like VATs and payroll taxes has increased. At the same time the use of income-related refundable tax credits at the bottom end of the income scale have increased progressivity there, effectively making the income tax system more like a negative income tax. To encourage participation and to dampen the effect of steeply rising marginal tax rates on work effort and saving, some countries have introduced refundable tax credit measures for low-income workers. The result is a negative marginal tax rate for the lowest income workers, followed by a steeper increase in marginal tax rates beyond low-income levels (Saez 2002b).

Notably, there are various nontax measures that are arguably much more effective policy instruments for redistribution than the income tax. These include stand-alone welfare transfer systems to the long-term unemployed and disabled, state pensions for the poor elderly, unemployment insurance for those temporarily out of work, in-kind transfers such as education, housing, and transportation subsidies, health insurance, care for the elderly, and minimum wages. A general consequence of these programs taken together is to make redistribution highly targeted on low-income and needy persons rather than being universal as some observers would advocate (Atkinson 1999; van Parijs 1995).

There remain some differences across countries. The United States tends to have a less progressive tax-transfer system than most other OECD countries, and provides a much lower level of social protection to those at the lower end of the income distribution, and to those facing ill health and unemployment. Some transitional economies have adopted linear progressive (flat) tax schedules. Some observers have attributed this to different societal attitudes to redistribution, to different beliefs about the source of inequality, that is, whether it is due primarily to luck or to individual effort (Alesina and La Ferrara 2005), to differences in political institutions, or to racial heterogeneity (Alesina, Glaeser, and Sacerdote 2001).

As can be seen, tax policy, like optimal tax theory, is constantly evolving, and the relationship between the two is neither obvious nor straightforward. One can find instances where innovations in tax theory led to broad tax reforms. At the same time tax policy has sometimes led tax theory. Even in these cases tax theory can be useful as a means of rationalizing or legitimizing past policy changes. These are among the themes I explore later. But, first, to complete our brief review, I summarize some of the challenges to current approaches to optimal tax theory that have come to the fore in recent years.

2.3 Challenges for the Theory of Tax Policy

It is possible that optimal tax theory was not always meant by its many founders to be policy relevant, but only to offer a systematic way of thinking about policy issues. The latter is certainly true. Nonetheless, some of the findings are at least suggestive of policy design, and tax policy specialists have not hesitated to draw on optimal tax theory to propose or defend particular policy prescriptions. Regardless, we ought to be aware that the standard analysis of optimal taxation that forms the basis for normative tax policy prescriptions, criticisms, and advice is built on a number of basic assumptions. These typically include, inter alia, common preferences and utility functions across all persons, a social welfare function based on welfarism such that individual utilities and only individual utilities count in social preferences, individual rationality, and social orderings based on normative criteria, including those that determine interpersonal utility comparisons. More specific simplifying assumptions are also typically built into given pieces of analysis, such as divisibility of commodities, a limited number of characteristics of persons, competitive production, a limited number of commodities, no household production, and so on.

Obviously specific results will depend on the particular assumptions made, so much turns on the acceptability of the assumptions and the extent to which they capture key elements of the real world in an abstract way. The ultimate question we want to address is whether the theory will survive relaxing some of the more important assumptions. Some issues that arise in that context and that will be explored in the following chapters are outlined here. Some of them arise from recent advances in economic analysis more generally that have made us think in new and challenging ways about individual and collective decision-making. Others challenge the normative principles on which the standard analysis is built.

2.3.1 Commitment
Standard normative second-best analysis assumes a particular order of decision-making by government and private agents in the economy. The government chooses its policies first, followed by private agents,

be they individuals or firms. In other words, the government is the principal, and the individuals and/or firms are agents. This is so despite the fact that some policies are not actually implemented until after some private actions are undertaken: the government is assumed to carry out its announced tax policies once private agents have irrevocably acted. The problem with this assumption is that in an intertemporal setting, government second-best optimal policy choices announced ex ante will generally not be time-consistent: given the opportunity, the government would change its announced second-best policies after the private agents have acted on at least some of their choices. For example, once assets have been acquired by saving or investment, the government can treat that as a fait accompli, knowing that whatever policies it now chooses (e.g., increasing taxes on assets or their income) will no longer influence private choices.

Note that time-inconsistency is a property of second-best policies, which is perhaps why it was not a concern in traditional welfare economics. First-best policies will be time-consistent, as shown by Hillier and Malcomson (1984) and Calvo and Obstfeld (1988). In a second-best setting, given that the government is benevolent, the ex post change in policies will only be implemented if it will cause social welfare to increase, so seemingly it is not a bad thing for the government to change its mind. However, it is reasonable to suppose that if the government cannot commit to announced second-best policies, private agents will anticipate that and will change their behavior accordingly. The time-consistent equilibrium, in which private agents correctly anticipate government ex post behavior and government policy chosen ex ante is time-consistent given agents' behavior, will be inferior to the second-best optimal policy that would apply if the government could commit, perhaps considerably so.

There are various policy environments in which the time-inconsistency of second-best policies is likely to arise. One could in fact argue that almost all second-best policies are time-inconsistent in principle. Even in the classical Ramsey static optimal tax problem, governments do not actually collect taxes until after labor is supplied, income earned, and goods purchased. Little is to prevent the government from changing their taxes after such decisions have been made. Apparently governments do not renege on tax policies applying to current labor supply and goods' purchases. For whatever reason, they can commit to these policies. Economists have instead focused on longer run choices made by private agents.

The classic optimal tax treatment of the problem is the two-period model by Fischer (1980)[20] where the distinction is made between labor supply decisions, as generating taxable income in the period in which labor supply occurs, and savings decisions, where assets are acquired that last and generate capital income for more than one period. Government tax policies announced before savings decisions are made can readily be changed in the following period when savings are sunk. In the simple representative-agent model, the government has an incentive ex post to obtain as much tax revenue as possible from capital income taxation and as little as possible from labor income taxation in the second period. In a time-consistent equilibrium, capital tax rates will be very high, discouraging saving and yielding a level of consumer utility that is highly inferior to the second-best level. In more reasonable settings, where individual lifetimes overlap, and where taxation cannot be age-specific, capital income taxes will apply to both the future income from current saving and past capital accumulations, so tax rates will not be as confiscatory as in the simple Fischer model. Nonetheless, capital income tax rates in the time-consistent equilibrium will be higher than in the second-best optimum.

The same problem applies to other sorts of asset accumulation besides individual saving. For example, it applies to human capital accumulation, to the purchase of real assets like housing, and to the investment decisions of firms. The latter includes intangible investments, like exploration for natural resources as we have seen, and product research and development more generally.

The observation that taxes on asset income are much higher than second-best policy would recommend suggests that these issues of commitment are potentially important. This is further supported by the fact that high tax rates on asset income coexist with various investment and saving incentives. The combination of high tax rates and incentives to acquire assets can be reconciled if one views the latter as ex ante devices to mitigate the commitment problem. Governments offer special incentives for investment, especially for resource firms, knowing that they cannot commit to lower tax rates on incomes generated in the future. This is particularly apparent in developing countries where tax holidays and other investment incentives are prevalent, while at the same time investment income by foreign firms can be taxed quite heavily.

---

20. The problem of dynamic inconsistency of optimal policy in a macroeconomic context was raised initially in the seminal work of Kydland and Prescott (1977).

Commitment issues should also be a concern with second-best redistribution policies. This is most apparent in the optimal nonlinear income tax problem of Mirrlees (1971), especially as restated by Stern (1982), Stiglitz (1982), and Guesnerie and Seade (1982) for the discrete-skills case. The analysis uses the revelation principle whereby individuals reveal their types by their choice of consumption–income bundles. Once types are revealed, the government ought to be able to use that information to apply lump-sum skill-contingent taxes and transfers. This possibility has been studied in multi-period models, where the information individuals reveal in one period can be used in subsequent periods (Roberts 1984; Apps and Rees 2006; Acemoglu, Golosov, and Tsyvinski 2010; Brett and Weymark 2008b; Krause 2009; Pereira 2009a, b). The same problem ought to arise in the design of transfer schemes where identifying those who are deserving is an important issue. Moreover the problem ought to apply in one-period static models, given that redistributive policies are only implemented once types have been revealed. In fact, even where the revelation principle is not invoked, such as in the standard optimal linear income tax model, individuals also reveal their types by their choice of an income–consumption bundle.

Unlike with asset income, there seems to be little evidence that the government exploits the information individuals reveal about their types to condition tax liabilities. Perhaps the explanation for this is that the simple one-characteristic model used in much normative optimal tax analysis is a caricature of reality. Once more than one type is allowed, or uncertainty exists, individual behavior may not reveal types unambiguously. For example, it may not be possible to distinguish low-skilled hard-working types from high-skilled lazy types.

From the point of view of normative analysis, the issue of commitment is an important one, if only because of the need to maintain the integrity of the analysis. In normative models, one can invoke the assumption that governments can commit as an analytical device. However, if the results of the analysis heavily rely on that assumption, going from analysis to lessons for policy might be suspect. The questions of whether governments can commit to announced policies and how they do so are important ones. However, they are still open questions that demand further research. Some recent work has suggested that there may be political economy forces that induce commitment by governments (Acemoglu, Golosov, and Tsyvinski 2010, 2011). But, as we will see later, this research is still at an early stage and uses assumptions that are still far-fetched and perhaps not convincing, such as infinitely lived voters and politicians, and voters that can commit to voting out of office politicians who will be replaced by other identical politicians.

Perhaps a more plausible explanation for why governments typically do not renege on their announced tax policies, except in the case of long-run investments like natural resources, is that changes in tax policy require legislation, and that takes time. This makes the setting of tax policy a long-run decision, which naturally leads to government tax policy decisions being taken before private agents commit themselves to investment, saving, or earning income. From this point of view, commitment problems are more likely to arise where policies are discretionary, such as deciding who is eligible for government transfer or social insurance programs.

In the real world a further problem is that even if the government could commit to its promises, commitments can only be made against foreseen policy circumstances. Policy-making is in fact based on promises by the government is analogous to incomplete contracting between private agents. Optimal policies should be based on the state of the world when the policies are implemented. It may simply be too complicated to specify the features of states of the world on which policy would ideally be contingent, or some of the features of the state of the world may not be easily verifiable when the policy is undertaken. In these circumstances, adjusting policy ex post may be a reasonable option (as in the case of sudden financial crises), and it may not be possible to distinguish between policies changed in response to unforeseen circumstances and those representing a failure to commit.

One final issue of commitment is relevant, and that concerns the ability of individuals to commit to future decisions. Recent behavioral economics literature has emphasized, among other things, that individual intertemporal choices sometimes exhibit time-inconsistency, at least in laboratory settings. This also poses important policy questions, given that time-inconsistent choices can lead to adverse long-run outcomes, such as addiction, undersaving, and other consequences of myopic decisions. I take this up later.

2.3.2 Heterogeneity of Individual Utility Functions
The assumption of identical utility functions is made for more than analytical simplicity than for realism. It also partly finesses one of the

key issues in applied normative analysis—whether in first- or second-best contexts—which is how to make interpersonal comparisons of welfare. In reality individual preference orderings differ, and one supposes that utility functions do as well, quite independently of differences in preferences. That is, some persons might get more utility from a given bundle of commodities than others even if they have the same preference orderings. Moreover some sources of utility gain may be problematic for inclusion in social welfare. All these factors cause potential problems for normative second-best analysis, so let me elaborate on them briefly here.

Different individuals make very different economic decisions in many dimensions. While differences in personal characteristics and circumstances may provide a partial explanation for this, it seems hard to avoid the conclusion that preference differences play a part. The many ways in which individuals make different choices include the bundle of goods and services they purchase; the amount of and type of labor to supply, including choice of occupation, effort, participation, retirement, and volunteer work; saving in financial assets, housing and human capital; risk-taking, and the purchase of insurance; voluntary income transfers, including bequests to one's heirs and donations to charity and nonprofit organizations; and family choices, including marriage, procreation, and divorce. This variety of choices complicates the choice of tax policy on various levels. A tax system that purports to be based on welfarist principles must take some view as to how heterogeneous outcomes translate into individual welfare: even comparing levels of welfare is controversial when different persons make different choices.

One potentially promising avenue that I will discuss further in later sections is to suppose that persons ought neither to be rewarded nor penalized for choices freely made but instead should be compared according to the opportunities they face that are beyond their control. Thus a distinction is made between the *Principle of Compensation*, whereby persons should be compensated for characteristics of their situation over which they have no control, and the *Principle of Responsibility*, which says that outcomes for which persons are themselves fully responsible (including possibly their own preferences) should not attract redistribution.[21] Such an approach would respect

21. The approach is presented in Fleurbaey (1995) and Roemer (1998), with a more technical survey in Fleurbaey and Maniquet (2010).

individual preferences and could lead to some prescriptions about the form of the tax system. For example, a uniform commodity tax (VAT) system would avoid discriminating against persons on the basis of their demand for particular goods and services (except if warranted on other grounds, such as externalities). A consumption tax would avoid penalizing high savers and risk-takers. A personal tax that ignores family circumstances would be neutral with respect to family formation. And a tax that taxes inheritances but ignores bequests and other income transfers would respect different preferences for giving. Of course, avoiding discrimination on the basis of preferences is one thing; the requirement to make interpersonal utility comparisons for the purpose of redistribution is another. This is complicated by preference heterogeneity.

It is also complicated by the fact that persons may differ in the ability to generate utility. Some may have different needs for particular goods or leisure for physical reasons. Persons may differ in their ability to generate utility from income, a possibility stressed by Sen (1973) that might be particularly relevant for the tax treatment of children, the disabled, and the elderly. This raises an important conflict between utilitarianism, which would favor redistributing resources in favor of those most able to generate utility, and more inequality-averse social welfare functions, which would favor the reverse. Apart from differences in the ability to generate utility, persons might simply differ in their happiness levels in ways that are affected by incomes (e.g., see Layard 2005).

More profound issues arise that question the foundations of welfarism itself. Should all sources of utility 'count' from a social welfare perspective? The issue is particularly relevant in the case of voluntary income transfers or gift-giving.[22] By revealed preference, one might presume that the transfer gives utility to the donor. But at the same time, it yields utility in the hands of the recipient. If both forms of utility count in determining the well-being of persons, the tax system will double tax the donation. Moreover, if double counting applies in the case of income transfers, consistency suggests it should also apply to interdependent utilities where no transfer occurs. Thus, if one person feels avarice or envy toward another, as the happiness literature might allege, this too would affect welfare in a way that is relevant for tax policy purposes, at least in principle. This has particularly important implications for the welfare generated by family or group membership. One presumes that some joy is obtained by all family members when,

---

22. This is discussed in detail in Cremer and Pestieau (2006).

say, a child member is made better off. Of course, on practical grounds, it is impossible to monitor the utility of persons in this broad sense. Even when there are income transfers involved, it is not clear that the donor obtains utility. The transfers may be involuntary, as in the case of unintended bequests, or, though voluntary, they may be given out of duty, to comply with social norms, or to signal something about the donor. Finally, welfarism may be in conflict with other social objectives, such as liberalism (Sen 1970) or nondiscrimination.

A more fundamental issue is at stake. One's view of the applicability of welfarism depends on how one interprets the meaning of utility itself. Some authors, most recently Kaplow (2008), take the view that at least in principle, utility is measurable and thus comparable across persons. That being so, the only value judgment that has to be made by the policy maker is how to aggregate these measurable utilities in a social welfare function, or equivalently, what should be the aversion to inequality. Even this might be avoided, according to Harsanyi (1955), if one appealed to von Neumann–Morgenstern principles to validate utilitarianism and simply added objective utility functions. Yet, if one takes a social choice point of view, following Arrow (1951), the only information one can have about persons is their preference ordering. Some value judgment must be made simply to measure utilities and make them comparable across households. Either point of view is compatible with the methodology of optimal tax analysis. In either case, there is a fundamental problem with how the value judgment is to be taken. As Arrow (1951) showed, if the only admissible information is the preference orderings of persons over social states, aggregation into a single social ordering is generally impossible without violating some reasonable axioms.

The way out adopted by optimal tax analysis is to allow more information in the form of measurability and comparability of individual utilities, as discussed in Sen (1977) and surveyed in Boadway and Bruce (1984). This involves value judgments, which in the simplest case often used in applied welfare economics can be distilled into a single parameter, the aversion to inequality.[23] The question is whose values are used

---

23. This is the approach used, for example, in the recent Stern Report (2007), as well as cost–benefit analysis manuals such as Dasgupta, Marglin, and Sen (1972) and Little and Mirrlees (1974). For a further discussion, see Boadway and Bruce (1984) and Drèze and Stern (1987). Some social choice theorists have studied the characteristics of optimal income taxation that can be obtained by eschewing the measurability of utility and relying solely on individual preference orderings and level comparisons across households. See, for example, Fleurbaey and Maniquet (2006, 2007).

for this purpose. This is the great unanswered question of normative policy analysis, and many qualitative results turn on it. For example, as we have mentioned, the degree of aversion to inequality determines whether one wants to redistribute resources to or from those who have less ability to generate utility. I will remain agnostic with respect to this question, instead highlighting, where relevant, which results depend on this parameter. Ideally the issue would be settled by some form of societal consensus determined in a fair and informative way. I will, however, assume that aversion to inequality is nonnegative. In many cases that is sufficient for making qualitative policy prescriptions.

2.3.3 Behavioral Issues

Normative second-best analysis typically adopts individualism as a working premise, that is, the assumption that social welfare functions should reflect individual preferences (or utilities, if those are taken to be objective measures). This seems to be eminently reasonable and lends weight to the Pareto principle. However, individualism is not a logical requirement. Some scholars have constructed social welfare orderings without necessarily invoking individualism, for example by imposing the planner's individual preference orderings to judge individual utility (Adler, forthcoming). Also, if preference orderings differ among individuals, it may be useful to invoke some reference preferences as an aid to making interpersonal comparisons (Schokkaert et al. 2004). In practice, there are some cases in which society apparently does overrule individual preferences: families take decisions on their children's behalf, the incapacitated elderly are dispatched to nursing homes against their will, the severely mentally ill and criminals are institutionalized, schooling is mandatory, and so on. However, these sorts of things are exceptions to the general rule that individualism should reign supreme, a rule that normative second-best analysis obeys.

Recently the literature on behavioral economics has called into question the merits of individualism as a general working hypothesis. There are various reasons for that, although, at the risk of oversimplification, three seem to be particularly relevant for normative policy analysis.[24] First, there is the problem of bounded rationality: decision-making may

---

24. See Bernheim and Rangel (2007) for a more detailed discussion of the implications of behavioral economics for public economics.

be too complicated and individuals may not be well enough informed to be able to take decisions in a fully rational way. Instead, they revert to shorthand techniques, like rules of thumb, adaptive behavior, and herd behavior. Of course, the incentive to become better informed will be greater the more there is at stake. But, for some types of decisions, the cost may simply be too high. One thinks of portfolio decisions, purchases of high-technology products and health care decisions. In these cases private agents may specialize in expertise and advise consumers about what is in their best interest, but there are likely to be agency problems in acquiring such advice that may cause serious market failure. The case for government intervention in the case of bounded rationality seems strong, assuming the government can inform itself. Governments do regulate financial instruments as well as product markets. In some cases governments do make portfolio decisions on behalf of households, for example, in funded public pension schemes.

Second, individual preferences may exhibit forms of irrationality in personal decision-making. They may be subject to status quo bias or loss aversion, or their choices may be affected by the manner in which choices are framed. They may react only to salient changes in policy. Especially relevant for public policy, they may be prone to making time-inconsistent intertemporal choices (Laibson 1997; Gul and Pesendorfer 2001, 2004). For whatever reason, individuals' current intertemporal preferences discount the future excessively in the sense that the rate of discount applying between today and the next period exceeds the rate of discount seen from today applying between two periods in the future. Effectively, preferences are changing over time. The general consequence is a tendency for one to be impatient or myopic relative to one's long-run preferences, leading to such things as undersaving, instant gratification, procrastination, binge consuming, and even addiction. To the extent that people recognize that their preferences are time-inconsistent, they may be able to take preemptive action to commit themselves to more far-sighted behavior. However, in general, the problem persists, and time-consistent behavior is suboptimal from the perspective of long-run outcomes without time-inconsistent preferences.

Governments apparently undertake measures on behalf of individuals to counter this form of myopia. Almost all governments mandate, or implement themselves, basic compulsory retirement savings schemes. Some encourage saving beyond the mandatory amounts by saving programs that individuals are automatically enrolled in unless they choose to opt out, so-called nudging policies (Thaler and Sunstein 2008). Addictive substances are regulated, taxed, and perhaps even banned. Education and seatbelts are mandatory, and so on. In all these cases governments are adopting paternalistic policies that override individual choices, albeit in the name of serving the long-run interests of individuals. Whether and when the government is justified in overriding personal choices is an important issue facing normative policy analysis.

Of course, individuals may take the "wrong" decision simply because they misconstrue the benefits or costs of the decision. They may overestimate the happiness that will be achieved by accumulating material possessions or underestimate the benefits of leisure time. More generally, they may simply not know the satisfaction they will achieve as a result of their actions. This may call into question the role of individual choice as a building block of welfare, although it is not obvious that the government policy has a natural role in addressing the problem.

Third, individual decisions may be based on factors other than their own self-interest. They may act in accord with social norms or to obtain social approval and acceptance (Akerlof 1980; Rabin 1993; Manski 2000; Fehr 2001). They may choose to act cooperatively when free-riding is an option (Ostrom 2000). They may act out of duty, such as when they provide caring services to their children and to needy relatives. Altruistic behavior might also be described as non–self-interested behavior, although economists commonly treat altruistic utility as a component of individual utility, not only for describing their behavior but also for determining their welfare for policy purposes as I have mentioned. Individuals may even act out of moral or ethical principles, which almost by definition involves acting against their own self-interest (Bordignon 1990, 1993; Baron 2010). Obeying the law might be a special form of such behavior. It can be convincingly argued that most individuals adopt law-abiding behavior as a matter of choice even though they may sometimes be better off by disobeying the law. For example, it can be argued that the standard theory of tax evasion that treats tax evasion as a decision under uncertainty akin to portfolio choice decisions is misleading since it ascribes no law-abiding motive to individuals. Indeed there would presumably be much more tax evasion than apparently occurs if everyone behaved as a simple expected-utility-maximizer. To put another perspective on it, individuals might be much more willing to engage in lawful tax avoidance by changing their behavior than tax evasion by misreporting their tax liabilities (Boadway, Marceau, and Mongrain 2007).

If individuals behave in nonselfish ways, the role of government becomes blurred. To the extent that individual choices are in accordance with society's consensual norms, individual choices reduce the need for coercive government action (Baron 2010). Moreover collectively imposed choices may be counterproductive in the sense that they crowd out private cooperative behavior (Frey 1994).

2.3.4 Responsibility and Compensation

Another major issue confronting normative optimal policy analysis, especially that involving redistribution, concerns the role of individuals' responsibility for determining outcomes affecting them, and correspondingly society's role in alleviating adverse outcomes. There are two elements of this. The first is that in a simple extension of the Mirrlees optimal nonlinear tax model where individuals differ from one another by a single characteristic—variously called productivity, skill, or ability that is reflected in the wage rate—outcomes may be determined not only by effort combined with ability, but also by luck. That is, ex post outcomes given the level of effort might be stochastic. In principle, this causes no conceptual concern for the Mirrlees welfaristic approach. However, the optimal degree of progressivity is undoubtedly affected by the relative importance of effort and luck in determining outcomes. In the standard optimal nonlinear tax approach, where effort is the only determining factor, income tax progressivity is surprisingly limited. Presumably luck enhances the argument for progressivity, although the technicalities have yet to be fully worked out (but see Sinn 1996; Low and Maldoom 2004). Since luck is likely an uninsurable risk, income taxation provides a form of insurance (Varian 1980; Golosov, Tsyvinski, and Werning 2007). Moreover, since luck is unrelated to individual behavior, utilitarian arguments for progressivity have special force. The balance between luck and effort in practice is unclear. However, some have argued that beliefs about the importance of luck versus effort are an important factor in explaining greater fiscal progressivity in Europe relative to the United States (Piketty 1996; Alesina and Glaeser 2004; Bénabou and Tirole 2006).

Another element involving personal responsibility has been emphasized in the equality of opportunity literature that I referred to earlier.[25] In this literature a distinction is made between personal characteristics that individuals have some control over versus those they do not. Thus one's preferences might be regarded as being at least partly a matter of one's choice, whereas native ability is not. A persuasive approach to dealing with this distinction is to posit that individuals should be compensated for adverse outcomes that result from characteristics over which they have control—the Principle of Compensation—but not for those for which they are responsible—the Principle of Responsibility.

Applying these two principles presents a challenge for normative public economics. For one thing, distinguishing those characteristics that one has control over from those that one does not is not a trivial matter. A common example used is preferences for leisure. If one is assumed to be responsible for one's aversion to work, one does not want to reward those whose low income is due to their free choice of low work effort. More important, as we will see later, there is a fundamental conflict between the two principles in the sense that even in a world of perfect information with lump-sum redistributive transfers, the government cannot generally satisfy the Principle of Compensation and the Principle of Responsibility together. Some compromise must be reached between the two principles, and the mechanics of that compromise are yet to be worked out.

2.3.5 Political Economy

Normative second-best policy analysis proceeds by maximizing some social objective function subject to a number of assumptions, policy variables, and constraints. The assumptions typically include producing firms operating to maximize their profits in competitive markets under given technological constraints and individuals maximizing their utility in the same markets. The government acting as a principal chooses its fiscal policies, such as taxes, expenditures, borrowing, and possibly price or quantity controls and other forms of regulation, taking into account how firms and individuals respond. In a first-best world, the government has full information about how agents behave and can identify all agents by type. This enables it to implement

---

25. The standard reference is Roemer (1998). Fleurbaey (1995a) provides a useful statement of the issues. See also Fleurbaey and Maniquet (2010) for a more technical survey of the issues.

lump-sum agent-specific taxes and transfers and to achieve a first-best outcome.

In a second-best world, additional constraints are imposed. There may be market imperfections (failure of the First Theorem of Welfare Economics), such as absence of competition, asymmetric information in the private sector, and missing markets or coordination failures that preclude efficient market clearing. And, as mentioned, the classical second-best analysis imposed arbitrary constraints that restricted the policy instruments that the government could deploy, such as linear taxes. Modern second-best analysis instead assumes that the government is imperfectly informed about either relevant characteristics of households or about their market transactions. For example, the government may not be able to observe individual incomes so must rely on self-reporting, which is subject to possible tax evasion.[26] However, they may be able to obtain information on market transactions anonymously (e.g., through firm self-reporting) and therefore able to tax such transactions using linear taxes (Guesnerie 1995).

Governments may also find it difficult to implement their preferred policies because of political pressures. There is now a vast literature on how politics affects economic policy outcomes.[27] The question is: Should political constraints be imposed on second-best normative policy analyses? The question has been explored in detail in Boadway (2002) and Dixit and Romer (2006), and is largely unanswered. My preferred approach is not to impose political constraints in normative second-best analysis. The grounds for this are varied. One is simply that normative policy analysis intends to suggest what ought to be done rather than what might be achievable from a political point of view. Thus normative analysis serves as a benchmark for actual policy decisions. Rather than supposing that normative outcomes are constrained by political factors, normative arguments should be used to persuade policy makers of what policies ought to be pursued.

More generally, it is not obvious what political constraints would be reasonable. They are ill defined in the literature, and it is not clear that there are hard and fast political constraints. Political processes are

---

26. The implications of tax evasion for optimal income tax policy have been explored in Cremer and Gahvari (1996), Marhuenda and Ortuño-Ortin (1997), Chander and Wilde (1998), and Boadway and Sato (2000), among others.
27. The modern literature can be traced to the two classic books by Downs (1957) and Buchanan and Tullock (1962). A recent survey is found in Persson and Tabellini (2002). See also Hettich and Winer (2005) and Besley (2006).

inherently complex. The actors are many, the objectives are mixed, and decisions are taken over matters that are highly heterogeneous. It is in fact somewhat presumptuous to suppose that political decisions can be captured in the relatively simple models that economists use. Abstract economic models can lead to important insights into the way in which markets behave, but political decisions are considerably more complicated and there is little consensus about which political economy model might be most appropriate.

There is a further problem. In virtually all the political economy literature, models of political choice lead to deterministic outcomes once the political mechanism is specified. That would seem to leave little room for normative policy decision-making. Moreover the deterministic outcomes are dictated by the specific model chosen, and the model may include value judgments implicitly.

All this is not to deny that normative analysis has its own problems. In particular, the objective function—typically a social welfare function—embodies a set of value judgments that will not reflect unanimous agreement. At most, there may be some consensus about broad objectives. Nonetheless, there is value in exploring the consequences of normative analysis under various judgments about, say, aversion to inequality as a way of informing the policy debate. No single model will ever be decisive in terms of generating policy advice, since by its very nature a model is an abstraction that is used to focus on one or more elements of a much more complicated picture. Still a model and its results can be informative if taken together with other models. Indeed it is the purpose of this study to explore how the past several decades of optimal tax analysis has helped inform actual tax policy debates and outcomes.

2.4 Optimal Analysis versus Reform Analysis

While the focus of my discussion is on the lessons learned from optimal tax analysis, some might argue that full optimality is too ambitious a benchmark. In the real world, policies seem to be a long way from optimal ones. Capital income is taxed nominally at a high rate, but with many exemptions and examples of preferential treatment. Business taxation is distortionary, with different types of financing and investment treated very differently, and losses treated differently than gains. The system of transfers and social insurance seems imperfectly targeted and leaves the least well off below poverty lines, and so on. To move from where we are to the optimum would involve policy changes that are so large as to be difficult to implement administratively and fairly, let alone politically. Almost any policy change involves winners and losers, and large policy changes would involve both large gains and large losses. Even on social welfare grounds, one might want to proceed incrementally if only to minimize the size of the losses during a transition.

There have been many attempts in the literature to rationalize the fact that policy reforms will create losses to some persons even if they are social-welfare-improving overall. A purist whose only criterion is social welfare would not be concerned with gainers and losers per se, only with whether the addition to social welfare from a policy change was positive or negative. However, this apparently does not sit well with all economists, especially those who worry about the force of value judgments that must be included in a social welfare function. Attempts to separate the efficiency from the equity effects of policy changes have reflected this unease.

The earliest attempts to separate efficiency from equity were the classical compensation criteria proposed by Kaldor (1939) and Hicks (1939). Kaldor suggested that a policy change might be acceptable if the gainers could compensate the losers after the change and still be better off. Hicks proposed the reverse test: a policy should not be undertaken if the losers could compensate the gainers for forgoing the change and still be better off. The compensation would take the form of a redistribution of the bundle of goods available in the post-change allocation (Kaldor) or the pre-change allocation (Hicks).

There were many refinements and caveats to, and arguments against, the Kaldor–Hicks criteria. A serious drawback is that it yields a significantly incomplete ranking of social outcomes, given that no social welfare judgments are admitted. Moreover, as Scitovsky (1941) showed, the rankings can be intransitive, since it may be the case that both the Kaldor test in favor of a policy change and the Hicks test against the same policy change can apply. The ordering can be expanded somewhat by expanding the notion of compensation to include income transfers rather than transfers of the outcome-specific bundle of goods, as Samuelson (1950) pointed out. However, the Scitovsky paradox still applies. More recently Coate (2000) has revisited the issue and has proposed a Kaldor–Hicks–Samuelson type criterion that takes account of second-best considerations. Specifically, Coate proposes what he calls an efficiency approach, whereby a proposed policy change is judged efficient if there is no other feasible policy change that would Pareto dominate it. This is in effect the analogue of the Hicks criterion where the compensation is restricted to second-best feasible alternative policies.

Compensation criteria suffer from other problems. One is that it is not clear how such criteria can be operationalized practically. The standard, and commonly used, justification for using the sum of compensating (or equivalent) variations to evaluate policy changes is that this somehow indicates whether or not a compensation test would be satisfied. Unfortunately, this rationalization is invalid. As Boadway (1974) and Blackorby and Donaldson (1990) showed, the sum of compensating variations is neither necessary nor sufficient to indicate whether a compensation test has been satisfied. This is quite apart from whether compensation tests are normatively convincing.

Perhaps the most serious case against compensation tests is that they rely on hypothetical transfers (or other forms of redistribution) to make their case. If the transfers are not consummated, it is not clear that their hypothetical possibility is sufficient to be convincing. Given this, some authors have tried to maintain the essence of the tests by accompanying them with judgments about the redistributive consequences of alternative allocations in addition to whether the compensation tests are satisfied. Thus Little (1957) proposed a joint test whereby a policy change was welfare improving if both the relevant compensation test was satisfied and the redistributive consequences of the change (in the absence of compensation) were judged to be favorable. To the extent that this resuscitated the compensation test as a useful device, it did so by reinstituting exactly the type of value judgments that the tests were meant to avoid. The efficiency approach of Coate (2000) is in the same spirit. He proposes to use the criterion to compare a proposed policy with other feasible policy changes that could achieve a given amount of redistribution. The choice of optimal redistribution is taken by those whose responsibility presumably includes making the requisite value judgments.

More recently Kaplow (2008), building on a result discovered by Konishi (1995) and refined by Laroque (2005) and Kaplow (2006), has proposed a two-step policy evaluation procedure that is very much in the spirit of Little (1957) and Coate (2000). (See also Gauthier and Laroque 2009.) The original Konishi–Laroque–Kaplow result was an extension of the Atkinson and Stiglitz (1976) finding that in an optimal nonlinear income tax world of many goods and leisure, if leisure is weakly separable from goods in the utility function, an optimal tax system involves only nonlinear income taxation and no differential taxation of goods. Their extension was to show that even if the income tax in place was not optimal, a reform from differential to uniform goods' taxation accompanied by a suitable revision of the income tax involving changes in income-specific tax liabilities would be Pareto improving and would satisfy both the government budget and information constraints.

Kaplow argued that this result could be applied to many other policy changes using a similar two-step decomposition in evaluating a policy change, one involving the policy change accompanied by lump-sum tax-transfer revisions to the existing income tax to establish whether a Pareto improvement was possible, and the other evaluating the redistributive effect of the policy change itself. In a sense, this procedure is more demanding than Coate's because it involves person-specific adjustments to the income tax system. Moreover, as in the Kaldor–Hicks–Samuelson tests, the adjustments in the income tax system need not be consummated. It is viewed as being sufficient to know that they could be made. And, as in Little, a social welfare function is needed to judge whether the redistributive step in the policy change is welfare improving.

The point is that if one is prepared to invoke a social welfare function to evaluate the redistributive effects of the policy change, it is not clear what is the point of disaggregating efficiency and equity effects in the first place. There are long-established procedures for evaluating policy changes in a single step using a social welfare function (Dasgupta, Marglin and Sen 1972; Little and Mirrlees 1974; Boadway 1976; Drèze and Stern 1987), and one might as well follow those from the beginning. Given that, policy reform analysis is as valuable as optimal tax analysis, and often gives qualitatively similar results. For example, the flavor of the original Corlett and Hague (1953) tax reform analysis continues to apply in the optimal tax analog of the same model (Harberger 1964).

Some caveats are, however, in order. For one, piecemeal policy analysis sometimes invokes constraints on policy instruments, although there is no particular reason for these constraints to apply in tax reform settings only. For example, the marginal cost of public funds approach to evaluation of government policies typically assumes linear taxes, since most tax systems are linear or quasi-linear to start with.[28] This can

---

28. For a recent detailed survey, see Dahlby (2008).

give quite different results compared with optimizing analyses when the government is free to change the tax structure discretely. To cite just one example, the marginal cost of public funds is typically greater than unity, perhaps much more so, when taxes are restricted to be linear, whereas when optimal nonlinear taxes can be used, the marginal cost of public funds can be effectively unity under some weak separability assumptions (Christiansen 1981; Boadway and Keen 1993). As well, from a theoretical point of view, optimal tax problems are typically not convex (Foster and Sonnenschein 1970; Harris 1977; Harris and MacKinnon 1979): there can be multiple optima. This is often ignored in policy analysis, but it can clearly lead to misleading results. A local policy reform that seems to be welfare improving may well from a global point of view be a move away from the global optimum.

2.5   Summary of Lessons for Tax Policy

The following chapters recount in more detail the contributions that normative tax analysis has made to our understanding of tax policy. Before turning to that, it might be worth summarizing some of the key tax reforms of recent years that have been in part inspired by, or at least supported by, theoretical contributions. Despite Tanzi's (2008) very critical appraisal of the usefulness of optimal tax theory, there seems to be plenty of evidence that the optimal tax way of thinking about tax policy has crept into both the thinking and practice of tax policy decision makers. What follows is a short list of important tax policy initiatives that have their counterpart in optimal tax analysis.

The VAT
The VAT has been adopted in over 100 countries worldwide. It is a form of taxation that guarantees production efficiency in the sectors it covers, as well as facilitating tax compliance, ideas that have been emphasized in optimal tax analysis. Production efficiency has also been an important factor in judging between maintaining trade taxes in developing countries or replacing them with a VAT, as well as informing techniques for cost–benefit analysis. More recently the multi-stage principles of the VAT have been proposed as a way of implementing carbon taxes in an efficient way (Courchene and Allan 2008).

The Personal Tax Base
Much of the recent work in extending optimal income taxation to a dynamic setting has lent support to maintaining some taxation of

capital income in the personal tax base. This represents a fundamental shift in thinking since the 1980s when personal consumption taxation was in favor. At the same time administrative considerations and arguments for the different treatment of capital and labor income have supported the move toward dual income taxation initiated in the Nordic countries whereby earnings are taxed progressively and capital income at a constant rate.

Refundable Tax Credits

Many countries have introduced refundable tax credits, or made existing tax credits refundable. This has provided another tax-based policy instrument for addressing redistributive and social policy goals. These credits have been targeted to low-income workers to provide them with an incentive (through a negative marginal tax rate) to participate in the labor force. This is supported by recent optimal income tax analysis that emphasizes the extensive labor supply margin (Saez 2002b). Refundable tax credits have also been used to offset the adverse equity effects of newly introduced VAT systems, and to target transfers to low-income families with children as part of an equality of opportunity policy agenda. At the same time stand-alone transfer programs have been maintained for the chronically unemployed and the disabled, where targeting by criteria broader than income is desired and where the self-reporting personal tax system cannot easily be used to administer transfers. The use of refundable tax credits also represents a potential movement from universal transfer programs to more targeted ones, especially since stigmatization and errors of administration are less evident than in conventional transfer programs.

Minimum Wages

One consequence of the optimal income tax literature, which emphasizes the information constraints that government faces, has been to lend support to policies that serve to improve the information available to government and help it target assistance to those most in need. In particular, the literature has emphasized the role of distortionary policies as ways of weakening the incentive constraint faced by government. This includes policies that in conventional first-best analyses would never be used because of the apparent distortions they impose. One such policy instrument is the minimum wage as a policy for targeting the least-skilled workers. An increasing literature has evolved in support of such instruments, especially where the extensive labor supply margin is important, despite the distortions that such policies otherwise impose. By the same token, other policies of price or income control have been advocated on the basis of the same principles of improved targeting, including rent controls, in-kind transfers, and workfare.

Efficient Business Taxation

As globalization has evolved and international mobility of capital has increased, pressures to rationalize the tax treatment of capital income have increased. The normative tax literature has contributed by suggesting ways of designing a business tax system that is neutral and so applies to the rents or pure profits of firms. The policy counterpart of this has been the ACE system recommended originally by the Institute for Fiscal Studies (1991) in the United Kingdom, and taken up in a number of countries. As personal tax systems rationalize their treatment of capital income, further reforms of business income tax systems will proceed apace. A sector in which efficient taxation is particularly important is natural resources. Many countries have implemented forms of rent taxation that have been inspired by normative tax analysis.

Environmental Taxation

A particular pressing tax policy problem concerns the pricing of carbon emissions that lead to global warming. The taxation of externalities has been a longstanding aspect of efficient tax design, as the term Pigouvian taxation implies. The actual design of a carbon pricing scheme must take into account many complicating features that have been studied by tax scholars. These include the second-best taxation of externalities as part of a broader system of distorting taxes (Sandmo 1975; Cremer, Gahvari, and Ladoux 1998), the relevance of the double dividend (Bovenberg and de Mooij 1994), the choice between carbon taxation and emissions trading systems or combinations of the two (Roberts and Spence 1976), the free-rider problem arising from the fact that emissions come from all countries (Stern 2007), the importance of intergenerational considerations given that the costs of abatement will be borne by current generations and the benefits by future generations (Stern 2007), and the interaction between carbon pricing policies and the incentives for suppliers of carbon fuels to extract more quickly (the so-called Green Paradox emphasized by Sinn 2008). Carbon pricing is obviously still a work in progress, but there is no doubt that normative analysis will continue to play an important role.

3   Policy Lessons from Optimal Tax Theory

Optimal tax theory, or normative second-best policy analysis more generally, cannot give categorical policy prescriptions. By necessity, theory is based on abstract models whose construction is designed to focus on particular factors to the exclusion of others as well as being either analytically or computationally feasible. Moreover computational feasibility itself may not be sufficient if the computations cannot yield some intuition about the mechanisms at work. Instead, normative analysis provides insights into the kinds of forces that lead to desirable outcomes. Different models provide different insights, and some judgment must be exercised in using these insights for actual policy prescription.

The potential pitfalls are many. Each model must be based on some assumptions, both about the structure of the model and about functional forms and reactions to policies. Some of these assumptions are difficult to verify, so one looks for qualitative results that do not rest on specific assumptions about the parameters of the economic environment. As well, normative models are necessarily based on some value judgments, and these too can affect the qualitative results. At the very least it is important to see how results vary with value judgments such as the aversion to inequality in the social welfare function or the treatment of persons with different preferences. Finally, one hopes that the results are at least partly robust to adding more complications to the model, although this may be difficult to be sure about in principle given the limitations involved in adding complexity to theoretical models. Put differently, one hopes that the results obtained from all models separately are not nullified when one imagines a more complicated world in which features of all the abstract models apply together.

These are powerful caveats to normative analysis. Of course, similar caveats apply as well to other forms of economic analysis, including empirical, institutional, historical, and policy analysis. Even though the caveats give us pause and force us to be suitably modest about our conclusions, theoretical normative analysis based on workable models with well-motivated assumptions is not only indispensable but also potentially valuable. It forces rigorous and systematic thinking about policy issues, and it indicates where particular assumptions lead to in terms of possible policy consequences. One does have to be prepared to make judgments about the relevance of the results based on the accumulation of various modeling approaches. In the context of optimal tax policy analysis, the results are suggestive enough to be reasonably convincing and to have an impact on the policy debate and policy outcomes.

A particularly important feature of normative policy analysis concerns the choice of objectives, constraints, and institutional environment for conducting the analysis. Some constraints are noncontroversial, such as the constraints on resources and technology. A competitive market environment is also assumed, although this is somewhat controversial and could be readily relaxed. More controversial is the objective function of the planner. This is typically assumed to be a welfaristic social welfare function that not only respects individual preferences but also notionally aggregates individual utility functions into a social welfare function. This aggregation obviously involves important value judgments that not all will agree on. For example, some may object to the standard assumption that all that counts are final outcomes and not initial positions. Those analysts who put more stock on property rights might insist that changes in social welfare should be evaluated taking into account deviations from initial positions. Sensitivity analysis can be conducted to identify how policy prescriptions vary with the value judgments made, especially the degree of aversion to inequality that affects the equity-efficiency trade-off. The normative government is also assumed to be constrained by information, and possibly by available policy instruments. Indeed it is precisely these types of constraints that make the analysis second best, and I will devote considerable attention to these contraints in this chapter.

Most controversially, in normative analysis the government is typically assumed to be benevolent and not subject to the constraints of politics. There is no doubt that in the real world, politics has an important influence on policy outcomes, so ignoring political constraints seems to be ignoring some aspects of reality. However, our view is that the role of normative analysis is to inform the political process. To impose political constraints would be to subvert that role. In fact it is not entirely clear how political constraints could be imposed, especially given our limited knowledge about such constraints. The political process is not really a constraint, but a mechanism for making decisions that is subject to the same constraints as in the normative analysis. What differs is the objective function. One may legitimately ask why the will of the people expressed through the political process ought to be second-guessed by a normative analysis using an objective function that may not conform with individual voter values. The answer is simply that, while the political process must be respected, voters and policy makers can legitimately be informed and perhaps persuaded by normative analysis. In the end, both the political process and the social values implicit in normative objective functions must draw on some social consensus. Normative analysis aims to help shape that social consensus. I return to this issue in the last chapter.

In this chapter, I focus on some of the main insights that we have learned from optimal tax analysis for policy, bearing in mind the caveats mentioned and aware of the fact that the literature is continuing to advance. Many of the insights I report have stood the test of time and of judgment, and to that extent can be treated with some gravitas. The insights are not listed in particular order of importance, although they are roughly in order of chronology of discovery. Most of the insights draw on the traditional optimal commodity tax literature and its extension to linear income taxes, as well as the more recent optimal nonlinear income tax literature. The ones I address are the following:

1. The classic question addressed by the optimal commodity tax literature is whether the rate structure should be uniform or differentiated. This is of obvious importance for the design of value-added taxation (VAT), which most countries in the world have adopted. The case for uniform taxes is surprisingly strong, quite apart from the administrative arguments for uniformity.

2. A main insight from the optimal commodity tax literature is the case for production efficiency, which is also relevant for, and adds further impetus to, a VAT system of commodity taxation.

3. There are some dynamic implications of optimal tax analysis to consider, especially the optimal taxation of capital income relative to earnings and its implication for the choice of a personal tax base. This has been a key concern in most tax reform proposals for over half a century.

4. Related is the question of progressivity of optimal taxation. What should be the rate structure of the personal tax system? There have been some important innovations in answering this question in recent years.

5. Asymmetric information has been a key feature of normative tax analysis, particularly the fact that the government is imperfectly informed about relevant characteristics of private agents. This precludes the government from achieving a first-best outcome using lump-sum taxes and transfers. There may also be asymmetric information among agents in the private sector that causes market failures. Government policy may be able to mitigate these market failures even if it is not better informed than private agents.

There are various features of the normative approach to policy analysis that are worth emphasizing at the outset, and that will appear in our discussion at various points. One is the importance of information constraints as the main deterrent to achieving the first best. The limitations on information impose significant constraints on the government in achieving optimal outcomes. This leads to two natural extensions of normative analysis. One is to seek nonconventional policy instruments, including various price and quantity controls and other distorting policy instruments, that might help mitigate information constraints. The other is to look for ways to improve the information available to the government. These extensions will be considered in the next chapter. Another important consideration that arises, especially in dynamic normative analysis, is the inability of the government to commit to future policies. When decisions of individuals and firms have long-term consequences, optimal government policies announced before such long-run decisions are taken will generally be time-inconsistent in the sense that even a benevolent government would choose to change them after long-run decisions have been made. Since individuals and firms will likely anticipate such changes, they will change their behavior accordingly, and the time-consistent outcome will be inferior to that which would be achieved if the government could commit. Attempts by government to mitigate these commitment problems will again include policies that would not otherwise be used. These too are discussed in the next chapter. Finally, normative analysis requires an objective function that reflects social values. Some of the issues that arise in choosing an objective function are discussed in chapter 5.

3.1 Uniformity of Commodity Taxes

In most countries the tax mix consists of both direct taxes and indirect taxes, with the latter most often taking the form of a VAT. While the latter could certainly have a differentiated rate structure across commodities, a uniform rate structure offers considerable administrative simplicity that mitigates both compliance and collection costs. This is particularly important given the multi-stage nature of the tax and the fact that all but the smallest firms must collect the tax. The conventional arguments for differentiated rates rely on both efficiency and equity considerations and the relation between them. Efficiency suggests that goods with less price-elastic demands be taxed at a higher rate, but those goods also tend to have low income elasticities of demand and thus comprise a greater share of expenditures of low-income persons. The balance between these two considerations should influence the optimal rate structure. A key finding of the optimal tax literature is that under some fairly weak conditions—weak separability of utility in goods versus leisure—the two effects balance one another so uniformity of rates is optimal. When these separability conditions are not satisfied, the direction of deviation or rates from uniformity is not at all obvious and is unlikely to conform with naive equity arguments for favoring goods that are necessities relative to those that are luxuries. To summarize these results, it is useful to review the development of the literature, beginning with the initial emphasis on efficient taxation.

The efficient structure of commodity taxes has been a preoccupation since Ramsey (1927), but it was not related to the broader tax structure until the work on direct versus indirect taxes by Little (1951), Friedman (1952), and Corlett and Hague (1953). I begin with the result of Corlett and Hague for the single-person case, generalized by Harberger (1964), and then turn to the multi-consumer case, where equity becomes a concern.

3.1.1 The Corlett–Hague Theorem

The issue studied by Corlett and Hague (1953) was whether it was more efficient to extract revenue from a household using differential commodity taxes or uniform commodity taxes, or equivalently, a proportional income tax. The insight from Corlett and Hague was prescient: they showed that for a representative consumer choosing three commodities (two goods and leisure), revenue-neutral deviations from a uniform tax on the two goods would improve the welfare of the individual if a higher tax rate were imposed on the good more complementary with leisure.

The analysis is as follows. Consider a representative individual with the utility function $u(x_1, x_2, x_0) = u(x_1, x_2, h - \ell)$, where the goods x_1 and x_2 bear consumer prices q_1 and q_2, h is the total time the individual has available, and the price of leisure x_0 or labor ℓ is w. The consumer faces a budget constraint $q_1 x_1 + q_2 x_2 = w\ell$ and maximizes utility to yield demand functions $x_i(q_1, q_2, w)$ ($i = 0, 1, 2$). The indirect utility function is written $v(q_1, q_2, w)$, and by the envelope theorem, $\partial v / \partial q_i = -\alpha x_i$, where α is the marginal utility of income.

The government raises revenues using taxes on the purchase of x_1 and x_2, with a tax on labor being suppressed because it is equivalent to a proportional tax on x_1 and x_2 and is therefore redundant. (If leisure could be taxed as well as the two goods, the government could effectively tax the consumer in a lump-sum way, and that is ruled out.) The government faces a budget constraint $t_1 x_1(q_1, q_2, w) + t_2 x_2(q_1, q_2, w) = R$, where R is its exogenous revenue requirement, the per unit tax on good i is $t_i = q_i - p_i$, and producer prices p_i are assumed fixed. In the Corlett and Hague exercise, feasible tax changes must satisfy the budget constraint, so by differentiation,

$$\left.\frac{dq_2}{dq_1}\right|_R = \left.\frac{dt_2}{dt_1}\right|_R = -\frac{x_1 + t_1 \partial x_1/\partial q_1 + t_2 \partial x_2/\partial q_1}{x_2 + t_1 \partial x_1/\partial q_2 + t_2 \partial x_2/\partial q_2} = -\frac{\partial T/\partial q_1}{\partial T/\partial q_2}, \tag{3.1}$$

where both the numerator and denominator are assumed to be positive, so we are on the rising portion of the Laffer curve and an increase in a tax rate increases tax revenue T.

Consider the effect on consumer utility of a change in t_1, with t_2 adjusting to keep revenue constant. Differentiating the indirect utility function and using the envelope theorem and (3.1) yields

$$\left.\frac{dv}{dq_1}\right|_R = \frac{\partial v}{\partial q_1} + \left.\frac{\partial v}{\partial q_2}\frac{dq_2}{dq_1}\right|_R$$

$$= \alpha \left[\frac{\partial T}{\partial q_2}\right]^{-1}\left[x_2\left(t_1 \frac{\partial x_1}{\partial q_1} + t_2 \frac{\partial x_2}{\partial q_1}\right) - x_1\left(t_1 \frac{\partial x_1}{\partial q_2} + t_2 \frac{\partial x_2}{\partial q_2}\right)\right].$$

Next use the Slutsky equation $\partial x_i / \partial q_j = s_{ij} - x_j \partial x_i / \partial m$, where $s_{ij} = \partial x_i / \partial q_j |_u$ is the compensated cross-price derivative, to obtain

$$\frac{1}{\alpha}\frac{\partial T}{\partial q_2}\frac{dv}{dq_1}\bigg|_R = x_2(t_1 s_{11} + t_2 s_{21}) - x_1(t_1 s_{12} + t_2 s_{22})$$

$$= x_1 x_2\left(\frac{t_1}{q_1}\frac{q_1}{x_1}s_{11} + \frac{t_2}{q_2}\frac{q_2}{x_1}s_{21}\right) - x_1 x_2\left(\frac{t_1}{q_1}\frac{q_1}{x_2}s_{12} + \frac{t_2}{q_2}\frac{q_2}{x_2}s_{22}\right)$$

$$= x_1 x_2(\tau_1\varepsilon_{11} + \tau_2\varepsilon_{12}) - x_1 x_2(\tau_1\varepsilon_{21} + \tau_2\varepsilon_{22}),$$

where $\tau_i = t_i/q_i$ is the ad valorem tax rate, ε_{ij} is the compensated elasticity of demand for good i with respect to the price of good j, and we have used the symmetry of the substitution effect $s_{12} = s_{21}$.

Finally, following Corlett and Hague, we evaluate this change in utility starting from equal proportional tax rates ($\tau_1 = \tau_2 = \tau$) and use the homogeneity of compensated demands, which implies $\varepsilon_{i0} + \varepsilon_{i1} + \varepsilon_{i2} = 0$:

$$\frac{1}{\alpha}\frac{\partial T}{\partial q_2}\frac{dv}{dq_1}\bigg|_R = x_1 x_2 \tau(\varepsilon_{20} - \varepsilon_{10}). \tag{3.2}$$

Thus a revenue-neutral increase in the tax on x_1 (and reduction of the tax on x_2) will increase welfare if $\varepsilon_{20} > \varepsilon_{10}$, that is, if x_1 is more complementary with leisure than is x_2. This is Corlett and Hague's main finding, and its intuition is compelling. Since leisure is untaxable, imposing a higher tax on the good more complementary with leisure is an indirect way of taxing it. For our purpose it is useful to emphasize another implication of these results. If $\varepsilon_{20} = \varepsilon_{10}$, so goods x_1 and x_2 are equally substitutable for leisure, welfare cannot be improved by deviating from uniformity of commodity tax rates. This result on uniform commodity taxation will be referred to as the *Corlett–Hague theorem*.

Harberger (1964) subsequently generalized this three-commodity case to the choice of an optimal commodity tax system. In this case the government chooses taxes on x_1 and x_2 to maximize utility $v(q_1, q_2, w)$ subject to its budget constraint. The Lagrange expression is $L = v(q_1, q_2, w) + \lambda((q_1 - p_1)x_1(q_1, q_2, w) + (q_2 - p_2)x_2(q_1, q_2, w) - R)$, from which we obtain the first-order conditions, which are, using $t_i = q_i - p_i$,

$$\frac{\partial v}{\partial q_k} + \lambda\left(x_k + t_1\frac{\partial x_1}{\partial q_k} + t_2\frac{\partial x_2}{\partial q_k}\right) = 0, \qquad k = 1, 2,$$

Using the envelope theorem for $\partial v/\partial q_k$, and the Slutsky equation as above, this becomes

$$\frac{t_1 s_{1k} + t_2 s_{2k}}{x_k} = -\left(\frac{\lambda - \alpha}{\lambda}\right) + t_1\frac{\partial x_1}{\partial m} + t_2\frac{\partial x_2}{\partial m} = -c, \qquad k = 1, 2,$$

or, using the symmetry of the substitution effect, $s_{ij} = s_{ji}$, we have

$$t_1 s_{11} + t_2 s_{12} = -c x_1, \quad t_1 s_{21} + t_2 s_{22} = -c x_2, \tag{3.3}$$

where c is the same for both equations. Eliminating c, we obtain

$$\frac{t_1}{t_2} = \frac{s_{22} x_1 - s_{12} x_2}{s_{11} x_2 - s_{21} x_1} = \frac{s_{22}/x_2 - s_{12}/x_1}{s_{11}/x_1 - s_{21}/x_2},$$

and, multiplying by q_2/q_1 and using the homogeneity property as above,

$$\frac{t_1/q_1}{t_2/q_2} = \frac{\tau_1}{\tau_2} = \frac{\varepsilon_{22} - \varepsilon_{12}}{\varepsilon_{11} - \varepsilon_{21}} = \frac{\varepsilon_{22} + \varepsilon_{11} + \varepsilon_{10}}{\varepsilon_{11} + \varepsilon_{22} + \varepsilon_{20}}.$$

Therefore, since $\varepsilon_{11} + \varepsilon_{22} < 0$, this says that $\tau_1 > \tau_2$ if $\varepsilon_{20} > \varepsilon_{10}$, that is, if x_1 is relatively more complementary with leisure than x_2, which is the optimal tax version of the Corlett and Hague analysis. Equivalently, uniform taxes are optimal if $\varepsilon_{20} = \varepsilon_{10}$, which is the Corlet–Hague theorem. These results on the three-commodity case are also reported in Diamond and Mirrlees (1971).

The Corlett–Hague theorem readily generalizes to any number of goods and leisure. In the case with n goods, $x_1, \ldots, x_n$, and leisure x_0, the conditions (3.3) generalize to

$$\sum_{i=1}^{n} t_i s_{ki} = -c x_k, \quad k = 1, \ldots, n,$$

or, after converting substitution effects s_{ki} to elasticities,

$$\sum_{i=1}^{n} \tau_i \varepsilon_{ki} = -c, \quad k = 1, \ldots, n.$$

This will be satisfied for uniform taxes, $\tau_i = \tau$ for all i, if

$$\tau \sum_{i=1}^{n} \varepsilon_{ki} = \varepsilon_{k0} = -c, \quad k = 1, \ldots, n,$$

which requires that $\varepsilon_{j0} = \varepsilon_{k0}$ for all j, k, so all goods must be equally complementary with leisure.

The conditions needed to satisfy this requirement for uniformity are quite stringent. It will be satisfied if the consumer expenditure function is implicitly separable, so that it takes the form $e(u, f(\mathbf{q}, u), w)$, where $\mathbf{q}$ is the vector of goods prices and w is the price of leisure x_0.[1] Differentiating this expenditure function, we obtain the compensated demand for good j to be $x_j(\mathbf{q}, w, u) = \partial e(\cdot)/\partial q_j = e_f f_j$, where subscripts refer to partial derivatives. The compensated elasticity of demand can therefore be written as follows (given that f_j is independent of w):

$$\varepsilon_{j0} = \frac{\partial^2 e}{\partial q_j \partial w} \frac{w}{x_j} = \frac{e_{fw} w}{e_f} = \varepsilon_{k0}.$$

A utility function satisfying this property is the weakly separable one of the form $u(f(x_1, \ldots, x_n), x_0)$ with the sub-utility function $f(\cdot)$ being homothetic (Sandmo 1976). Intuitively, preferences for goods are independent of leisure. An increase in the tax on w will therefore decrease labor income available for spending on goods, and since preferences are homothetic, the demand for all goods will decrease proportionately. A proportional tax on all goods will be equivalent to a tax on leisure and will cause the demand to fall proportionately thereby not imposing any distortion in demand patterns.

When the model with linear taxes is extended to heterogeneous households, equity considerations now become relevant. Suppose that these are captured by using a social welfare function as the government's objective function. Remarkably the Corlett–Hague theorem extends to this case with some revision. Suppose now that the tax mix can involve not only indirect taxes on all goods but also a poll subsidy. (The latter was simply assumed away in the representative consumer context since it would obviously dominate indirect taxes.) Uniform commodity taxes combined with a poll subsidy would be equivalent to a linear progressive income tax. Uniformity again might apply under certain preference forms (always assuming for now that all individuals have the same preferences but differ in their wage rates). For example, Deaton (1979) shows that if preferences are weakly separable as above and goods have linear Engel curves with identical slopes across individuals, indirect taxes will be uniform and can be dispensed with entirely in favor of a linear progressive income tax.[2] (The proof follows

---

1. Implicit separability and its properties are summarized in Blackorby, Davidson and Schworm (1991a).
2. Linear Engel curves apply for the Stone–Geary utility function, of which the Cobb–Douglas is a special case. More generally, Engel curves are linear for the Gorman (1961) polar form utility function, whose expenditure function for person i takes the form $e^i(\mathbf{q}, u^i) = g^i(\mathbf{q}) + u^i f(\mathbf{q})$, where $\mathbf{q}$ is the vector of consumer prices and $f(\mathbf{q})$ is the same for all persons.

an analogous procedure as for the optimal tax version of the Corlett–Hague theorem above.) This is only a sufficient condition, and there may be others, although they are not at all obvious.

Two points might be noted about this extension of Corlett and Hague to a heterogeneous-population setting. First, Deaton's sufficient conditions for uniformity put lie to the argument that equity considerations require that necessities should bear a lower tax rate than luxuries. His conditions are perfectly consistent with income elasticities of demand being very different among goods. What is more important, as in the Corlett–Hague theorem, is the complement-substitute relation of goods with leisure. This will become clearer in the next subsection.

Second, if the relevant sufficient condition is not satisfied, then both direct and differential indirect taxes should be deployed in this world. Note, however, that the tax mix is indeterminate in the sense that the level of indirect and direct taxes are indeterminate: a proportional increase in goods' taxes combined with a reduction in the income tax rate will have no effect. In other words, only relative commodity tax rates are determined, not absolute.

As mentioned above, weak separability and linear, parallel Engel curves do not rule out the fact that some goods can be luxuries and others necessities. As long as the linear progressive tax is optimal, commodity tax rates on all goods should be uniform. However, if the income tax rate is suboptimal, preferential commodity taxation of necessities can be welfare improving. Boadway and Pestieau (2011) show this in a simple two-good example where there is a luxury good and a necessity good. Specifically, let preferences take the quasi-linear form $u(x_1 + b(x_2) - h(\ell))$, so that x_2 is a necessity with zero income effects and x_1 is a luxury. Since all income changes go to x_1, $dx_1/dm = 1/q_1$. Since $dx_2/dm = 0$, the slopes of Engel curves are linear and the same for all households. Therefore the Deaton conditions apply.

Suppose that there are n_i persons with wage rate w_i, $i = 1, \ldots, r$, and let us denote their commodity consumption by x_{1i}, x_{2i} and labor ℓ_i. The government imposes a linear progressive income tax with a marginal rate t and lump-sum component a, and a commodity tax θ on x_2. (The tax on x_1 can be arbitrarily set to zero.) Households maximize utility subject to a budget constraint $x_{1i} + (1+\theta)x_{2i} = (1-t)w_i\ell_i + a$. This yields $x_{2i}(1 + \theta)$ and $\ell_i((1-t)w_i)$ and indirect utility $v_i(\theta, t, a)$, where $v_{i\theta} = -u_i'x_{2i}$, $v_{it} = -u_i'w_i\ell_i$, $v_{ia} = u_i'$ by the envelope theorem.

The government maximizes a social welfare function,

$$W(\theta, t, a) = \sum_i n_i v_i(\theta, t, a),$$

which is assumed to be utilitarian for simplicity, subject to a fixed budget constraint

$$B(\theta, t, a) \equiv \sum_i n_i(\theta x_{2i}(1+\theta) + tw_i \ell_i((1-t)w_i) - a) = R.$$

If only a linear progressive income tax is used, the effect of a change in the tax rate t on social welfare with a balancing the budget is given by

$$\left.\frac{dW}{dt}\right|_{\theta=0} = \sum_i n_i\left(v_{it} + v_{ia}\frac{da}{dt}\right) = \sum_i n_i\left(v_{it} - v_{ia}\frac{B_t}{B_a}\right),$$

where B_t and B_a are the derivatives of the government budget constraint. Using the envelope results from the household's problem, the government budget, and $y_i = w_i \ell_i$, we can rewrite this as

$$\left.\frac{dW}{dt}\right|_{\theta=0} = \sum_i n_i u_i' \sum_i n_i y_i - \sum_i n_i y_i u_i' + \sum_i n_i u_i' \sum_i n_i t \frac{dy_i}{dt}$$

$$= -\text{Cov}[u'y] + tE[u']E\left[\frac{dy_i}{dt}\right].$$

The first term represents the equity benefits of increasing the tax rate, with the lump-sum transfer a increasing to balance the budget. The second term reflects the efficiency costs of increasing t. In an optimum, this term is set to zero, and we obtain the well-known optimal tax result of Sheshinski (1972):

$$t^* = \frac{\text{Cov}[u'y]}{E[u']E[dy_i/dt]}.$$

Consider now the tax reform exercise of increasing the tax rate on x_2, starting at $\theta = 0$, holding a and thus the degree of progressivity fixed, and reducing the income tax rate t to keep revenues constant. Starting at arbitrary levels of t and a, we obtain

$$\left.\frac{B_t}{x_2}\frac{dW}{d\theta}\right|_{\substack{a=\bar{a}\\\theta=0}} = -\sum_i n_i u_i' \sum_i n_i\left(y_i + t\frac{dy_i}{dt}\right) + \sum_i n_i y_i u_i'$$

$$= \text{Cov}[u'y] - tE[u']E\left[\frac{dy_i}{dt}\right].$$

This result has two implications. First, if the income tax rate had been set optimally at t^* to begin with, the welfare effect of a change in θ would be zero, confirming Deaton's result that differential commodity taxes should not be used in this case. However, if $t < t^*$, so that the income tax is less progressive than optimal, a reduction in θ would be welfare improving. Equivalently the necessity good x_2 should be treated preferentially in a commodity tax system (and vice versa if the income tax is overly progressive). Thus the relevance of the Deaton result depends on the income tax being set optimally.

Naturally, if the Deaton conditions do not apply, then differential commodity taxes will be useful even if the linear income tax is set optimally. However, that does not imply that preferential tax rates should apply to necessities. They may turn out to be more complementary with leisure than are luxuries, although that would have to be determined by reliable empirical analysis that does not yet exist. Given that, a default position of uniformity is reasonable if income taxes are set optimally.

3.1.2 The Atkinson–Stiglitz Theorem

The simple setting with linear commodity and income taxes is restrictive, but its methodology has served as a useful starting point for more general cases. The most remarkable extension is that of Atkinson and Stiglitz (1976). They consider a standard optimal nonlinear income tax setting in which individuals differ only in their wage rate, supply labor and consume $n > 1$ goods, and in which the government observes individual incomes and anonymous transactions so can apply a non-linear income tax and indirect taxes on goods to maximize a social welfare function. The *Atkinson–Stiglitz theorem* states that if utility is weakly separable in leisure and goods so that utility takes the form $u(f(x_1, \ldots, x_n), x_0)$, optimal commodity tax rates should be uniform regardless of the properties of the sub-utility function in goods. This is a powerful result, and imposes relatively weak requirements on the utility function. Before turning to its proof and the consequences of its violation, some general remarks are in order.

The Atkinson–Stiglitz theorem seems to offer much stronger support for uniform taxation than the Corlett–Hague theorem. However, as should become clear, this is somewhat misleading. The conditions for uniformity are weaker in Atkinson and Stiglitz than in Corlett and Hague and its multi-person extensions, but that is because the government has available stronger redistributive policy instruments (nonlinear taxation versus linear progressive taxation). That difference, however, is a matter of degree rather than a fundamental difference. In both settings there is no presumption for imposing higher taxes on goods that form a larger proportion of the budgets of high-income persons, that is, those with higher income elasticities of demand. On the contrary, as we will see, deviations from uniformity are based more on substitute–complement relations among various goods and leisure, and it is not apparent which goods should be preferred on those grounds. Exceptions might be found in an intertemporal setting or in a setting where the consumption of goods is time intensive, as we will see later.

The Atkinson–Stiglitz theorem is highly suggestive in its own right, and also as it applies to other situations, as discussed below. It is worth at this point highlighting some extensions and caveats to the approach. Despite the fact that there are many caveats to the Atkinson–Stiglitz theorem and many circumstances in which it will not apply, it is none-theless a powerful and useful result. It sets a benchmark for studying optimal tax results that is quite intuitive. As a benchmark it is also useful as an organizing device for highlighting deviations from it. From a policy perspective, it provides a prime facie case for a uniform com-modity tax system even in a world where equity is an important concern. Even though households of different income levels consume different proportions of goods, as long as separability applies it is better to pursue redistribution through the nonlinear income tax than through the differential taxation of luxuries and necessities.[3] Given the admin-istrative costs of imposing differential commodity taxation, there are natural advantages to uniformity, as proponents of a single-rate VAT argue. The onus is on detractors to show that violations of the Atkinson–Stiglitz theorem are important enough to warrant deviations from uni-formity. Deviations from uniformity become especially relevant in an intertemporal context where the same good consumed at different dates constitutes different goods for tax purposes.

The intuition for the Atkinson–Stiglitz theorem follows from the fact that the main constraints on redistribution in the optimal nonlinear income tax model are the incentive constraints that preclude individu-als of a given wage rate from mimicking those of a lesser wage rate.

---

3. Even if nonlinear commodity taxation could be applied, separability would be suffi-cient to rule out using differential commodity taxes as the original proof of the theorem by Atkinson and Stiglitz (1976, 1980) shows.

Differential commodity tax rates will weaken the incentive constraint if persons with a higher wage rate devote relatively more of their disposable income to the more highly taxed commodities. Given that higher wage persons mimicking the income of lower wage persons will consume more leisure, this will be the case if the highly taxed commodities are relatively more complementary with leisure than other commodities are. Alternatively, if goods are weakly separable from leisure in the utility function, two individuals that have the same disposable income but differ in the leisure they enjoy will consume the same bundle of goods. This will be the case for a person with a given wage mimicking the income and aggregate consumption of a person with a lower wage. This incentive constraint cannot be weakened by imposing differential taxes. They can only make all persons worse off.

The proof of the Atkinson–Stiglitz theorem is best seen in the context of the Mirrlees (1971) optimal nonlinear income tax model, and can be found in Atkinson and Stiglitz (1980) and Christiansen (1984). Consumers differ only in their exogenously given productivity reflected in the wage rate w, which follows the distribution function $F(w)$ for $\underline{w} \leqslant w \leqslant \overline{w}$, where $\underline{w} \geqslant 0$, $\overline{w} \leqslant \infty$. Producer prices for all goods are normalized to be unity. Consumer prices are given by $q_i = 1 + t_i$ for $i = 1, \ldots, n$, where t_i is an indirect tax with the normalization $t_1 = 0$ (since the absolute level of indirect taxes does not matter, so one tax can be normalized to be zero). Consumers face a nonlinear income tax schedule $T(w\ell)$, and choose goods and labor to maximize $u(x_1, \ldots, x_n, \ell)$ subject to the budget constraint $\sum_{i=1}^{n}(1+t_i)x_i = w\ell - T(w\ell)$. This yields the first-order conditions

$$\frac{u_k}{u_j} = \frac{1+t_k}{1+t_j} = \frac{q_k}{q_j}, \quad \frac{wu_k}{u_\ell} = -\frac{1+t_k}{1-T'} = -\frac{q_k}{1-T'}.$$

The government maximizes a social welfare function $\int_w W(u)f(w)dw$, assumed to be additive, subject to two constraints. One is the budget constraint, or the economy's resource constraint, $\int_w (w\ell - \sum x_i)f(w)dw = R$, where R is the revenue requirement. The other is a set of incentive constraints that take the form $\dot{u}(w) = -\ell u_\ell / w$ for all w, where $\dot{u} \equiv du/dw$. The incentive constraints require that each wage type w prefer the consumption–income bundle chosen by the planner for him rather than that chosen for any other wage-type w', or $u(\mathbf{x}(w), y(w)/w) \geqslant u(\mathbf{x}(w'), y(w')/w)$, where $\mathbf{x}(w)$ is the consumption bundle intended for a type w person and $y(w)/w = \ell(w)$ is labor supply. The incentive constraint

$\dot{u} = -\ell u_\ell / w$ is a sufficient condition for this to be satisfied. Formally, the incentive constraint can be written, with some abuse of notation, as $0 = u(w) - u(\mathbf{x}(w), y(w)/w) \leqslant u(w') - u(\mathbf{x}(w), y(w)/w')$. Choosing w' to minimize the right-hand side and evaluating it at $w' = w$ yields the incentive constraint.

The control variables for the government's problem are $x_2, \ldots, x_n, \ell$ with x_1 determined by inverting the utility function, $x_1 = (x_2, \ldots, x_n$ $\ell, u)$. The state variable is u. The Hamiltonian can be written

$$H = (W(u) + \lambda(w\ell - \sum x_i - R))f(w) - \frac{\gamma \ell u_\ell}{w}.$$

Since we are interested in indirect tax rates, we can concentrate on the first-order conditions on x_k for a type-w individual:

$$-\lambda \left(1 + \frac{\partial x_1}{\partial x_k} \Big|_u \right) f(w) - \gamma \frac{\ell}{w} \left(u_{\ell k} + u_{\ell 1} \frac{\partial x_1}{\partial x_k} \Big|_u \right) = 0$$

Using $\partial x_1 / \partial x_k |_u = -u_k / u_1 = -(1 + t_k)$, this can be written

$$t_k = \frac{\gamma \ell u_k}{\lambda w f} \left(\frac{u_{\ell k}}{u_k} - \frac{u_{\ell 1}}{u_1} \right), \quad \text{or} \quad \frac{t_k}{q_k} = \frac{\gamma \ell \alpha}{\lambda w f} \left(\frac{d(\log(u_k / u_1))}{d\ell} \right),$$

where α is the consumer's marginal utility of income. Then it follows directly that if utility takes the weakly separable form $u(f(\mathbf{x}), x_0)$, we obtain $t_k / q_k = 0$ for all $k = 1, \ldots, n$, which is the Atkinson–Stiglitz theorem. Moreover $t_k / q_k > 0$ if and only if x_k is more complementary with leisure than x_1 in the sense that its relative valuation increases with labor supplied. As can be seen, this bears an uncanny resemblance to the Corlett–Hague theorem in the two-good case.

Note, however, that the expression above is derived for a type-w person, and the optimal indirect tax t_k will differ for each type if weak separability does not apply. As Atkinson and Stiglitz (1976) show, the optimal tax structure can then be implemented if nonlinear commodity taxes are deployed. If we restrict the government to the same linear commodity tax rates for all individuals, the same qualitative results apply: higher taxes should be imposed on goods that are more complementary with leisure.

Some intuitive insight can be seen for this result if we consider the discrete-type optimal income tax case pioneered by Guesnerie and Seade (1982), Stern (1982), and Stiglitz (1982), and frequently used in what follows. Following Edwards, Keen, and Tuomala (1994) and Nava,

Schroyen, and Marchand (1996), consider the simplest case of two wage types w_1 and w_2, with $w_2 > w_1$, and two goods x_1 and x_2 plus leisure or labor. The government can observe pre-tax income $y_i = w_i / \ell_i$ but not w_i or ℓ_i as in the standard optimal income tax literature. As well, it cannot observe individual demands for x_1 and x_2, but it can tax transactions anonymously. The government can therefore impose a nonlinear tax on income y as well as indirect commodity taxes on goods. As above, normalize the tax on x_1 to be zero, so that the only indirect tax will be t_2 on x_2. Continue to assume producer prices are unity, so that $q_1 = 1$, $q_2 = 1 + t_2$. Imagine disaggregating consumer decision-making into two stages, given the tax system in place. In the first stage, the choice of ℓ_i determines y_i and disposable income $c_i = y_i - T(y_i)$, and in the second, disposable income c_i is allocated between x_1 and x_2.

Begin with stage 2, where disposable income and pre-tax income are given. A type-i individual chooses x_1 and x_2 to maximize $u(x_1, x_2, y_i / w_i)$. Since $c_i = x_1 + q_2 x_2$, the consumer chooses x_2 to maximize $u(c_i - q_2 x_2, x_2, y_i / w_i)$. The solution gives $x_2^i(q_2, c_i, y_i)$, which is decreasing in q_2. Let the value function for this stage be $v^i(q_2, c_i, y_i)$, with the associated envelope theorem properties $v_q^i = -x_2^i u_x^i$, $v_c^i = u_x^i$, $v_y^i = u_y^i / w_i$. A type-2 person might also have been tempted to mimic a type-1 in stage 1. If so, the problem at stage 2 becomes to choose $\hat{x}_2$ to maximize $u(c_1 - q_2 \hat{x}_2, \hat{x}_2, y_1 / w_2)$, where a "hat" is used to denote the mimicker's choices. This yields the demand $\hat{x}_2^2(q_2, c_1, y_1)$ and indirect utility $\hat{v}^2(q_2, c_1, y_1)$.

Note that in stage 2, the type-1's and the mimicking type-2's have the same disposable and pre-tax incomes (c_1, y_1), but differ in labor supply, $\ell_1 > \hat{\ell}_2$ since type-2's have a higher wage rate. If the utility function is weakly separable, $u(f(x_1, x_2), \ell)$, then $x_2^1 = \hat{x}_2^2$. If instead x_2 is more complementary with leisure than is x_1, then $x_2^1 < \hat{x}_2^2$.

In stage 1, individuals choose labor supply, and therefore income. Following Stiglitz (1982), this choice can be treated as the outcome of a direct mechanism whereby the government chooses (c_i, y_i) for each of the types, such that these choices maximize social welfare while being incentive compatible and satisfying a revenue constraint. The government also chooses the indirect tax rate t_2 (recall that $t_1 = 0$ by normalization). Assuming a utilitarian social welfare function (which does not affect the results of interest), the government maximizes $n_1 v^1(q_2, c_1, y_1) + n_2 v^2(q_2, c_2, y_2)$, where n_1 and n_2 are the numbers of the two types. The revenue constraint is $n_1(y_1 - c_1 + t_2 x_2^1(q_2, c_1, y_1)) + n_2(y_2 - c_2 + t_2 x_2^2(q_2, c_2, y_2)) = R$, and the binding incentive constraint is $v^2(q_2, c_2, y_2) = \hat{v}^2(q_2, c_1, y_1)$.

The first-order condition on t_2 reduces after some manipulation to the following:

$$\gamma \hat{v}_c^2 (\hat{x}_2^2 - x_2^1) + \lambda t_2 \left(n_1 \frac{\partial \tilde{x}_2^1}{\partial q_2} + n_2 \frac{\partial \tilde{x}_2^2}{\partial q_2} \right) = 0,$$

where $\tilde{x}_2^i$ is compensated demand for x_2 by person i, $\gamma > 0$ is the Lagrange multiplier on the incentive constraint, and $\lambda > 0$ is the multiplier on the revenue constraint. Therefore the optimal tax rate t_2 can be written

$$t_2^* = -\frac{\gamma \hat{v}_x^2 (\hat{x}_2^2 - x_2^1)}{\lambda \left(n_1 \partial \tilde{x}_2^1 / \partial q_2 + n_2 \partial \tilde{x}_2^2 / \partial q_2 \right)} \gtreqless 0 \quad \text{as} \quad \hat{x}_2^2 \gtreqless x_2^1.$$

The denominator is an efficiency effect showing that the tax rate will be higher the smaller are the compensated demand responses to tax changes. This is intuitive. The numerator involves the incentive constraint. It will be zero if the utility function is weakly separable so the mimicker demands the same amount of x_2 as does the type-1 person. This is the Atkinson–Stiglitz theorem. Alternatively, if x_2 is relatively complementary with leisure, the indirect tax on it should be positive, and vice versa. Intuitively, if $\hat{x}_2^2 > x_2^1$, then mimicking is made more difficult by imposing a tax on x_2. More specifically, the intuition is as follows. Suppose that $\hat{x}_2^2 > x_2^1$. Starting at $t_2 = 0$, increase t_2 and adjust the income tax paid by the two types so that $dT_i = -x_2^i dt_2$. This will leave $v^i(\cdot)$ as well as government revenue unchanged. However, $\hat{v}^2(\cdot)$ is reduced, so the incentive constraint is relaxed and social welfare can be increased.

As cautioned earlier, this is a result about the structure of the tax system, not the tax mix, that is, the share of tax revenues obtained from direct and indirect taxes. A given structure of commodity and nonlinear income tax rates is compatible with any tax mix, since a proportional increase in indirect tax rates combined with a proportional decrease in direct tax rates will have no effect. To nail down the tax mix, some feature must be added to the model to cause levels of tax rates to be relevant and not just their structure. One obvious candidate might be tax evasion. Since indirect and direct taxes are typically administered separately, if only because they involve separate taxpayers, and since the incentive to evade taxes might be expected to increase with the tax rate,[4] it would be welfare-improving to spread a given tax burden

---

4. But it is by no means clear that evasion is increasing in the tax rate. In the simple model of Allingham and Sandmo (1972) where the penalty is based on the amount of

across more than one tax base so as to keep the rate low on each base.[5] Work remains to be done on the topic of the tax mix, especially given how important it is to real-world tax policy decisions.

The Atkinson–Stiglitz theorem involves the choice of *optimal* tax rules, particularly the choice of commodity tax rates when the nonlinear income tax is set optimally. This might be thought to be restrictive, since income taxes are almost certainly not being set optimally. One seemingly straightforward extension to deal with this issue has been proposed by Konishi (1995), Laroque (2005), and Kaplow (2006) and generalized by Gauthier and Laroque (2009). It was briefly mentioned earlier. They show that whatever arbitrary income tax system is in place, if one starts from a differentiated commodity tax structure, a reform to uniform commodity taxes accompanied by a suitable change in the income tax levied on each skill type that raises at least the same amount of revenue as before and that satisfies all incentive constraints will be Pareto improving as long as preferences are weakly separable. This extension, which is discussed in detail in Kaplow (2008), would seem to add considerably more policy relevance to the Atkinson–Stiglitz theorem.

However, some caution is in order (Boadway 2010). This generalization of the Atkinson–Stiglitz theorem assumes that as part of the proposed reform, the income tax can be changed at will by income-specific changes in tax liabilities. If the commodity tax reform is not accompanied by these income tax reforms, the Pareto improvement will not materialize. In effect there is the potential for a Pareto improvement analogous to the potential Pareto improvements indicated by Kaldor–Hicks–Samuelson compensation tests discussed in the previous chapter. All the objections that applied to those compensation tests will apply here. Moreover the kinds of reforms of the income tax required for the Konishi–Laroque–Kaplow result to apply will typically go well beyond the form of the nonoptimal income tax that is in place.

For example, suppose that for whatever reason the income tax is constrained to be linear progressive. We know, as discussed above, that the conditions required for commodity tax uniformity in this case are

---

income not reported, the effect was ambiguous: there is a substitution effect favoring evasion, and an income effect working in the opposite direction. Yitzhaki (1974) shows that if the penalty is based on the shortfall in taxes, the substitution effect vanishes and an increase in the tax rate reduces evasion.

5. Boadway, Marchand, and Pestieau (1994) develop a rudimentary theory of the direct–indirect tax mix along these lines.

more restrictive than in the nonlinear tax case: in particular, weak separability is not sufficient. Given that, moving to uniformity on the basis that preferences are weakly separable will not generally be welfare improving even if the linear progressive tax is set optimally to begin with. The hypothetical income tax changes needed to engineer a Pareto improvement would require deviating from linearity. The same argument would obviously apply if the income tax were restricted to be piecewise linear progressive, which is a form commonly used. More generally, if the government could make the changes to the income tax system required to generate a Pareto-improving move to commodity tax uniformity, there is seemingly little to preclude it from going to the fully optimal nonlinear income tax, in which case the Atkinson–Stiglitz theorem already applies.

Despite these seemingly serious reservations, we do learn something from the Konishi–Laroque–Kaplow approach, if only about the limits of the Atkinson–Stiglitz theorem. Perhaps the more important question about the relevance of the Atkinson–Stiglitz theorem concerns the policy implications resulting from failure of the theorem either because preferences are not weakly separable or because optimal income taxation is not in place. In the former case, the theory tells us that relatively higher taxes should be imposed on goods that are more complementary with leisure. However, there is limited evidence on that, particularly when one takes into account the many forms that leisure time can take. In particular, there is no presumption that necessities should be taxed more lightly than luxuries. In the latter case, the direction of deviation from uniformity is not obvious: it depends on the form of the income tax in place and what one assumes about the prospects for income tax reform. In either case, one can argue that uniformity is a reasonable policy choice. The costs of deviating from the optimum are likely strictly convex, so if one does not know in which direction to deviate, expected losses are minimized by implementing uniformity.

Besides the requirement for optimal income taxation to be in place, there are several other caveats or extensions to the Atkinson–Stiglitz theorem. Many of these involve expanding the arguments in the utility function in various ways or changing their properties. In what follows, we discuss briefly each of the following cases: different needs for particular commodities across the population, different preferences, the allocation of time by individuals to nonmarket labor or to the consumption of purchased goods, the emission of an externality by one or more goods, imperfect substitutability of different skills of labor, wage uncertainty, and dynamic optimal taxation. In each case the assumption of weak separability of goods from leisure is retained so that we can focus on other possible violations of the theorem.

Needs for Goods or Leisure

Consider a simple case where individuals vary in their needs for a particular good. This can be captured in a simple extension of the weakly separable utility function used above, $u(f(x_1, \ldots, x_{n-1}, x_n - r), x_0)$, where r is the basic requirement or need for good x_n, which can vary among individuals.[6] The factor r could also be interpreted as an initial endowment of good x_n following Cremer, Pestieau, and Rochet (2001), or more generally a taste factor. Individuals can now differ in two dimensions, wage rates and needs. Whether the Atkinson–Stiglitz theorem applies depends on the joint distribution of w and r, as well as on whether r is observable.

If r is observable, matters are straightforward and instructive. Suppose that there are a finite number of values for r: as few as two would suffice, say, high need and low need. The population of taxpayers can then be divided into two identifiable need groups, those with high and low needs. Effectively, needs serve as a signal or tag, as in Akerlof (1978), Parsons (1996), Immonen et al. (1998), and Boadway and Pestieau (2006). In an optimum a separate nonlinear income tax structure should be imposed within each needs group, and there can be lump-sum transfers (possibly implicit) between the two groups. Since within each group, the same separable utility function is operative, the Atkinson–Stiglitz theorem applies. The lump-sum transfer between the two groups should be sufficient (1) to compensate for differences in needs per capita between the two groups and (2) to compensate for differences in the share of high-skilled workers between the two groups. The latter will involve a transfer from the group with a larger proportion of high- to low-skilled persons to the group with the smaller proportion.

If needs are not observable, the Atkinson–Stiglitz theorem generally does not apply. Consider the simplest case in which the wage rate w and needs r are perfectly correlated. If needs are increasing with the wage rate, there should be a differential commodity tax on good n alongside an optimal nonlinear income tax. Intuitively, higher wage

---

6. This formulation of needs follows Rowe and Woolley (1999) and Boadway and Pestieau (2003). Note that basic needs could apply for all n goods, as in the Stone–Geary utility function, but we assume that only for good n do they differ across households. For other goods, needs can be suppressed from the utility function.

persons will demand more of good n for a given level of income, so taxing x_n relaxes the incentive constraint. The opposite applies if needs fall with the wage rate. More generally, if needs apply to more than one good, or if they are only imperfectly correlated with the wage rate, the Atkinson–Stiglitz theorem will still not apply, but the characterization of the optimal commodity tax system will be more complicated.[7]

Needs could also apply to leisure rather than goods. In the simple case of additive needs, the separable utility function would take the form: $u(f(x_1, \ldots, x_n), x_0 - r)$, where r is the need for leisure and can vary across individuals. In this case the Atkinson–Stiglitz theorem applies regardless of whether r is observable to the government, and that will be true for more general forms of interaction between r and x_0, such as multiplicative, $u(f(x_1, \ldots, x_n), rx_0)$. Because of separability, the demand for commodities depends only on disposable income: a high-wage person mimicking the income of a low-wage person will consume the same commodity bundle, so differential commodity taxes serve no purpose. Of course, the form of the nonlinear income tax will be affected by leisure needs, possibly in complicated ways. If needs are observable, they serve as a tag, and a different income tax structure can apply for different needs groups. If needs are not observable, the optimal income tax problem becomes a two-dimensional screening problem, so the pattern of incentive constraints is ambiguous. In either case the redistributive of treatment of persons of different needs is not clear as the following case shows. Nonetheless, no differential commodity taxes are needed.

Different Preferences

Related to differences in needs are differences in tastes or preferences. Saez (2002a) studies the applicability of the Atkinson–Stiglitz theorem in this case. He shows that differentially high commodity taxes should be imposed on goods that are demanded more by higher skilled persons. (See also Blomquist and Christiansen 2008 for a related analysis.) The intuition follows directly from that outlined above for the case of nonseparable preferences. Such a tax can weaken the incentive constraints and facilitate greater redistribution to lower skilled persons.

---

7. If needs are observable, but the government is constrained to apply a common income tax schedule and credit for needs to all persons, the credit for needs should overcompensate for needs if there is a higher proportion of low-skilled in the needy group, and vice versa. If the credit for needs can differ by skill or income class, the tax credit for needs should over-compensate the low-skilled and undercompensate the high-skilled persons.

Saez also provides an interpretation of this result for the intertemporal case in which goods consumed in different periods are different goods, and preference differences take the form of differences in the utility discount rate. His results in this case hinge on whether the utility discount rate varies systematically for persons of different skills. This case is of some relevance for the issue of taxing capital income (savings), which we consider below. As we will see, if the utility discount rate is lower for higher skilled persons, the latter will have higher saving rates. A tax on capital income will therefore serve as an indirect way of redistributing from the high-skilled to the low-skilled, thereby augmenting the redistributive labor income tax.

It is worth noting in passing how persons with different preferences are aggregated for social welfare purposes, since this is an issue to which we will return. Saez uses as a social objective function a weighted average of persons of different preference classes, where the weights are not specified. His results then turn on how social welfare weights vary with consumption. How social welfare weights should vary with tastes, if at all, is an open question. The point here is simply that, whatever weights apply to persons with different preferences, the Atkinson–Stiglitz theorem will generally be violated. Of course, as with other violations of the Atkinson–Stiglitz theorem due to nonseparability of preferences, it is not at all clear how to generally identify those goods that should bear a higher tax rate. That depends both on unidentified preferences and substitute–complement relations of goods with leisure about which empirical uncertainty exists.

Allocation of Time by Individuals

In the standard analysis an individual's time endowment h is divided between labor supplied to the market ℓ and general leisure x_0. We could have written utility in a general form $u(x_1, \ldots, x_n, \ell, x_0)$ where both labor and leisure affect utility separately. However, since ℓ and x_0 are related through the time constraint, $\ell + x_0 = h$, we can write the utility function either as $u(x_1, \ldots, x_n, \ell, h - \ell)$ or as $u(x_1, \ldots, x_n, h - x_0, x_0)$, or in shorthand form and abusing notation, either $u(x_1, \ldots, x_n, \ell)$ or $u(x_1, \ldots, x_n, x_0)$. Similarly the budget constraint can be written in terms of labor, $\sum_{i=1}^{n} q_i x_i = w\ell$, or leisure, $\sum_{i=1}^{n} q_i x_i + wx_0 = wh$. It does not matter whether utility is taken to be a function of goods and labor or goods and leisure. All the standard results can be obtained.

Two realistic extensions are relevant. First, the individual may devote labor to nonmarket activities, either household production or the informal sector. Second, the individual may also devote time to the consumption of various goods. Consider each of these in turn.

Nonmarket Labor

Suppose that the labor supplied by the household ℓ—total time available h less time devoted to leisure x_0—is divided between market and nonmarket uses, ℓ_m and ℓ_n, respectively. We can treat utility as a function of goods and labor, and write the weakly separable form of utility function as $u(f(x_1, \ldots, x_n), \ell_m, \ell_n)$. Market income is given by $y_m = w\ell_m$, where w is the wage rate. As usual, we assume that y_m is observable. If the nonmarket income represents household production, ℓ_n produces some unobserved nonmarketed goods or services that differ from those purchased on the market. Suppose that the benefit of this household production is included in the argument ℓ_n in the utility function. In this case the Atkinson–Stiglitz theorem still applies: for a given level of disposable income, individuals allocate it among market goods identically regardless of either ℓ_m or ℓ_n.

Of course, if household production produces a good that is not separable from purchased goods in the utility function, the Atkinson–Stiglitz theorem will not apply. Presumably higher tax rates will be preferred for goods that are complementary with nonmarket goods. The nonlinear income tax structure—perhaps even the direction of the incentive constraint—will be affected by labor devoted to household production. Precisely how the income tax is affected would depend on the details of the technology of household production, including the productivity of high- and low-skilled persons in household production. Such details remain to be worked out in the literature.

Alternatively, the nonmarket labor might be supplied to the informal or hidden sector where income, which can be used to purchase market goods, is hidden from the government. A full treatment of this case would involve consideration of the chances of being caught and punished, but the intuition can be seen by supposing that the cost of supplying informal labor implicitly takes into account these considerations.[8] The same form of the separable utility function as in the household production case applies, except that ℓ_n now takes account of both the costs and benefits of working informally. The important point is that income earned in the informal sector, y_n, is hidden from the government and can be used to purchase market goods. The Atkinson–Stiglitz

---

8. For further discussion, see Slemrod and Yitzhaki (2002) and Sandmo (2005).

theorem will therefore be violated: a high-wage person mimicking the market income of a low-wage person will generally have different total income, so will consume different bundles of goods, even if utility is weakly separable. If, for example, high-wage persons have higher non-market incomes, y_n, they will consume proportionately more of those goods that have higher income elasticities of demand. Those goods should bear a higher tax rate.

Time Taken for Consumption

Next suppose, following Becker's (1965) seminal analysis, that time must be allocated to the consumption of at least some goods and services, as well as being used for labor and pure leisure. (We assume that there is pure leisure as well as time spent consuming, although this could be assumed to be zero.) Assume that time per unit of commodity i consumed is fixed at a_i. The time constraint faced by the household is then $\ell + x_0 + \sum_{i=1}^{n} a_i x_i = h$. In general, household utility depends on the quantities of all goods consumed and the various uses of time: $u(x_1, \ldots, x_n, x_0, a_1 x_1, \ldots, a_n x_n, \ell)$. Whether the Atkinson–Stiglitz theorem is violated in this case depends on how time and the consumption of goods interact.[9] A distinction can be made between consumption time that is substitutable for leisure and that is substitutable for labor (Boadway and Gahvari 2006). In the former case, time spent consuming gives pleasure (attending a concert), while in the latter it is unpleasant (scrubbing floors). To make a clearcut distinction, consider the extreme cases where consumption time is perfectly substitutable for either labor or leisure.

If time spent consuming all n goods is a perfect substitute for leisure, utility can be written $u(x_1, \ldots, x_n, x_0 + \sum a_i x_i, \ell)$. Using the time constraint, we can rewrite this as $u(x_1, \ldots, x_n, h - \ell, \ell)$, or equivalently (and again with some abuse of notation) as simply $u(x_1, \ldots, x_n, \ell)$. The household budget constraint can be written $\sum q_i x_i = w\ell - T(w\ell)$, where q_i are consumer prices and $T(w\ell)$ is the nonlinear tax function. Effectively, time spent consuming can be suppressed from the problem and the standard optimal tax analysis applies. In particular, if goods are weakly separable from the various uses of time in the utility function, that is, $u(f(x_1, \ldots, x_n), x_0 + \sum a_i x_i, \ell)$, the Atkinson–Stiglitz theorem applies and no differential commodity taxes are required.

---

9. Christiansen (1984) has also studied the applicability of the Atkinson–Stiglitz theorem in a simple version of the Becker model in which one good is a leisure-using good and the other is not. He finds that a tax on the leisure-using good is warranted if the good and leisure are strong technical complements.

At the other extreme, suppose that all consumption time is a perfect substitute for labor. In this case, using the time constraint, we have utility take the form $u(x_1, \ldots, x_n, x_0, \ell + \sum a_i x_i) = u(x_1, \ldots, x_n, x_0, h - x_0)$. Now the household budget constraint (in terms of leisure rather than labor in this case) can be written, using the time constraint, as $\sum q_i x_i = w(h - x_0 - \sum a_i x_i) - T(h - x_0 - \sum a_i x_i)$.[10] As Boadway and Gahvari (2006) show using methods analogous to earlier, even with weakly separable preferences, the Atkinson–Stiglitz theorem does not apply in this case. A differential commodity tax should be used alongside optimal nonlinear taxes, with higher tax rates imposed on goods with a higher time requirement a_i.

It is apparent that the Atkinson–Stiglitz theorem will also generally fail if consumption time is only an imperfect substitute for labor, and again a relatively high tax should be placed on goods with a higher time requirement. The theorem will likewise fail if time spent consuming is an imperfect substitute for leisure, although the relative tax rates are a bit more complicated in this case.

Externalities

Externalities provide an independent reason for commodity taxes besides revenue raising. Even in a first-best setting with optimal personal lump-sum taxes, Pigouvian taxes would be applied to commodities whose use in production or consumption emits negative externalities. The question is what happens to corrective taxes in a second-best world, and more generally to other commodity taxes. Does some version of the Atkinson–Stiglitz theorem continue to apply? The issue of second-best commodity taxes in the presence of externalities has been around at least since the seminal paper by Sandmo (1975). More recently much attention was devoted to the implications of second-best considerations for the double-dividend hypothesis (Bovenberg and de Mooij 1994; Auerbach and Hines 2002; Cremer, Gahvari, and Ladoux 2001; and Boadway and Tremblay 2008). The issue has taken on greater relevance with interest in carbon taxation schemes to address global warming.

Consider the simple case where the consumption of one of the n goods, say good x_1, emits a negative externality on all individuals. The

---

10. In the representative consumer case with only commodity taxes, the constraint can be written $\sum \tilde{q}_i x_i = w(h - x_0)$, where $\tilde{q}_i = 1 + t_i + w a_i$ is the effective price of good i, including the unit producer price, the per unit tax rate t_i and the time cost. The effect of consumption time is to increase the optimal Ramsey tax rates more for goods with a higher time cost. See Gahvari and Yang (1993) and Kleven (2004) for an analysis of this case.

separable utility function in our otherwise standard multi-commodity model may now be written $u(f(x_1, \ldots, x_n), x_0, e(X_1))$, where $e(X_1)$ is the quality of the environment and is decreasing in aggregate consumption of the "dirty" good denoted X_1. Thus, if p is the population indexed by j, then $X_1 = \sum_{j=1}^{p} x_1^j$.

In a first-best world, the optimal corrective, or Pigouvian, tax t_c is set equal to the sum of the marginal damages to all individuals evaluated at their own marginal utilities of income, or

$$t_c = \sum_{j=1}^{p} \frac{1}{\alpha^j} \frac{\partial u^j}{\partial e} e'(X_1),$$

where α^j is the marginal utility of income of individual j. The government imposes redistributive lump-sum taxes to equalize the marginal social utilities of income among all individuals. Thus, if the social welfare function is a weighted sum of individual utilities, $\sum \rho^j u(f(x_1^j, \ldots, x_n^j), x_0^j, e(X_1))$, lump-sum redistributive taxes would equate $\rho^j \alpha^j = \rho^k \alpha^k$ for all j, k.

In a second-best world where the government observes only individual incomes and market transactions, an optimal nonlinear income tax can be used in addition to commodity taxes. A restrictive and natural form of the Atkinson–Stiglitz theorem applies. Given a weakly separable utility function of the form above, no differential taxes should be applied to nonpolluting goods $x_2, \ldots, x_n$ (Cremer, Gahvari, and Ladoux 1998).[11] The tax on the dirty good x_1 plays a dual role, partly as a Pigouvian corrective tax and partly as a component of the commodity tax system used for revenue-raising purposes. Although it is not possible to separate these two roles in general, it is useful to use as a benchmark for the latter the same uniform tax as on the nonpolluting goods. The residual optimal tax on x_1 can then be regarded as the corrective component. Given this interpretation, the form of the corrective tax differs from the first-best Pigouvian tax. The government is now unable to equate marginal social utilities of income among individuals since lump-sum redistributive taxes are no longer available, and the corrective tax takes this into account. In particular, the corrective tax equals the sum of marginal social damages evaluated at the marginal utility of government revenue, where the latter is an average of marginal social utilities of income (Boadway and Tremblay 2008).

---

11. Pirttilä and Tuomala (1997) also investigate the design of tax and environmental policies in a second-best world.

For example, consider the simple case where there are two skill types, $w_2 > w_1$, whose populations are n_1 and n_2. Assume that the social welfare function is utilitarian, so that $\rho_1 = \rho_2$. The tax on good x_1 is given by $t_1 = t + t_c$, where t is the tax rate imposed on the nonpolluting goods, and t_c is the corrective component, given by

$$t_c = n_1 \frac{1}{\lambda} \frac{\partial u^1}{\partial e} e'(X_1) + n_2 \frac{1}{\lambda} \frac{\partial u^2}{\partial e} e'(X_1).$$

In the second-best optimum, marginal utilities are not equated across individuals as they would be in the first-best utilitarian optimum. Instead, we can show that $\alpha^1 > \lambda > \alpha^2$, which is intuitively plausible. Equivalently, relative to the first-best corrective tax, the second-best corrective tax puts more weight on the marginal social damages of low-wage persons than high-wage persons. This is reminiscent of a result of Sandmo (2006) for global externalities in the absence of optimal international income transfers.

If preferences are not weakly separable in the n goods, so the Atkinson–Stiglitz theorem would otherwise not apply, the optimal taxes on nonpolluting goods would no longer be uniform: higher taxes would apply on goods more substitutable with leisure. This would also be reflected in the tax rate on the polluting good x_1. It would include not only a corrective component along the lines just discussed but also a component reflecting the relative complementarity of x_1 with leisure compared with the other $n - 1$ goods, as in Cremer, Gahvari, and Ladoux (1998).

Skills Are Imperfect Substitutes

The basic optimal income tax model of Mirrlees (1971) assumes that workers of different skills are perfect substitutes in production. Effectively, different skills lead to different effective units of labor supply for each hour worked. As Stiglitz (1982) pointed out, this assumption has a bearing on the optimal income tax rate structure. He showed that in a two-skill-type model if high- and low-skilled workers are imperfect substitutes, the optimal marginal tax rate on the high-skilled persons should be negative. Intuitively, a negative marginal tax rate increases labor supply by the high-skilled persons, and this induces an increase in the low-skilled wage rate in general equilibrium as the ratio of high- to low-skilled labor rises.

Extending this version of the optimal income tax model to include more than one good, Naito (1999) showed that the Atkinson–Stiglitz theorem may no longer apply. In particular, if the production of different goods uses different ratios of skilled and unskilled labor, a differential tax on the good that is most skill-intensive will increase the ratio of wage rates in favor of the unskilled. The decline in demand resulting from the tax on the skill-intensive good will create an excess supply for the high-skilled by releasing a relatively large amount of skilled labor into the workforce to be absorbed by less skill-intensive firms. A small tax will have only a second-order distortionary effect, but the induced change in wage rates will have a first-order welfare effect.

Subsequently Saez (2004) showed, in a striking result, that this breakdown in the Atkinson–Stiglitz theorem hinges on the labor supply assumption used in the standard optimal income tax model. Naito and Stiglitz, following Mirrlees, assume that labor variability resulting from changes in the after-tax wage consists entirely of changes in the amount of time worked. The marginal tax rate affects labor supply through its effect on effort. Saez refers to this as the short-run labor supply response. He shows that if workers are also allowed to choose occupations—the long-run labor response—the Atkinson–Stiglitz theorem applies, even if relative wages are endogenous.

The intuition leading to the restoration of the Atkinson–Stiglitz theorem by Saez is as follows. In the Stiglitz and Naito models of endogenous wage rates, workers can only change their income by varying their effort, which is what Saez refers to as the short-run response. In these circumstances the government can use differential commodity taxes to increase the wage of low-skilled workers without violating the incentive constraint of the high-skilled. Saez's model incorporates a long-run response whereby workers are free to switch occupations: high-skilled workers can choose to work in low-skilled jobs and earn the same incomes as the latter. Given this possibility, an indirect tax aimed at increasing low-skilled wages will induce high-skilled workers to switch occupations. In these circumstances there is no advantage to using commodity taxes in addition to a nonlinear income tax to redistribute income, so the Atkinson–Stiglitz theorem applies.

A further implication of Saez's occupational choice approach is that the formulas for the optimal nonlinear income tax do not depend explicitly on the degree of substitution between high- and low-skilled labor in the production function as they do in Stern (1982) and Stiglitz (1982). The difference in results can be explained by each model being a distinct interpretation of the Mirrlees (1971) model. If the Mirrlees model is interpreted as an hours of work model where skills are fixed, then the optimal tax formulas are not robust to the relaxation of perfect substitutability as in Stern (1982) and Stiglitz (1982). However, if the Mirrlees model is interpreted as an occupational choice model, where individuals choose over a continuum of occupations, the degree of substitutability has no bearing on the optimal tax formulas.

Wage Uncertainty

Cremer and Gahvari (1995) have considered the Atkinson–Stiglitz theorem in an economy in which wage rates are uncertain, and individuals must make some consumption decisions before they know their wage rate. Given the sequencing of decisions, one might think that a dynamic approach would be appropriate. However, the intuition of their result can be shown in a static model in which decisions are taken sequentially. The setting is similar to that used by Low and Maldoom (2004), discussed later to study the effect of uncertainty on the progressivity of the income tax. (Below we return to optimal non-linear income taxation in an explicitly dynamic, uncertain setting.) Individuals are identical ex ante but face uncertain wage rates. There are some goods that must be purchased before the uncertainty is revealed—characterized as housing and other consumer durables— while other goods are purchased and labor supplied after wage rates are known. The government can impose a nonlinear tax on ex post incomes, as well as commodity taxes on consumer purchases when they are made. If all goods' purchases are made ex post, so that there are no durables, the government's problem would be identical to the standard Atkinson and Stiglitz (1976, 1980) problem and the Atkinson–Stiglitz theorem would apply: no differential commodity taxes are necessary if goods are weakly separable from leisure in the utility function.

However, when some goods are purchased before uncertainty is resolved, the Atkinson–Stiglitz theorem fails. Although no differential taxation is called for among goods purchased ex post, those goods purchased ex ante bear a different tax. As Cremer and Gahvari show, the latter will typically bear a lower tax rate. The intuition is that inducing all persons to increase their consumption of the durable good makes it more difficult for those who turn out to have higher skills ex post to mimic those with low skills, since ex post consumption requirements are higher. Cremer and Gahvari argue that this provides some justification for the preferential treatment that is offered to housing and consumer durables in many income tax systems: in both cases the imputed rent to the consumer goes untaxed. This argument is closely related to those in favor of taxing capital income in a dynamic setting when there is wage uncertainty, which is discussed below (Golosov, Tsyvinski, and Werning 2007; Diamond 2007).

Dynamic Optimal Nonlinear Taxation
The Mirrlees optimal nonlinear income tax model is a static one. Recently the "new dynamic public finance" literature has extended the Mirrlees model to an intertemporal setting in which heterogeneous households live for several (maybe infinite!) periods, consume and supply labor in each period, and carry saving from one period to the next. (See Golosov, Tsyvinski, and Werning 2007 for a selected survey of results using simple models.) The dynamic analogue of the Atkinson–Stiglitz theorem has been investigated in these models by Golosov, Kocherlakota, and Tsyvinski (2003). They consider the case where lifetime utility is the discounted sum of per period utilities, where the latter are weakly separable functions of labor and the vector of per period consumption. The skill distribution evolves arbitrarily with each period, and a person's own skill level in each period is revealed privately at the beginning of the period. The government maximizes an intertemporal social welfare function which is the weighted sum of individual lifetime utilities with (arbitrary) weights based on initial skills. The government is constrained by a per period resource constraint, and by a set of incentive constraints. The latter reflect the fact that the government can condition policy in each period on the full history of information learned in all previous periods (including past skill levels). Thus individual incentive constraints apply on a lifetime basis: each person must weakly prefer his lifetime consumption–income allocation to that of any other. The problem is solved using a direct mechanism by which the government chooses consumption bundles and income for all households in each period. It is important to note that the government can commit ex ante to the direct mechanism that solves the social planning problem, or equivalently to an optimal tax system.

Golosov, Kocherlakota, and Tsyvinski focus on two dimensions of the problem. One is the characterization of so-called intertemporal wedges—the extent and direction of distortions of intertemporal consumption/saving decisions that influence the tax on savings or capital income. We return to that below. Our immediate interest is in the taxation of goods in each period. The authors show that the per period analogue of the Atkinson–Stiglitz theorem applies. In each period the marginal rate of substitution between any pair of goods equals its marginal rate of transformation for all persons. Thus indirect taxation can be dispensed with. The intuition is very much similar to the static case.

This result does, of course, rely on some heroic assumptions, such as full commitment by the government and a direct tax system that at any point in time depends on past history. Nonetheless, it is not obvious that relaxing these assumptions would affect the case for uniform commodity taxation.

These various extensions indicate the richness as well as the shortfalls of the Atkinson–Stiglitz theorem as a benchmark in the optimal tax literature. One is left with a reasonable strong case for a simple commodity tax system with uniform rates. The case for deviating from uniformity rests on the presumption that some goods are more complementary with leisure than others, and there is little a priori reason to suppose that will be the case for particular goods. The mere fact that some goods are luxuries while others are necessities does not generally imply complement–substitute biases. The commonplace argument, often found in actual VAT systems, that necessities should bear lower tax rates than luxuries is not supported by the theory. While equity arguments alone might support that point of view, efficiency arguments tend to go the other way. The theory suggests relying on the direct tax system for redistribution.

As we will see below, the Atkinson–Stiglitz theorem also has interpretive implications for direct taxation, particularly for the treatment of capital income. First, we turn to the next important general result from the optimal tax literature, which is also one that has implications for the form of the commodity tax system.

3.2 Production Efficiency: Implications and Caveats

The majority of transactions in a modern economy are between firms (including public firms) for the purchase of intermediate inputs and capital goods. An important question is whether and how such transactions should be taxed. In their classic paper on optimal commodity taxation in a static general equilibrium world with heterogeneous individuals, Diamond and Mirrlees (1971) showed that if commodity taxes were imposed optimally and all pure profits were taxed, production should be efficient, which we can refer to as the *production efficiency theorem*. The argument clearly applies to the case with nonlinear income taxes as well. To the extent that this theorem is valid in more realistic settings, it has potentially important policy implications, complementing those of the subsequent Atkinson–Stiglitz theorem just discussed.

The intuition of the production efficiency theorem is quite straightforward. If the economy is operating inside the production possibilities frontier, in principle more of some goods could be produced without producing less of others. Producing more of some goods without producing less of others should be a good thing, and in a first-best world could lead to a Pareto improvement if accompanied by appropriate lump-sum tax changes. The issue is whether production efficiency is also desired in a second-best setting when the government does not have access to lump-sum taxes. Diamond and Mirrlees' answer is yes, and the intuition is as follows. Given that the government controls all commodity taxes, it effectively controls consumer prices. Moreover, if pure profits are taxed fully, individuals' utility depends only on consumer prices. In particular, a reduction in the price of a good that is being consumed by all individuals will increase the utility of all. Given this, the government can reform taxes such that the price of such a good falls, causing the demand for that commodity and utility to rise. Since the economy is inside the production possibilities frontier, resources can be reallocated to meet that demand—and taxes adjusted to accommodate the change in producer prices from the reallocation—without reducing the supply of any other good. Consumers are therefore better off, so a Pareto improvement has occurred.

More formally, the argument is as follows. Let $v^j(\mathbf{q})$ be person j's indirect utility function obtained as the value function for the problem of maximizing utility $u(\mathbf{x}^j)$ subject to the budget constraint $\sum_{i=1}^{n} q_i x_i^j = q_0^j(h - x_o^j)$, where we assume all consumers face the same goods prices, so exchange efficiency is satisfied, but they may face different leisure (or labor) prices, q_0^j.[12] Then, let $\mathbf{y}^k \in \mathbf{Y}^k$ be producer k's vector of production, where $\mathbf{Y}^k$ is k's feasible production set, which can then be used to satisfy both private demands $\mathbf{x}^j$ and commodities used by the public sector, denoted $\mathbf{g}$. We assume for now that the vector $\mathbf{g}$ includes only private commodities produced for the public sector (or

---

12. There could also be a uniform poll subsidy obtained by all persons, though that would not affect the result.

alternatively produced by public sector producers), not public goods. Market clearing implies the resource constraint $\sum_j x^j + \mathbf{g} = \sum_k \mathbf{y}^k \in \sum_k \mathbf{Y}^k$. The chosen production vector determines the set of relative producer prices $\mathbf{p}^k$, which we take to be competitively determined so that they correspond with relative marginal costs (marginal rates of transformation). Given that consumer demands are homogeneous of degree zero in consumer prices $\mathbf{q}$, and production for each producer is homogeneous of degree zero in $\mathbf{p}^k$, consumer and producer prices can be normalized independently. Equivalently, commodity taxes can be normalized by, say, setting one of them to zero. The government maximizes some social welfare function $W(v^1(\mathbf{q}), \ldots, v^h(\mathbf{q}))$ subject to the resource constraint.

Suppose now that $\sum \mathbf{y}^k$ lies in the interior of $\sum \mathbf{Y}^k$; that is, production is inefficient, so $\mathbf{p}^k$ differs across producers. It is possible to increase the output of some commodities without reducing the output of any others. Since the government can choose $\mathbf{q}$ independently of $\mathbf{p}^k$, it can reduce the price for some good that has a positive net demand by consumers, say, q_i. Social welfare will therefore rise by the envelope theorem, and given the initial production inefficiency, the increase of production is feasible. This implies that in an optimum, $\sum \mathbf{y}^k$ must be on the boundary of $\sum \mathbf{Y}^k$. In other words, all producers face the same producer prices ($\mathbf{p}^k = \mathbf{p}$ for all producers k).

Note the importance of taxing pure profits at a 100 percent rate. In an economy where individuals own the shares in firms, any untaxed pure profits will accrue to them. Therefore individual utilities will depend not only on consumer prices but also on the distribution of untaxed pure profits, and correspondingly on producer prices. The intuition above then fails. Starting with production inefficiency, a reduction in the consumer price of a good that all persons consume will initially cause their utility to rise, but the reallocation of production that makes it possible to meet the increased demand without reducing the output of other goods will generally cause the pattern of profits to change. In these circumstances one cannot be certain that a Pareto improvement is possible. If the government could implement firm-specific profit taxes, it could always ensure that a move to the production frontier is Pareto-improving provided it accompanied the change in commodity taxes with changes in firm-specific profit taxes (Dasgupta and Stiglitz 1972; Mirrlees 1972b; Hahn 1973). However, that is a rather tall order. If the government can only tax profits at a constant rate, the production efficiency theorem will generally fail, except under some specific patterns of share ownership by individuals (Blackorby and Murty 2009). Unfortunately, if the production efficiency theorem is violated, it will generally be difficult to know which producer taxes should be relatively high. One might have to fall back on the principle of insufficient reason and simply assume production efficiency.

Two implications of the production efficiency theorem immediately stand out. The first is that in a second-best optimum, no differential taxes should be imposed on intermediate inputs of different firms. This can be assured by a VAT system that, although it taxes all transactions, gives full credit to firms' purchases. The same effect can obviously be achieved by a single-stage retail sales tax that applies on consumer purchases alone. However, it is practically impossible for sellers who charge the tax to distinguish consumers from firms. So, despite the extra compliance cost associated with the much greater number of transactions taxed under a VAT, the crediting system does preserve production efficiency. It also apparently has some value in creating a paper trail of transactions that can be used to monitor compliance.

The second implication arises from the fact that production efficiency should apply across both private and public sectors of the economy. That is, relative producer prices (marginal rates of technical substitution) should be the same for private and public producers. This has the implication, exploited by Little and Mirrlees (1974), that in evaluating public projects prices used to value inputs purchased (or sold) in the market by the public sector (so-called shadow prices) should be producer prices. This contrasts with the more complicated shadow pricing rules developed by Harberger (1971), Dasgupta, Marglin, and Sen (1972) among others that attempt to adjust prices used to evaluate public projects to compensate for tax distortions in private markets.[13]

These implications for evaluating public projects applies for private commodities used or produced in the public sector. Suppose that public goods are produced as well. Clearly, they should be produced efficiently, but the rule determining what quantity of public goods to produce cannot itself be deduced from production efficiency. Since public goods must be financed by tax revenues, the deadweight loss

13. This contrast might be more apparent than real. Dasgupta (1972) and Boadway (1975) showed how weighted-average shadow pricing rules could be converted to world prices by a change in price normalization.

associated with raising those revenues must generally be taken into account in determining the decision rule for public goods, even if taxes are levied optimally (Atkinson and Stern 1974). We will see in the next chapter such decision rules, which involve the marginal cost of public funds indicating the cost of raising incremental amounts of tax revenue when a distorting tax system is in place. These rules determine how to allocate society's resources between the public and private sectors, but do not affect the validity of the production efficiency theorem.

Like the Atkinson–Stiglitz theorem, the production efficiency theorem serves as a useful benchmark. It leads to appealing and simple policy implications when it applies, and serves as a basis for judging outcomes in more realistic settings. As a fallback position, it has some attraction, if only because, as mentioned, it is not obvious in which ways one should deviate from production efficiency in the real world. There are, however, several caveats to its applicability that are worth noting explicitly.

The first is that taxes are almost certainly far from optimal. In the Diamond–Mirrlees world where only commodity taxes are used, they may be set nonoptimally if only because there may be restrictions on the number of tax rates that apply to the different commodities. For example, in the typical VAT system, there is a uniform rate applying to most goods and services, with different rates applying to a limited number of other commodity groups, such as through zero rating or exemption. Clearly, the prerequisites of the production efficiency condition are violated assuming that the VAT rate structure is not optimal, and the same applies in the more general setting with nonlinear income taxes. The practical policy implications of that violation are, however, far from clear. Presumably, there will be some third-best tax policy that involves imposing differential taxes on commodities used in the production process, but no clear qualitative guidelines have been proposed for what determines the nature of the production distortion.

The problem is analogous to the so-called piecemeal policy problem in classical second-best analysis posed by Lipsey and Lancaster (1956–57). They pointed out that in a setting where some markets are distorted because of monopoly, tariffs, taxes, and so on, it will generally not be optimal to set consumer prices equal to (or even proportional to) producer prices in other markets. One can derive circumstances in representative individual settings in which it is efficient to pursue piecemeal (nondistorting) policies in some sectors, for example, if some separability conditions (i.e., implicit separability) between distorted and nondistorted commodities are satisfied (Boadway and Harris 1977; Jewitt 1981; Blackorby, Davidson, and Schworm 1991a). But, in economies with heterogeneous individuals, additional aggregation conditions are required, but they are highly unlikely to be satisfied (Blackorby, Davidson, and Schworm 1991b). One is then left with agnostic results for piecemeal policy in the classical second-best context, and for tax policy in the optimal tax context. It is tempting to adopt the fallback position that the production efficiency theorem should be adopted in these less favorable circumstances. The principle of insufficient reason applies again here with some force since one does not know which way to deviate, and the expected efficiency costs of deviating are positive because of the convex nature of welfare costs of distortions.

There are in fact some circumstances in which violations of production efficiency are unambiguous. Newbery (1986) showed a rather remarkable result. Suppose that commodities can be used both as final consumption goods and as inputs into production. Suppose that the consumption of only a subset of commodities can be taxed optimally. Newbery showed that starting from the case where no production taxes are in effect, imposing a tax on the production of one of the untaxed commodities will be social welfare improving. Moreover imposing a tax on the production of one of the commodities whose consumption is already being taxed will also be welfare improving. These results apply with almost no important restrictions (apart from the fact that taxes are being imposed optimally on a subset of commodities). One possible implication of the analysis is that in a world in which a subset of commodities is in an informal nontaxed sector, it will be optimal to impose some taxes on production (or tariffs).

One recent instance where the implications of restricted policy instruments have been important concerns the debate over the best tax structure for developing countries. In this context the restriction on taxes arises largely from the existence of a large informal sector in which producers do not register as taxpayers. Emran and Stiglitz (2005) argued provocatively that given this informal sector, reliance on trade taxes for most of their revenue needs might be more efficient that adopting a VAT as advocated by international organizations. This was based on the idea that informal traders could not avoid paying trade taxes, which are collected at a small number of border points, but they were outside the VAT net. This was disputed by Keen (2008), who pointed out that informal traders were in fact paying VAT on their intermediate input purchases (and could not claim a rebate), and this in reasonable circumstances could outweigh the alleged advantage of trade taxes. The issue was taken up by Boadway and Sato (2009) in a small open economy version of a Diamond and Mirrlees (1971) world with intermediate inputs and trade taxes, with an informal sector of endogenous size, and without full taxation of economic profits. They argued that both trade taxes and VATs had advantages and disadvantages. For example, the VAT unlike trade taxes preserved production efficiency in the formal sector, whereas trade taxes served to tax economic rents or profits indirectly, something the VAT did not do. In principle, either revenue regime could dominate, although the VAT would provide the government with a greater incentive to improve tax administration.

Policy agnosticism also applies when other caveats are considered. As mentioned, the production efficiency theorem requires that economic or pure profits be fully taxed, and it is apparent that this is not achieved in practice. For whatever reason, governments do not explicitly try to tax away pure profits, despite the fact that there are possible fiscal instruments for doing so, as discussed below. There may be various reasons for this. Governments may face informational constraints that preclude learning about firm profits because of the need to rely on self-reporting. They may worry about mobility of the factors generating pure profits. Or, there may be institutional factors such as property rights or political constraints that preclude full profit taxation. Whatever the reason, the existence of untaxed pure profits implies that production efficiency is generally not desired for the reasons mentioned above, so the production efficiency theorem fails. But, as with other restrictions on taxes mentioned above, it is not entirely clear how production efficiency should be violated on this account. As one example, however, taxes on business inputs might be desired to the extent that they indirectly impinge on pure profits (Boadway and Sato 2009).

It may also be efficient to violate production efficiency if workers of different skills are imperfect substitutes in production. Naito (1999) illustrated this for a model consisting of a public and a private sector. The public sector can affect the ratio of unskilled to skilled wages by increasing its relative demand for unskilled labor, even if this causes production inefficiency between the public and private sectors. As in the case of the Atkinson–Stiglitz theorem discussed above, Saez (2004) showed that this argument for deviating from production efficiency would be vitiated if workers could freely choose their occupations. The

Naito argument relies on the fact that if the government can indirectly affect the ratio of unskilled to skilled wage rates, this can make the unskilled better off without violating the incentive constraints on the skilled. However, if the skilled can choose to work in unskilled occupations, measures that increase the unskilled wage rate will induce skilled workers to take unskilled jobs, thereby defeating the purpose of the policy, which is to improve the lot of low-skilled persons. The implication is that measures that interfere with production efficiency are not necessary to the extent that labor variability takes the form of occupational choice.

Somewhat related, Blackorby and Brett (2004) show that production inefficiency is optimal if wages are for some reason fixed and the production technology is strictly concave. However, the motivation for assuming fixed wages in this context is not at all clear.

Finally, the production efficiency theorem was developed by Diamond and Mirrlees for the case of a national economy, whether open or not. There has been a tendency for policy purposes to extend the reach of the theorem to an international context. Keen and Wildasin (2004) identify three international tax policy prescriptions that have been rationalized by the production efficiency theorem: the destination-based VAT, residence-based capital income taxes, and free trade. All three preserve common relative producer prices for traded commodities across countries, which is the condition for production efficiency. As they point out, these international policy prescriptions are unfounded since the production efficiency theorem has only been shown for production within a country rather than between. They investigate the conditions for Pareto efficiency in an international economy, allowing for country-specific commodity taxes and tariffs, full taxation of profits on an origin basis, and crucially country-specific budget constraints. They show that production efficiency is generally not desirable in this setting, and attribute this result mainly to the requirement for country-by-country budget balance rather than a single international budget constraint, or equivalently, the absence of international transfers. More generally, this implies that production efficiency cannot be used to validate the three policy prescriptions.[14] The danger, as with other findings that social values are generally not reflected

---

14. A similar result in a different context is reported in Sandmo (2006). He shows that in the absence of international transfers, the optimal carbon tax should be higher in high-income countries than in low-income countries, implying global inefficiency in abatements.

properly in market prices in a second-best setting, is that the finding might lend support to interventionist policies that would only be warranted in specific circumstances.

Perhaps one need not be quite so pessimistic when considering the effects of the violation of the production efficiency theorem for production efficiency across the public and private sectors. Shadow-pricing techniques have been devised to take account of distortions in the market economy in public sector project evaluation methods. These methods are outlined in detail by Drèze and Stern (1987), as well as by the other works just cited, and are suitable for general contexts.

3.3 Capital Taxation and the Personal Tax Base

One of the main tax policy issues is the choice of a base for the personal tax. It was the preoccupation of key tax reform reports, such as the US Treasury (1977), the Meade Report (1978), and the President's Advisory Panel on Federal Tax Reform (2005). The main issue differentiating alternative proposals is the treatment of capital income, and this is borne out in the recent background study by Banks and Diamond (2010) for the Mirrlees Review in the United Kingdom. As we have discussed earlier, the treatment of capital income is what distinguishes the three main contenders for the personal tax base—income, consumption and dual income—as well as what distinguishes other broad-based taxes, such as VAT and payroll taxes, from personal taxes. Considerable insight has been gained into the optimal tax treatment of capital income from results in static optimal tax analysis, particularly the Corlett–Hague theorem and the Atkinson–Stiglitz theorem. Indeed both the US Treasury Blueprints and the Meade Report relied for their analytical underpinnings on these results, particularly the Corlett–Hague theorem. At the same time the tax treatment of capital income raises important additional issues of a dynamic nature that deserve special attention, and these have been treated by a separate literature. These have yielded insights that have informed the more recent normative tax policy literature. In this subsection, I draw attention to some of these insights.

It is useful to distinguish between results derived in models of linear taxation, where the focus is largely on efficiency, from those involving nonlinear income taxation. Unique insights into the tax treatment of capital income come from each of these perspectives.

3.3.1 Linear Taxation in a Dynamic Setting

The dynamic analogue of the Ramsey optimal tax problem involves treating goods consumed in different time periods as different goods. We can first learn something from the two-period equivalent of the Corlett–Hague model of a representative individual who lives for two periods of equal length and whose utility depends on three goods: first-period consumption (x_1), second-period consumption (x_2), and first-period leisure (x_0). The second period can be thought of as retirement. Leisure is naturally also enjoyed in retirement, but it is fixed and not a matter of choice, so can be suppressed. In the first period, the individual makes a labor–leisure choice as well as a saving decision, while in the second period, consumption is financed by interest-augmented saving. Assume initially that capital markets are perfect, there is no uncertainty, individuals have perfect foresight, and the government chooses its taxes at the beginning of the first period to maximize the representative individual's utility subject to a given revenue requirement in present value terms.

As there are three goods, there are two relative prices and the government can control them using two taxes. These can be taxes on first- and second-period consumption, or taxes on wage income and capital income, or other combinations. Taking the first case for illustration, it is clear that the Corlett–Hague theorem applies directly. The consumption tax should be higher on the good that is most complementary with (first-period) leisure.

This reasoning has a number of implications. If the intertemporal utility function takes the weakly separable form, $u(f(x_1, x_2), x_0)$, with $f(x_1, x_2)$ homothetic, proportional consumption taxation is efficient. Equivalently wage taxation alone is efficient since in this context a proportional wage tax is equivalent to a uniform goods tax system that yields the same present value of revenue. Alternatively, if second-period consumption is more complementary with leisure, it should face a higher tax. In principle, this could be achieved by a differential commodity tax system, but in practice, this is virtually impossible to implement by indirect taxation. It is simply not feasible to impose a higher indirect tax on goods consumed by older individuals. Instead, the differential taxation of second-period consumption, if desirable, can be achieved by a wage tax combined with a tax on capital income, since the latter constitutes a differential tax on second-period consumption.

As an aside, the indeterminacy of the exact tax structure even in this simple model is a first illustration of the *implementation problem*. An optimal tax outcome can be characterized by an allocation of resources and a set of "wedges" showing how relative consumer evaluations (marginal rates of substitution) or relative consumer prices q_i/q_j should differ from marginal rates of transformation, or relative producer prices p_i/p_j, on the production side. In an intertemporal setting there are different ways of implementing these relative price wedges using a tax system. In particular, a relative price wedge applying on the intertemporal margin need not imply a tax on capital income (Kocherlakota 2004). The same effect can be achieved by other taxes or combinations of taxes, such as differential taxes on consumption in different periods as the above example illustrates. Nonetheless, it is often useful for pedagogical purposes to equate intertemporal wedges with taxes on saving or capital income. Equivalently it is useful to infer that there need be no tax on capital income if the intertemporal wedge is zero.

It might be thought that first-period consumption should be more complementary with variable leisure, which also occurs in the first period. After all, it takes time to consume, so first-period leisure and first-period consumption naturally go together. If that were the case, the tax system would treat second-period consumption preferentially, which is equivalent to a subsidy on saving. However, that characterization of preferences is by no means certain. If leisure is enjoyed for its own sake and so is consumption, there is no apparent reason based on pure preferences, that the two should be complementary. In general, it does not seem obvious whether first- or second-period consumption should be more complementary with first-period leisure.

This simple three-good, two-period model illustrates the difficulties of constructing an efficiency case for or against capital income taxation. There is no presumption that second-period consumption will be more of a complement with first-period leisure than is first-period consumption. On the contrary, one could expect the opposite. Even if second-period consumption is more complementary with leisure, it is highly unlikely that the extent of complementarity will be such that capital income and labor income be taxed at the same rate. In other words, the case for income taxation as well as consumption taxation is ambiguous at best.[15] The case for a dual income tax system that sets

---

15. However, if it is equally likely that x_2 will be a substitute or complement with x_0, expected welfare would be maximized by taxing x_1 and x_2 at the same rate. That is because deadweight loss is, roughly speaking, strictly convex in the tax rate.

the tax rate on capital income separately from that on labor income might be more tenable. (Note that a dual income tax system can be implemented either directly by a combination of taxes on labor and capital income or indirectly by a tax mix consisting of a uniform tax on first- and second-period consumption combined with an income tax system that taxes capital and labor income at the same rate.) However, it is not clear what the tax rate on capital income should be, or even if it should be positive. This agnosticism is further reinforced when we add more complications to the simple dynamic model, some of which enhance the case for capital taxation, while others detract from it.

Consider first the case where the above two-period model with three goods is embedded into an overlapping generations model. Optimal second-best policy now involves using intergenerational transfers alongside taxes on goods in the first and second period of each life cycle to maximize an intergenerational social welfare function. Intergenerational transfers can equivalently be seen as influencing the rate of capital accumulation to steer the economy's capital–labor ratio toward its optimal long-run level. Suppose, however, that such transfers are not available, and that the only policy instruments the government has at its disposal are capital and labor income taxes. Atkinson and Sandmo (1980) and King (1980) independently demonstrate that, if the interest rate exceeds the rate of growth of the economy so that the capital–labor ratio is too low from a long-run perspective, the usual Corlett–Hague-type tax structure should be augmented by a term that calls for an increase in the tax on capital income.[16] The reason is that a revenue-neutral shift from wage taxation to capital income taxation encourages saving, despite the relative price effect, since capital income tax is collected in the second period of the life cycle while labor income tax is collected entirely in the first period. Of course, this effect would be mitigated to the extent that consumption taxes are used as well, since consumption taxes generate more saving than labor income taxes, based again on life-cycle timing effects (Summers 1981). If intergenerational transfers are allowed, such as public debt, the corrective term disappears and the Corlett-Hague tax structure applies, since the capital stock can now be controlled independently (Pestieau 1974).

---

16. This result relies on individual preferences taking a Cobb–Douglas form. Pestieau (1974) makes a similar point in a more general model that includes public investment.

Things become more complicated when variable labor also occurs in the second period. Consider the taxation of a representative household in this context with two periods and four commodities: a consumption good and leisure in each period. In such a setting there are at least five potential types of taxes: commodity taxation in each period, labor income taxation in each period, and capital income taxation. However, since there are only three relative prices, only three taxes need be used from among the five possible. If both labor and commodity taxation can be made age-specific, capital income taxation can be dispensed with entirely. However, if one or the other cannot be age-specific, capital income taxation will be required except under particular circumstances. That is because there are now two intertemporal wedges: one on goods consumed in the two periods, and one on leisure.

Suppose, for example, that commodity taxes cannot be differentiated over time, which is reasonable, but labor income taxes can. Then no capital income tax is needed if it is optimal to tax the consumption good uniformly over time. This will be the case, for example, if the utility function takes the form $u(f(x_1, x_2), \ell_1, \ell_2)$ with $f(\cdot)$ homothetic.[17] Alternatively, if there are no taxes on labor income, but differential taxes on goods, the optimal tax on capital income is zero if it is optimal to tax labor income in the two periods at the same rate. The sufficient condition for this is that the utility function be separable in first- and second-period leisure, and homothetic in the latter two variables.[18]

If neither wage nor consumption taxes can be varied over time, the second-best optimal tax structure can generally not be implemented except in special circumstances. However, the problem has a particularly simple and relevant solution if (1) the utility discount factor equals the interest rate, (2) the wage rate is the same in both periods, and (3) preferences are additively separable and identical over time, as is often assumed, so that $u(x_1, x_2, \ell_1, \ell_2) = u(x_1, \ell_1) + \beta u(x_2, \ell_2)$. In this case it is optimal not to tax capital income, and to have time-independent tax rates, whether consumption or labor income taxes

17. More generally, it will be optimal to tax consumption uniformly over time if the individual expenditure function can be written in the following implicitly separable form: $e(A(q_1, q_2, u), (1 - t_{w1})w_1, (1 - t_{w2})w_2, u)$, for some function $A(\cdot)$, where q_1, q_2 are consumer prices in the two periods and w_1, w_2 are wage rates with taxes t_{w1}, t_{w2} (Boadway and Keen 2003).

18. Equivalently, it is sufficient that the expenditure function take the implicitly separable form $e(q_1, q_2, u, B(w_1, w_2), u))$.

are used. Moreover both consumption and labor supply are constant over time, and there is no saving.[19]

Intuitively this setup corresponds with the steady state to which the economy approaches in a Ramsey (1928) optimal savings model of a representative infinitely lived individual whose intertemporal utility function is $\sum_{t=0}^{\infty} \beta^t u(x_t, \ell_t)$. Chamley (1986) shows that in such a context, if the planner is restricted to labor and capital income taxes, the capital income tax rate will approach zero in the long run.[20] More generally, given a stock of capital at the beginning of the planning period, inherited from the past, the social planner will initially set a relatively high capital income tax rate, and then gradually replace it with a labor tax as time goes by. The high capital tax rate arises because of the fact that the taxation of "old" capital has no deadweight loss, but as time goes by, the amount of "new" capital rises relative to "old" capital. In fact Chamley (1986) also shows a stronger result. If the per period utility function takes the form $u(x, \ell) = x^{1-\sigma}/(1-\sigma) + v(\ell)$, the optimal capital tax should be zero in all periods after the first one. See Erosa and Gervais (2001) for a simple proof.

This result of a zero capital income tax rate in the long run has been influential. However, it is based on some strong assumptions. Two in particular are worth noting and controversial. The first involves the validity of the representative agent model as a way of capturing the efficiency effects of capital taxation. This is based on the so-called Ricardian equivalence notion of an overlapping generations model of representative individuals in each period who make operative bequests to their immediate heirs based on altruism. In such a model, the path of consumption over all cohorts can be replicated by maximizing a dynastic utility function subject to an intertemporal budget constraint (Barro 1974). This dynastic model depends on a number of far-fetched

---

19. This can be demonstrated as follows. Let consumer prices for goods and leisure be $q_1 = 1$, $q_2 = p_2 + t_{c2}$, $\omega_1 = w_1 + t_{w1}$, $\omega_2 = w_2 + t_{w2}$, where producer prices are $p_1 = 1$, p_2, w_1, w_2. The first-order conditions from the consumer's utility maximization yield $u_c^1 = \alpha$, $\beta u_c^2 = \alpha q_2$, $u_\ell^1 = -\alpha \omega_1$, $u_\ell^2 = -\alpha \omega_2$. From these, the consumer's budget constraint can be written $u_c^1 c_1 + \beta u_c^2 c_2 = -u_\ell^1 \ell_1 - \beta u_\ell^2 \ell_2$. The government's optimal tax problem is to maximize $u(c_1, \ell_1) + \beta u(c_2, \ell_2)$ subject to the consumer's budget constraint and the economy's resource constraint $w_1 \ell_1 + w_2 \ell_2 - c_1 - p_2 c_2 = R$. By the stated assumptions, $p_2 = \beta = 1/(1 + r)$ and $w_2 = \beta w_1$, the first-order conditions yield $q_2 = p_2$, implying no tax on capital income, and $q_2/q_1 = w_2/w_1$, so labor taxes are the same over time. As well, $c_1 = c_2$ and $\ell_1 = \ell_2$.

20. See also Judd 1985. Bernheim (2002) argues that one way to account for the result is that in a multi-period context, any positive capital income tax rate implies a growing distortion between present consumption and consumption in the distant future.

assumptions. Some of them involve technical issues such as the existence of a fully operative bequest motive that operates both positively
and negatively, perfect foresight and certainty, and so on. Importantly,
the utility discount factor of the representative agent must be the same
as that of the intergenerational social planner. That is, the weight put
on the utility of future generations must be dictated by the extent of
altruism alone. More critically, the Ricardian model depends on being
able to aggregate all individuals in any cohort into a representative
agent whose bequest motive applies to the representative agent of the
next cohort. Bernheim and Bagwell (1988) show the implausibility of
such an aggregation. Once one takes account both of biology—each
child has two parents—and of anthropology—parents come from different families—the bequest motive becomes effectively dissipated.
The heirs of any given person of the current cohort are shared indirectly
with all other persons of the same cohort, so making a bequest amounts
to making a voluntary contribution to a national public good. In these
circumstances bequests will be underprovided and an efficiency case
can be made for subsidizing them (Marglin 1963; Sen 1967).

The point is simply that the Ricardian model is logically inconsistent. Given its maintained assumptions, the equilibrium is at least as
likely to resemble an overlapping generations model without bequests.
In such a model, the zero capital-tax-rate result no longer generally
applies, as Erosa and Gervais (2001, 2002) show. The circumstances in
which it does apply include the following. First, if the individuals'
discount rate equals the government's discount rate, and if consumption and labor supply are constant over the life cycle, no capital
income tax is required. In effect the overlapping generations economy
replicates the steady state of the Ricardian model. This case is not
particularly appealing since with labor supply and consumption both
constant over the life cycle, there is no individual saving. Any capital
is owned by the government. In the real world, where there are productivity changes over the life cycle as well as retirement, this case
cannot apply. Moreover it is not obvious why each individual's utility
discount rate should equal the discount rate used by the planner to
discount lifetime utilities of different cohorts. A second case where the
zero capital tax is obtained is when the per period utility function
takes the additively separable form with constant elasticity of the
utility of consumption as above: $u(x, \ell) = x^{1-\sigma}/(1-\sigma) + v(\ell)$. In this case
capital income taxes should be zero in an optimal tax outcome after
the first period.

However, even this result is more restrictive than it first appears. It requires that the government be able to levy age-dependent labor income taxes over the individual's life cycle. If this is not possible, capital income taxes will generally be required as an indirect way of affecting age dependency. For example, Alvarez et al. (1992) show in a related context with the wage rate constant over the two-period life cycle, optimal labor income taxes for the representative household should decline with age if the interest rate exceeds the utility discount factor, and vice versa. However, if labor income taxes cannot be made age specific, there should be a positive interest income tax if the interest rate exceeds the utility discount factor, and vice versa. Alternatively, as mentioned above, Bernheim (2002) shows that in a multi-period life-cycle context, a constant capital income tax rate is equivalent to an increasing tax on consumption over time. In these circumstances, if consumption taxes cannot be made age specific, a positive capital tax will be welfare improving if it is optimal for the tax on consumption to increase with age. Similarly capital income should be subsidized if the optimal tax on consumption falls with age.

Moreover capital market imperfections can affect the case for capital income taxes. Hubbard and Judd (1987), using an overlapping generations model, consider the case where there are liquidity constraints that preclude borrowing against future labor income (see also Bernheim 2002). A typical life-cycle pattern of optimal asset accumulation would involve individuals borrowing when they are young when their earnings are relatively low and their demand for assets like housing and consumer durables is high. If they are precluded from doing that, consumption will be closely related to current income, so a tax on earnings will be doubly distortionary since it tightens that constraint. Under these circumstances a tax on capital income whose liability falls later in life can be welfare improving.

Aiyagari (1995) shows that the same result applies in a model more closely related to the Chamley–Judd setting. This model has been more recently used in the new dynamic public finance literature. It has a continuum of infinitely lived agents subject to idiosyncratic productivity shocks. The absence of insurance markets and borrowing constraints give rise to capital income taxation in a second-best optimum. Specifically, the risk of hitting a borrowing constraint in the future leads individuals to self-insure by accumulating precautionary savings. These precautionary savings are suboptimal since there is no aggregate risk, and taxing capital income mitigates the welfare loss.

Conesa, Kitao, and Krueger (2009) argue, using simulations in a general equilibrium model with overlapping generations of finite-lived individuals calibrated to US data, that the combination of liquidity constraints and wage uncertainty (along with the absence of age-dependent taxation) can lead to significant capital income tax rates, of the order of 36 percent. Importantly, their analysis allows for the choice of an optimal progressive earnings tax system along with the linear capital income tax, in other words, a dual income tax system of the Nordic variety.

The second main assumption underlying the Chamley–Judd result is that the government can and will implement a tax plan to apply into the indefinite future based on what is optimal from the point of view of the initial period. The assumption that the government can commit to a future path of optimal tax rates is a very strong one, especially given the assumption that in the initial period, the government taxes all previously cumulated capital at a high rate of tax. The same logic would seem to suggest that sometime into the future, if given the chance to re-optimize, the government would once again choose a relatively high capital income tax rate. There seems to be no compelling reason to assume that the government can commit to future tax rates. If it cannot, the full commitment solution, including the zero capital-tax-rate result, is time inconsistent in a second-best setting.[21]

Fischer (1980) first characterized the commitment problem in a simple two-period Ramsey optimal tax setting. The representative individual saves from a given income endowment in the first period and supplies labor in the second (variable labor supply in the first period being nonessential to the argument). The government raises a fixed amount of revenue in the second period using labor and capital taxation. In a second-best optimum where the government announces its tax structure at the beginning of the first period, it will generally be the case that both labor and capital should be taxed, although it is possible that the optimal tax on capital is nonpositive depending on individual preferences. Once the first period has gone by, the government will prefer to renege on the announced second-best tax system since capital is now fixed and taxing it will be nondistortionary. In this representative-individual setting the government will want to tax capital at the highest possible rate and labor, which is still variable, at as low a rate

---

21. No such problem arises in the first best, as Hillier and Malcomson (1984) long ago showed.

as possible. If individuals anticipate this, they will reduce their saving. Not surprisingly, the time-consistent (subgame perfect) equilibrium involves an excessively high tax rate on capital income, given the incentive to impose a high tax rate on capital already accumulated, and a level of welfare that can be much lower than the second-best optimal tax. Notably this consequence is not due to any nonbenevolence on the part of the government: even a fully benevolent planner faces the problem. Rather, the problem is an inability to commit.

Not surprisingly, the literature has suggested a number of ways of mitigating the effects of the inability to commit. These might involve limits on the policy instruments of government. For example, consumption taxation might be preferred to income taxation, especially dual income taxation, as a way of constraining the government from overtaxing capital.[22] The government might choose particular policy instruments to overcome commitment problems. Thus it might mandate saving, social insurance or training to overcome its inability to commit ex ante to future transfers—the so-called Samaritan's dilemma (Bruce and Waldman 1991; Coate 1995). Or, it might provide public unemployment insurance to counter its inability to commit to a macroeconomic policy to control unemployment (Boadway and Marceau 1994). The government may underinvest in tax enforcement technology or administration as a way of mitigating the consequences of excessively high capital income taxes in the future (Boadway and Keen 1998).[23] Finally, the government might provide up-front incentives to private sector agents to mitigate the fact that taxation will be unavoidably high in the future. These can be savings incentives for households (e.g., tax-sheltered savings for retirement) or investment incentives for firms (e.g., tax holidays, investment tax credits). The use of investment incentives is widespread, but it is particularly prominent in developing countries that rely on investment by foreign firms (Vigneault 1996; Wen 1997) and that rely heavily on revenues from natural resource investments with long time horizons (Boadway and Keen 2010; Osmundsen 2010).

---

22. Rogers (1987) has shown that in a two-period representative individual setting with consumption and labor in both periods, consumption taxation might be preferable to wage taxation in a time-consistent equilibrium, even though the preference is reversed in a second-best optimum.

23. Arozamena, Besfamille, and Sanguinetti 2008 argue instead that the government cannot commit to an audit intensity, and they study how this affects optimal tax and penalty policy.

These examples help account for the fact that in the real world, governments sometimes undertake policies that would be anathema in a first-best setting: regulations, quantity controls, subsidies of private activity, public provision, and so on. Moreover even benevolent governments might rationally engage in such policies. As we will see later, it is not just commitment problems that might induce benevolent governments to intervene in nonconventional ways. Information constraints can induce the same types of policies. One does not need to resort to political economy arguments or nonbenevolent governments to rationalize such policies, although no doubt those factors have explanatory value as well.

3.3.2   Nonlinear Taxation in a Dynamic Setting

We have so far focused on capital tax issues in economies with linear taxation. When we move to the unrestricted policy case where the government is free to use nonlinear taxation, matters change substantively. The relevant constraint faced by the government is an information constraint: its inability to observe individuals' characteristics, like their ability of skills. The dynamic setting not only complicates the implications of information constraints, it also exacerbates the problem of commitment. If the government is constrained only by information, the choice of an optimal nonlinear income tax satisfies the revelation principle in a separating outcome in which all downward incentive constraints are binding. In a static setting, it is implicitly assumed that the government commits to the tax structure it announces (i.e., to the bundles of income and disposable income it offers) and implements them. In an explicitly dynamic setting, this commitment assumption is particularly strong. If individuals reveal their types in the first period, why should the government not use that information in the following period(s)?

In the dynamic optimal income tax literature, this problem has been addressed in one of two ways. First, it may simply be assumed that the government can commit (Golosov, Tsyvinski, and Werning 2007; Diamond 2007). This parallels the assumption made in the static model, where commitment is no less important. Second, information learned in the first period may not be fully informative about individual types in the second. For example, wage rates may be stochastic (Golosov, Kocherlakota, and Tsyvinski 2003). This does not fully solve the commitment problem unless the government is unable to make use of a person's past history in determining current tax liabilities. Nonetheless, it mitigates it since past information is less informative about individuals' current and future propects.

In what follows, we take the first route and simply assume that the government can commit to an intertemporal optimal nonlinear tax. Although this is somewhat of a heroic assumption, it is instructive nonetheless (and is the one adopted by Banks and Diamond 2010). We return later to providing some rationalization for the assumption that the (benevolent) government can commit. Following Diamond (2007), most of the intuition can be obtained from simple two-period models, so we restrict attention to those. Since our focus is on capital income taxation, we begin with a simple benchmark case.

A Dynamic Atkinson–Stiglitz Theorem

It is useful to begin with a case where the Atkinson–Stiglitz theorem carries over directly to an intertemporal setting.[24] Adopting the three-good model to a two-period setting with two wage types suffices to make the point. Suppose that lifetime utility is given by the additive utility function $u(x_1) - h(\ell_1) + \beta u(x_2)$, where x_1 and x_2 represent composite consumption in the two periods and ℓ_1 is labor supplied in the first period. For a person with wage rate w, lifetime utility can be written in terms of income and consumption as $u(x_1) - h(y_1/w) + \beta u(x_2)$, where $y_1 = w\ell_1$ is income earned in the first period. Note that this function satisfies the weak separability requirement of the Atkinson–Stiglitz theorem, so it is not surprising that the theorem is satisfied. The earlier proof follows directly. Suppose that the government can observe income but cannot observe how that income is divided between the two goods: present and future consumption. An indirect tax can be levied on, say, second-period consumption, by taxing capital income paid by financial institutions. If the government sets the nonlinear income tax optimally, there is no need for an indirect tax on capital income because of the weak separability of preferences. In this context that implies that the government can apply a nonlinear progressive tax on labor income and leave capital income untaxed.

The literature typically assumes that the government can observe saving, or equivalently first- and second-period consumption. Although the Atkinson–Stiglitz theorem survives this generalization, it is useful

---

24. This intertemporal version of the Atkinson–Stiglitz theorem should be distinguished from the applicability of the theorem within each period in a multi-period model by Golosov, Kocherlakota, and Tsyvinski (2003), discussed above.

for our subsequent discussion to specify the capital tax issue in this context. Consider the simplest case in which there are two skill-types, with skills now denoted $w^2 > w^1$, so that superscripts denote skills and subscripts are used for time periods. Also assume that the social welfare function is utilitarian, although similar results are obtained with any quasi-concave social welfare function in individual utilities. The optimal nonlinear tax problem of the government is now to choose consumption levels x_i^j and incomes y_i^j to maximize $n^1[u(x_1^1) - h(y_1^1/w^1) + \beta u(x_2^1)] + n^2[u(x_1^2) - h(y_1^2/w^2) + \beta u(x_2^2)]$ subject to a revenue constraint, $n^1[y_1^1 - x_1^1 - x_2^1/(1+r)] + n^2[y_1^2 - x_1^2 - x_2^2/(1+r)] = R$, and an incentive constraint, $u(x_1^2) - h(y_1^2/w^2) + \beta u(x_2^2) \geqslant u(x_1^1) - h(y_1^1/w^2) + \beta u(x_2^1)$. The incentive constraint is defined on a lifetime basis: a high-skilled person who mimics a low-skilled person must choose first- and second-period consumption and incomes of the latter (x_1^1, y_1^1, x_2^1). From the first-order conditions, one obtains the following intertemporal wedge expression:

$$\frac{u'(x_1^1)}{\beta u'(x_2^1)} = \frac{u'(x_1^2)}{\beta u'(x_2^2)} = 1 + r,$$

which says that the intertemporal marginal rate of substitution in consumption for both skill-types should equal the intertemporal marginal rate of transformation. This implies that there should be no tax on capital income or savings, which is equivalent to a tax on second-period consumption. The government can rely solely on a nonlinear income tax, which has the same properties as in the static model.

Some interpretive remarks are, however, in order. First, to the extent that this two-period representation is meant to capture the working and retirement periods of a person's life cycle, the nonlinear income tax must apply to income earned over the entire working period. Given that actual income tax systems are annual, this would require a lifetime system of averaging. It would also require a high degree of commitment by the government.

Second, the incentive constraint bears some attention. The optimal nonlinear income tax allocation involves the government offering menus of income, y_1, and disposable income, say, c_1, to the individuals in the first period of their lives. The choice of (y_1, c_1) by an individual represents the choice of a point along the lifetime budget constraint, $c_1 = y_1 - T(y_1)$, where $T(y_1)$ is the income tax function. Individuals then use their disposable income to finance first- and second-period consumption according to their budget constraint $c_1 = x_1 + x_2/(1 + r)$. Given the separable utility function we have chosen, high-wage individuals will choose the same consumption profile as low-wage individuals if they have the same disposable income. This in turn implies that high-wage types mimicking low-wage types will choose the same (x_1, x_2) bundle, and it is this that renders differential taxation of present and future consumption useless as a policy instrument alongside the nonlinear income tax.

Finally, the fact that individuals have some capital income in the second period would make it tempting for the government to tax it, just as in the linear tax case. The assumption of commitment is thus important to preclude this from happening. Of course, just like in the linear tax case of Pestieau (1974) and Atkinson and Sandmo (1980), if one incorporates these individuals into an overlapping generations setting, there will be another motive for taxing capital income if the government cannot control the rate of aggregate savings directly. For an analysis of this case with a two-period life-cycle model with first-period labor supply, see Stiglitz (1987). He also shows that if the relative wage rates of the high- and low-skilled workers vary with the capital stock, it will be optimal to control the latter. If the only instrument available is taxation or subsidization of capital income, that constitutes another argument for capital income taxation.

Suppose now that we allow for labor supply in both periods, so that the assumed intertemporally and intratemporally separable utility function becomes $u(x_1) - h(\ell_1) + \beta(u(x_2) - h(\ell_2))$. The income tax system becomes more complicated now because there are taxes in both periods. As mentioned, this case strains the assumption of commitment since individuals will reveal their types in the first period. If the government could not commit, one of two outcomes could occur. Either individuals reveal their types in the first period, and the government uses that knowledge to implement a lump-sum redistributive tax in the second, or there is a pooling equilibrium in the first period in which neither type reveals their skills, followed by a standard one-period optimal nonlinear tax in the second. Either outcome could be preferred by the government depending on the parameters of the model.[25] Roberts

---

25. See the analysis in Pereira (2009a, b). Krause (2009) showed that there is a third possibility. Assuming that there are many high-wage and low-wage types, it may be optimal for the government to induce a portion of the high-wage types to reveal themselves in the first period, while the rest do not.

(1984) considered the implications of the inability of the government to commit in a multi-period Mirrlees setting.[26] He showed that as the number of periods increases and the discount rate falls, all persons pretend to be the worst type every year. They supply the lowest amount of labor and receive the lowest amount of consumption, which is clearly a highly nonoptimal outcome. Indeed in some circumstances the time-consistent equilibrium might even be inferior to the no-intervention (laissez-faire) outcome. See Boadway, Marceau, and Marchand (1996) and Konrad (2001) for examples of this when households can improve their skills through education.

We focus instead on the case where the government can commit. The government can impose a nonlinear labor income tax in each period, and in addition a differential commodity tax on first- and second-period consumption, or equivalently a capital income tax or subsidy.[27] Remarkably, when the government can impose optimal nonlinear labor income taxes in both periods, no capital income taxation should be imposed (or, equivalently, no differential taxation of first- and second-period consumption), given the separable form of the utility function.[28] This result applies even if wage rates for the two types vary over the two periods. However, this assumes that the government can impose age-specific tax systems.

The nature of those per period optimal nonlinear income tax systems is of independent interest. In the case of the high-ability persons, the marginal tax rate at the top is zero in both periods, which Golosov, Tsyvinski, and Werning (2007) and Diamond (2007) refer to as a tax-smoothing result. Of course, that does not imply that the average tax rate is the same in both periods: given that the wage rate differs over periods, the average tax rate almost certainly does as well. In the case of the low-wage persons, they face a positive marginal tax rate, as usual, and that tax rate will generally vary between the two periods.

---

26. See also Berliant and Ledyard (2005), Apps and Rees (2006), and Brett and Weymark (2008b).

27. If the government can observe individual saving as above, it could impose a nonlinear tax/subsidy on it. We ignore that complication for now since it adds no additional insight.

28. The analysis is a straightforward extension of the above analysis where there are only first-period earnings. Now the government chooses consumption and income in both periods (x_i^j, y_i^j) for $i, j = 1, 2$. The lifetime incentive constraint is $u(x_1^2) - h(y_1^2/w^2) + \beta[u(x_2^2) - h(y_2^2/w^2)] \geqslant u(x_1^1) - h(y_1^1/w^2) + \beta[u(x_2^1) - h(y_2^1/w^2)]$. From the first-order conditions, we find that there is no intertemporal distortion on consumption for either skill type.

An exception is if relative wages of the two types are the same in both periods, and the utility of labor supply is constant elasticity, as shown by Diamond (2007). If the age-earnings profile rises more rapidly for the high-wage types, the marginal tax rate for the low-wage types will tend to rise over the life cycle, and vice versa.

While these results are suggestive, they also rely on somewhat strong assumptions. They require that governments deploy age-dependent tax rates. However, income tax systems are typically not age dependent, although there may be some age-related components, such as tax credits or deductions based on age. It would be worth investigating the consequences of restricting the income tax to be non–age dependent. In the linear income tax case, that restriction provided a rationale for capital income taxation or subsidization (Alvarez et al. 1992). Presumably that would be the case with nonlinear taxes as well. Why income taxes are not age dependent is an open question. As Banks and Diamond (2010) note, it is hard to argue that it is a matter of nondiscrimination or horizontal equity since all individuals experience different ages, unlike with other characteristics like gender, race or physical attributes.

If wage rates in the two periods are endogenous over the life cycle, the pattern of marginal tax rates is qualitatively affected. Krause (2009) has considered the case where second-period wages for both high- and low-wage types are affected by the amount of labor supplied in the first period. He refers to this highly plausible experience effect as learning by doing. In the case where the government can fully commit to a two-period nonlinear tax policy, the marginal tax rate on the high-wage types is zero in both periods, as usual. The optimal marginal tax rate on the low-skilled is positive in the second period when commitment is not an issue. However, it may be optimal to impose a negative marginal tax rate on the low-wage types in the first period. This encourages labor supply and therefore increases second-period wages for the low-wage types, and this may actually weaken the lifetime incentive constraint imposed on the high-skilled types.

In the case where the government cannot commit, outcome will differ depending on whether the high-wage types reveal themselves in the first period. If they do, so lump-sum taxation can be applied in the second period, the marginal tax rate on the low-wage types in the first period can again be negative. If there is pooling in the first period, the marginal tax rate on the low-wage types will be negative and on the high-wage types positive, and the average marginal tax rate will be overall negative. Note that Krause assumes that individuals do not save: they consume their income in each period. This simplifies the analysis, and apparently does not affect the intuition of the results.

Other Complications in the Two-Period Setting

There are a number of complications that could be considered in a dynamic setting, some of which I have hinted at already. I discuss four complications briefly here. The first two emerge from the dynamic macroeconomic public finance literature (Golosov, Tsyvinski, and Werning 2007; Diamond, 2007), and have been stressed as arguments for capital income taxation by Banks and Diamond (2010). They are uncertainty over wage rates and systematic differences in intertemporal preferences. The third involves the implications of human capital accumulation for capital income taxation, and the fourth considers the interaction between redistributive taxation and social insurance in retirement.

Wage Rate Uncertainty

Suppose, first, that there is some uncertainty about second-period wage rates. The key results can be obtained by focusing on the simplest case where individuals have a common wage rate in the first period, but can either be high-wage or low-wage in the second period. There is no aggregate uncertainty, so a given proportion of the population turns out to be high-wage and the rest are low-wage. Individuals learn their wage type at the beginning of the second period before they have chosen their labor supply (but after first-period labor supply and savings have been chosen). Crucially, although wage uncertainty is in principle insurable, it is assumed that insurance markets do not exist, possibly because of information constraints facing insurers. Individuals' welfare is captured in a lifetime expected utility function, $u(x_1) - h(\ell_1) + \beta \sum_{j=1,2} \pi^j (u(x_2^j) - h(\ell_2^j))$, where π^1 and π^2 are the proportions of population who are of types 1 (low wage) and 2 (high wage).

The government imposes a common lump-sum income tax in the first period since all persons are indistinguishable then. In the second period a nonlinear labor income tax can be imposed as well as a tax on capital income (based on first-period saving). The only incentive constraint is in the second period. The government announces its tax

structure at the beginning of the first period, and as usual is assumed
to be able to commit to it. If there were no incentive constraint, the
government that maximizes per capita expected utility would redistribute lump sum in the second period such that consumption is equalized ($x_2^1 = x_2^2$).

In the first-best setting the government provides full consumption
insurance through the tax system. However, the incentive constraint in
the second-best setting results in underinsurance ($x_2^1 < x_2^2$): high-wage
persons must be given more consumption to preclude them from mimicking the low-skilled. Moreover it becomes optimal to tax capital
income. Intuitively, reducing saving makes it more costly for the high-
wage types to mimic the second-period income of the low-wage types
(by reducing the amount of second-period consumption made available by saving). This intuitive result carries forward to the case when
individuals are heterogeneous in the first period (Golosov, Kocherlakota,
and Tsyvinski 2007).[29]

Formally, the government maximizes expected utilities (equiva-
lently, the sum of utilities), $u(x_1) - h(\ell_1) + \beta \sum_{j=1,2} \pi^j [u(x_2^j) - h(\ell_2^j)]$, subject
to the revenue constraint, $y^1 - x^1 + (1+r)^{-1} \sum_{j=1,2} n_2^j (y_2^j - x_2^j) \geq R$, and a
second-period incentive constraint, $u(x_2^2) - h(y_2^2/w_2^2) \geq u(x_2^1) - h(y_2^1/w_2^2)$.
From the first-order conditions, we obtain

$$\frac{u'(x_1)}{\beta \sum_j n_2^j u'(x_2^j)} < 1 + r.$$

This says there is a positive intertemporal consumption wedge, implying that there should be a positive tax on saving.

Heterogeneous Discount Rates
Next suppose that individuals have different utility discount rates. The
simplest case to consider is that in which discount factors are perfectly
correlated with wage rates. The utility function of a type-j individual
now becomes $u(x_1) - h(\ell_1) + \beta^j (u(x_2) - h(\ell_2))$, where $\beta^2 \neq \beta^1$. This case is
a simple extension of the one considered above in deriving the dynamic
Atkinson–Stiglitz theorem. The utilitarian objective function becomes
$\sum_{j=1,2} n^j [u(x_1^j) - h(y_1^j/w^j) + \beta^j u(x_2^j)]$,   and   the   incentive   constraint   is

29. Stiglitz (1982) considered the case where uncertainty was not over the wage rate, but
over output given the wage rate. In this context he showed that there should be 100
percent taxation for the top wage earners, that is, full insurance.

$u(x_1^2) - h(y_1^2/w^2) + \beta^2 u(x_2^2) \geqslant u(x_1^1) - h(y_1^1/w^2) + \beta^2 u(x_2^1)$. From the first-order conditions, the intertemporal wedge conditions become

$$\frac{u'(x_1^2)}{\beta^2 u'(x_2^2)} = 1 + r \gtrless \frac{u'(x_1^1)}{\beta^1 u'(x_2^1)} \text{ as } \beta^2 \gtrless \beta^1.$$

Intertemporal decisions of the high-skilled types remain undistorted, while those of the low-skilled are distorted if $\beta^2 \neq \beta^1$. Saez (2002a) and Diamond and Spinnewijn (forthcoming) argue that the evidence suggests a positive correlation between wage rates and the weight individuals put on future utility, so $\beta^2 > \beta^1$. In this case, where high-wage types tend to have higher savings rates than the low-skilled, a positive capital income tax should be imposed on the low-skilled.

If savings is not observable but could be taxed indirectly at a constant rate, it is straightforward to show that the tax rate on capital income should be positive if $\beta^2 > \beta^1$ (Diamond and Spinnewijn, forthcoming). They also show that this is the case if skills are imperfectly, but positively correlated with the weight put on the utility of future consumption. This lends some credence to a dual income tax system, albeit credence that is based on the presumed correlation between the wage rate and β (and on the ability to levy an age-specific nonlinear earnings tax). Related to this is the argument that skills are positively related to expected longevity (Cremer, Lozachmeur, and Pestieau 2010). The high-skilled will also save more on this account, so a tax on capital income will be part of an optimal tax package.

The difference in discount rates will also have an implication for the progressivity of the income tax. However, precisely how progressivity is affected is conceptually questionable. If individuals have different preferences, it is not clear how to weight their utilities in a social welfare function. Simply adding the utility function above for the two types as we have just done will give arbitrarily heavier weight to those with higher β's. We return to this issue in chapter 5.

Human Capital Investment

As a third complication, suppose that we make earnings endogenous by allowing individuals to invest in human capital accumulation as well as to save. From the perspective of capital income taxation, human capital accumulation can be viewed as an asset in the individual's portfolio alongside financial assets and real assets, such as housing and personal business capital. Tax systems typically treat these various forms of assets quite differently. For example, in typical income tax systems, most financial income is taxed (apart from savings dedicated to supporting income in retirement), while housing and human capital investment are tax-sheltered. Given the difficulty of taxing the returns on these latter assets, second-best considerations would lead to a case for preferential taxation of capital income relative to earnings so as to mitigate inter-asset distortions.

Anderberg (2009) generalizes the simple wage uncertainty setting discussed above to the case where wages rates are the outcome of uncertain returns to human capital investment. In particular, second-period wages are determined by the wage function $w(z,\theta)$, where z is the amount of human capital investment in the first period (assumed to be forgone earnings) and θ is a stochastic parameter reflecting states of the world. Policies now include both an optimal nonlinear tax and taxes or subsidies on education and saving. The intertemporal consumption wedge is positive as in the model just discussed, so there should be a tax on saving or capital income. The optimal education policy depends on whether education increases or decreases wage risk, that is, whether education increases the wage outcome of good productivity shocks relative to bad productivity shocks. Formally, if $w_z(z, \theta)/w(z, \theta)$ is increasing in θ, increasing z will increase the wage of an individual with a better shock relative to that of an individual with a worse shock, which Anderberg interprets as saying the education increases wage risk. Policy should distort human capital investment downward (i.e., tax human capital investment) if the latter increases wage risk, and upward if it decreases wage risk. Suppose that education increases wage risk. By imposing tax on education, the utility cost to an individual with a good productivity shock pretending to have had a bad productivity shock is higher than that of an individual who actually had a bad productivity shock. This way the incentive compatibility constraint can be relaxed.

Jacobs and Bovenberg (2010) make another point. They observe that a progressive earnings tax will discourage investment in human capital since the marginal tax rate on increased earnings exceeds the marginal tax rate on current forgone earnings. This will induce individuals to substitute financial capital for human capital if the returns on financial capital go untaxed, as in a consumption tax system. In these circumstances, a positive tax rate on capital income will mitigate the disincentive to accumulate human capital by making financial assets less attractive.

Interaction with Social Insurance

Our final complication involves the relationship between the tax system that redistributes from high- to low-skilled persons and social insurance schemes that also redistribute across the life cycles of taxpayers. Bovenberg, Hansen, and Sørensen (2008) observe that a substantial portion of income taxes paid are used to finance social transfers that redistribute income over an individual's life cycle rather than across individuals of different incomes. For example, they estimate using Danish data that three-quarter of taxes levied finance public transfers so effectively finance life-cycle redistribution. The financing of transfers over the life cycle from general tax revenues imposes significant efficiency costs as well as perhaps compromising the redistributive intents of the tax-transfer system. This finding validates the earlier consideration of schemes that rationalize the integration of income and social insurance schemes.

Bovenberg and Sørensen (2004) address the broader issue of the inefficiency of tax financing of social insurance. They show how in a simple model a Pareto improvement can be achieved by the introduction of mandatory lifetime savings accounts. A shift from general revenue financing to actuarially fair individual accounts to finance social transfer schemes (unemployment/disability insurance, early retirement and parental leave programs, etc.) removes the distortion on labor supply that results from funding transfers through the tax system, a point that was also made by Feldstein (2005). The accounts work as follows. A proportion of each person's income tax bill is replaced by a mandatory contribution to a personal lifetime savings account. Whenever the individual receives a social benefit, the account is debited. At the statutory retirement age, if the account balance is positive, the balance is transferred into an annuity that supplements the publicly funded pension plan. If the balance is negative, the account is canceled and the individual receives a guaranteed annual income through the public pension. Thus the initial tax contributions are vested in the individual and the source of the labor supply distortion is eliminated. This approach is used in Singapore for health care savings accounts with some success.

To deal with the redistributive issue, Bovenberg and Sørensen (2006) study an optimal lifetime income taxation and disability benefit system using a two-period model. Workers may be either high-skilled or low-skilled and face an exogenous probability of becoming disabled in the second period of life. The government wants to redistribute income both from high-skilled to low-skilled and from able to disabled workers using a linear income tax, retirement benefits and disability insurance. The optimal tax-benefit scheme has the disability benefit increasing more strongly with previous income than the standard pension benefit. In addition, the optimal disability benefit does not fully insure individuals (even though moral hazard is absent from the model). Both these features improve incentives to supply first period labor, so the distortion from taxing income is ameliorated. Since the disability benefit depends on the individual's income history, this implies that it is optimal to tax incomes on a lifetime rather than annual basis.

The various extensions discussed above provide some support for some tax on capital income, though not necessarily for a comprehensive income tax as opposed to, say, a dual income tax. Whether these arguments for capital taxation based on fairly simple abstract theoretical models are sufficient to warrant recommending capital income tax in practice is a matter of judgment. They are at least suggestive, and lend support to other, perhaps more telling arguments. For example, to the extent that unobserved wealth endowments contribute significantly to unequal levels of consumption, taxing capital income on such wealth is an indirect way of getting at consumption that would otherwise go partly untaxed (Boadway, Marchand, and Pestieau 2000). A direct tax on bequests would serve a similar purpose.

3.4 The Issue of Progressivity

The issue of the rate structure is a difficult one, especially since it involves some value judgments about the form of the social welfare function. Even in a first-best world where the government can implement lump-sum transfers based on individual characteristics, there is considerable ambiguity concerning the degree of progressivity. Indeed there is no presumption that the individual tax will be progressive even if the government is highly inequality averse. Take the extreme case of a maximin social welfare function in the standard two-type optimal income tax setting where individuals differ only in skills or wage rates, and where the government has to raise a given amount of revenue. Under lump-sum taxes utility levels would be equalized for the two types, and this would entail a higher tax on the high-wage individuals. However, as Sadka (1976) shows, this does not necessarily imply that the average tax rate—the tax as a proportion of income—is higher for the high-wage individuals. The reason is that it is optimal for high-wage persons to supply more labor than low-wage persons. That reduces their utility, and they must be compensated for that by having higher consumption relative to the low-wage types. Depending on the shape of indifference curves relating consumption to labor supplied, the average tax rate can rise or fall with income.

Surprisingly, in this first-best case, the tax will actually be more progressive in the utilitarian case where there is no aversion to inequality (assuming consumption and leisure are normal). This is because high-wage individuals will be worse off than low-wage individuals in the first best (Mirrlees 1974). This can be readily seen in the case where preferences are additively separable, so $u(x, \ell) = b(x) - h(\ell)$ with $b' > 0 > b''$ and $h', h'' > 0$. In a utilitarian optimum, marginal utilities of consumption, $b'(x)$, are equalized across individuals, which implies consumption is as well. At the same time, consumption and labor supply satisfies the individual optimization condition $h'(\ell) = wb'(x)$. Since $b'(x)$ is the same for all persons, ℓ must be increasing in w to satisfy this condition. Therefore higher wage persons obtain the same consumption as lower wage persons but supply more labor, so are worse off.

Adding other factors to the standard model makes the ambiguity about progressivity even more striking. If individuals differ in their ability to generate utility, perhaps because of different needs for consumption goods, the direction of redistribution can depend crucially on aversion to inequality. A highly inequality-averse government will want to redistribute toward those with greater needs so as to make utilities more equal, while for very low aversions to inequality, the emphasis will be on generating more aggregate utility, which will entail redistributing toward the less needy (Sen 1973; Kaplow 2008). Similarly, if individuals differ in preferences for leisure, the direction of redistribution can be ambiguous and depends on the relative weight the government puts on these preferences (Boadway et al. 2000; Cuff 2000).

Thus, even in a first-best setting, the question of how progressive the tax-transfer system should be is vexing. In a second-best setting where the government faces the additional constraint of not being able to observe individuals by type, one might expect the structure of the rate schedule to be even more ambiguous. Nonetheless, if one focuses on the standard second-best optimal income tax setting in which individuals vary mainly according to skills, some suggestive qualitative results are obtained. A number of rather stylized qualitative results stand out, many of which are found in Mirrlees (1971) and Tuomala (1990). Most of the results are based on the schedule of optimal marginal tax rates by skill level. Some of them are derived analytically for particular cases, while others follow from simulations using reasonable modeling assumptions.

The formal model commonly used has evolved from the one initially proposed by Mirrlees. The basic approach was briefly outlined earlier when discussing the Atkinson–Stiglitz theorem, and can be summarized as follows. Individuals differ only in their wage rate w, and are distributed over $w \in [\underline{w}, \bar{w}]$ according to the distribution function $F(w)$, with density $f(w) = F'(w)$, where $\underline{w} \geq 0$, $\bar{w} \leq \infty$. Since there are no scale effects, we can normalize the total population to unity. Individuals of wage-type w consume an amount $c(w)$, supply labor $\ell(w)$ and earn income $y(w) = w\ell$. Their utility functions in c, ℓ are identical. Transforming the utility function into one with c and y as arguments, the utility of a type-w person can be written $u(w) = v(c(w), y(w), w)$. The government maximizes an additive and quasi-concave social welfare function, $\int_{\underline{w}}^{\bar{w}} W(u(w)) f(w) dw$ subject to two constraints. One is a budget constraint, $\int_{\underline{w}}^{\bar{w}} (y(w) - c(w)) f(w) dw = R$. The other is an incentive constraint, which as we have seen takes the form $\dot{u}(w) = -\ell u_\ell / w$.[30] There are three variables in this problem, $c(w)$, $y(w)$ and $u(w)$, but $c(w)$ can be treated as a function of $y(w)$ and $u(w)$ by the utility function $u(w) = v(c(w), y(w), w)$. Therefore the government problem has one control variable, $y(w)$, and one state variable, $u(w)$.

The first-order conditions involve dynamic optimization techniques. Let us focus, following Diamond (1998), on the special case of quasi-linear preferences, so for a type-w person $u(c, y/w) = c + b(1 - y/w)$, where $b(\cdot)$ is the utility of leisure and is strictly concave and increasing. The first-order conditions are as follows (see Diamond 1998):

$$(w - b')(\lambda f)^2 = \left(\frac{b'}{w} - yb'' \right) \int_w^{\bar{w}} (\lambda - W') f(w) dw \qquad \forall w,$$

30. This is the so-called first-order incentive constraint because it is a necessary condition for individuals to be choosing the consumption–income bundle intended for them rather than mimicking another wage type. It is not, however, sufficient. Sufficiency requires that income be nondecreasing, $\dot{y}(w) \geq 0$, the second-order incentive constraint. Where the latter constraint is binding, individuals of different w will be bunched at a common consumption–income level. (See Ebert 1992 for a careful discussion.) We ignore this problem in our discussion.

where λ is the Lagrange multiplier on the government revenue constraint (the shadow value of revenue) and we have suppressed all arguments of functions for simplicity. To interpret this condition in terms of the tax function, note two things. First, given an income tax function $T(y)$, a type-w individual's optimal choice of income (or labor supply) satisfies $b' = (1 - T'(y))w$.[31] Second, for the quasi-linear utility function, which implies there are no income effects on labor supply, the elasticity of supply of labor can be written $\varepsilon = -wb'/(yb'')$. Using these and following Diamond (1998), the first-order conditions can be written in terms of the marginal tax rate as follows:[32]

$$\frac{T'(y)}{1-T'(y)} = \frac{1+\varepsilon}{\varepsilon} \cdot \frac{\int_{w}^{\bar{w}}(1-W'/\lambda)f(s)ds}{1-F(w)} \cdot \frac{1-F(w)}{wf(w)} \qquad \forall w.$$

The intuition follows from considering the social benefit of an increase in the marginal tax of a type-w person, holding all other marginal tax rates constant. The immediate effect on the type-w's is to increase the distortion on their labor supply, the effect being greater the higher is the elasticity of labor supply ε. This is picked up in the first term on the right-hand side. Next, when the marginal tax rate increases at w, the tax paid by all persons at higher wages increases by a lump-sum amount since their marginal tax rate remains constant. The value of this transfer of revenue to the government per person above w (since $1 - F(y)$ is the number of persons above w) is picked up in the second term. Since W', marginal social utility, is decreasing with w, this term will be increasing in w. These two terms are weighted by the third term reflecting the distribution of skills.

This formulation illustrates three commonly cited features of the optimal income tax structure. First, if there is an upper bound to the skill distribution (so $\bar{w} < \infty$), the marginal tax rate at the top should be zero. This follows from the fact that the middle term is zero at the top. Second, the marginal tax rate at the bottom is zero as well, provided that there is no bunching. This follows because the value of the shadow price of government revenue satisfies $\lambda = \int_{\underline{w}}^{\bar{w}} W'f(w)dw$. That is, in an

---

31. This is the first-order condition for the problem $\max_y y - T(y) + b(1 - y/w)$.

32. One may wonder why the marginal tax rate appears as $T'(y)/(1 - T'(y))$ here and in the following instead of just $T'(y)$. The reason is that the tax is defined as a function of y, so $T'(y)$ is the marginal tax rate applied to a tax-inclusive tax base y. One can interpret $T'(y)/(1 - T'(y))$ as the marginal tax rate applied to the net-of-tax base, c.

optimum, the value of a euro to the government equals the value of transferring a euro to all persons in a lump-sum way (which does not affect their labor supply in the quasi-linear case). Therefore the second term is again zero. Third, the marginal tax rate for all persons with w > 0 will be positive, since all three terms in marginal tax rate expression are positive. If there is bunching at the bottom, the marginal tax rate will be positive at the end of the bunching range. These features all apply in the case of preferences more general that quasi-linear.

More generally, there are conflicting factors influencing the pattern of tax rates, and results depend on the specific features of the economy. Nonetheless, the literature stresses various qualitative results. Broadly speaking, the optimal nonlinear income tax is not all that progressive. For much of the interior of the skill distribution, marginal tax rates change at only a moderate rate, so the system does not differ much from linear progressive. Mirrlees and Tuomala found that marginal tax rates tended to rise moderately, but Boadway and Jacquet (2008) showed, without resorting to simulations, that for a maximin social welfare function, marginal tax rates will decline under mild assumptions. Sufficient conditions are that (1) preferences be additive in consumption and labor, (2) the disutility of labor be isoelastic, and (3) aggregate skills be nondecreasing in the skill level.[33] These maximin results are partly driven by the fact that for this case, the marginal tax rate for the least-skilled persons is positive, unlike with other social welfare functions. Figures 3.1 and 3.2 depict typical patterns of marginal tax rates reported in Brewer, Saez, and Shephard (2010) and Boadway and Jacquet (2008).

At the upper end of the skill distribution, as we have seen the marginal tax rate falls abruptly to zero at the upper bound (if there is one). If there is assumed to be no upper bound to skills, one can get odd patterns for marginal tax rates, given some specific assumptions. For example, Diamond (1998) argues, using the above quasi-linear formulation, that at the upper end of the income or skill distribution, a U-shaped pattern can be obtained. However, this is crucially dependent on the absence of an upper bound to skills; that is, if there is such a bound, then the marginal tax rate at the top falls to zero (Boadway, Cuff, and Marchand 2000).

---

33. Aggregate skills are $wf(w)$, where w is the wage or skill level and $f(w)$ is its density. Note that the solution for the maximin case effectively involves maximizing the amount of tax revenue obtained from all those above the lowest wage level.

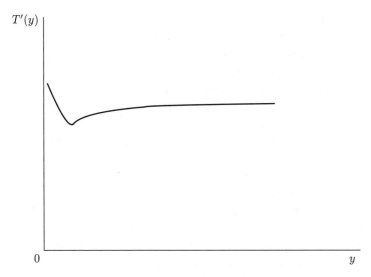

Figure 3.1
General pattern of marginal tax rates (Brewer, Saez, and Shephard 2010)

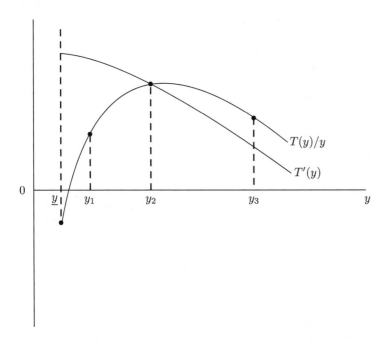

Figure 3.2
Average and marginal tax rates under maximin (Boadway and Jacquet 2008)

At the lower end, much depends on whether there is bunching, that is, whether persons of more than one skill level choose the same consumption-income bundle. With no bunching, as mentioned the marginal tax rate is zero for the least-skilled, unless the social welfare function is maximin, and rises steeply for low skills. However, bunching at the bottom is likely in practice, assuming those at the bottom have very low skills. In principle, the bunching could entail low-skilled individuals earning positive, but small, amounts of income, but it is more likely the case that a nonnegative income constraint at the bottom is binding. In either case the marginal tax rate applying at the end of the bunching range will be positive, and will again generally rise sharply for lower skill levels above the bunched range (except in the maximin case).

An alternative approach was developed by Saez (2001) and provides more intuition about the derivation of the optimal tax formula. Saez translates the analysis from wage space to income or earnings space. Let $H(y)$ represent the distribution of individuals by income y, with density $h(y)$. Note that income, which equals $w\ell$, is endogenous, unlike w. Using $y = w\ell$, preferences can be written as

$$v(c, y) = c - \frac{1}{1+(1/e)}\left(\frac{y}{w}\right)^{1+(1/e)}.$$

Given the budget constraint, $c = y - T(y)$, the optimal choice of income yields $y = w(1 - T'(y))^e$, so e is the elasticity of income with respect to its "price," $1 - T'(y)$:

$$e = \frac{dy}{d(1-T'(y))}\frac{1-T'(y)}{y}.$$

Suppose now that the optimal income tax is in place, and consider an increase in the marginal income tax rate at a given level of income, holding all other marginal tax rates constant. In the optimum, that change should not affect social welfare. Formally, perturb the income tax function by increasing incrementally the marginal tax rate at y (over the interval $y + dy$), holding the marginal tax rates unchanged elsewhere. This has the following effects, corresponding to the effects identified by Kaplow above.

For all those with incomes $y' > y$, their tax liabilities rise by $dT'dy$. Since their marginal tax rate does not change, the income they earn does not change because there are no income effects on labor supply because of quasi-linearity. There are $1 - H(y)$ of these persons, so government revenue rises by $(1 - H(y))dT'dy$. This represents a transfer from these taxpayers to the government. In an optimum, the value of a unit of government revenue is unity, since the government could make an equal lump-sum transfer to all households. Let $G(y)$ be the average social value of giving a unit of income to all those with $y' > y$. It will be decreasing in y, and less than unity except at the minimum value of y since the government values redistribution. Therefore the net value of the revenue obtained from those with incomes $y' > y$ is $(1 - G(y))(1 - H(y))dT'dy$. (The term $1 - G(y)$ is the equivalent of the second term on the right-hand side of the expression above for the optimal marginal income tax rate.)

There is also an effect on those in the interval $y + dy$ whose marginal tax rate has increased. Using the expression for elasticity e above, their earnings fall by $-dy = -eydT'/(1 - T')$ each, so tax revenue falls by $-T'(y)dy$ each. Since there are $h(y)$ persons at income level y, the loss in tax revenues from them is

$$-\frac{eydT'}{1-T'}h(y)T'dy.$$

(Their loss in welfare is negligible since they are optimizing their earnings when the small change is introduced.)

When the tax structure is optimized, the net gain from the revenue obtained from those with $y' > y$ must just offset the loss in revenue from those with income y, which leads to

$$\frac{T'(y)}{1-T'(y)} = \frac{1}{e}\cdot\frac{1-H(y)}{yh(y)}\cdot(1-G(y)).$$

This is the equivalent of the optimal tax formula derived earlier and has a similar interpretation. The tax is decreasing in e and $G(y)$, as expected. It is increasing in $1 - H(y)$, which is the number of persons whose tax payments go up when the marginal tax rate on y rises, and decreasing in $yh(y)$, which is the total output of those at income level y. Of course, this new equation is derived under some strong assumptions, including quasi-linearity of preferences and constant elasticity of earnings with respect to $(1 - T'(y))$. Nonetheless, the intuition carries through to more complicated settings.

These results are for the standard model of optimal nonlinear income tax pioneered by Mirrlees (1971). Qualitatively different results for the marginal tax structure are obtained under different assumptions. One important and policy-relevant caveat to the standard results arises when individual labor supply behavior is altered. The standard model assumes that labor supply variability is along the intensive margin: individuals vary their intensity of work effort. A complementary approach is to assume that they make discrete decisions, about whether to participate in the labor market (the extensive margin), and if so, in what sort of employment. This approach is isolated by assuming that hours of work are fixed, following Diamond (1980) and Saez (2002b), and exploited by Brewer, Saez, and Shephard (2010). In the pure extensive margin approach, workers of any skill simply choose whether to work for an income commensurate with their skill, or not to work. Preferences for work vary across the population, so for any skill level some will choose to work, and others will not. (The government cannot observe preferences for work.) In such a setting, if the government has a redistributive motive, marginal tax rates will be negative at the bottom, except in special circumstances.[34] This result implies that low-income workers will receive a greater transfer than the unemployed, a result that stands in stark contrast with the standard model where marginal tax rates are always nonnegative at the bottom. The result might be taken to rationalize the existence of refundable tax credits for low-income workers that are found in several countries, such as Canada, the United Kingdom, and the United States, and which if large enough can imply a negative marginal tax rate (or higher transfers if working) at the lowest skill levels.

To see this result, consider the simple case drawn from Saez (2002b). Individuals are endowed with a skill level w_i drawn from a discrete distribution, with $w_i > w_{i-1}$ for $i \leqslant I$. If they choose to work, they do so at a job specific to their skill level, supply one unit of labor and obtain earnings w_i. These earnings are observable to the government. If they choose not to work, their earnings are zero, though they will receive a transfer from the government. Denote by $w_0 = 0$ the earnings of those who choose not to work, regardless of their skill level. Individuals of a given skill level differ in their preferences for leisure versus work. Some will choose to work and earn w_i, and other will choose not to work and earn $w_0 = 0$. The number of workers who choose to work in

---

34. Wage subsidies at the bottom can be rationalized in other ways. For example, they can be optimal if there are fixed costs of working, as shown in Boadway, Marceau and Sato (1999). See also the wide-ranging discussion in Keen (1997).

occupation i is denoted n_i, and those who choose not to work comprise n_0, where $\sum_{i=0}^{I} n_i = 1$. While the government can observe earnings, it cannot observe the preferences for work of a given person. Therefore taxes can be conditional only on earnings, and are denoted t_i for $i = 0, \ldots, I$, where t_i can be positive or negative. Consumption levels are then given by $c_i = w_i - t_i$.

Suppose preferences are quasi-linear in consumption. This implies that labor choices depend only on the return from choosing to work and not on income. The number of workers of type i who choose to work can then be written as $n_i(c_i - c_0)$, where $n_i' > 0$. Define the elasticity of labor supply of type i's as

$$\eta_i(\cdot) = (c_i - c_0) \frac{n_i'(\cdot)}{n_i(\cdot)}.$$

It reflects the distribution of preferences for leisure among persons of skill-type i.

The government needs to raise a given amount of revenue R using taxes on earnings. The budget constraint is $\sum_{i=0}^{I} n_i(\cdot) t_i = R$. The government objective is assumed to be to redistribute from higher to lower skill persons. Following the logic of the standard approach, suppose that in a second-best optimum, the social value of consumption is declining in skills, $W'(c_i) > W'(c_{i+1})$ for $i > 0$. The case of $i = 0$ is more contentious. Those earning $w_0 = 0$ include persons of all skill levels. They have chosen not to work either because they have a high preference for leisure or because they find working more difficult because of some disability. It could reasonably be assumed that either $W'(c_0) < W'(c_1)$ or the opposite. It will become clear in what follows that the same qualitative results apply in either case, as long as $W'(c_0)$ is not too high relative to all others. In any case, in the optimum, the values of $W'(c_i)$ will satisfy $\sum_{i=0}^{I} n_i W_i' = 1$. Intuitively, a uniform lump-sum transfer to all individuals will have the same value as an additional euro in the hands of the government since, with no income effects, the reward from working and therefore labor supply behavior n_i is unaffected by a uniform transfer.

It is straightforward to infer that the optimal tax structure in this case will satisfy the following simple condition (Saez 2002b; Brewer, Saez, and Shephard 2010):

$$\frac{t_i - t_0}{c_i - c_0} = \frac{1 - W'(c_i)}{\eta_i} \quad \text{for } i \geqslant 1. \tag{3.4}$$

This represents the participation tax faced by a type-i person. The numerator is an equity effect—the social benefit of transferring a euro from a type-i worker to the government—while the denominator is an efficiency effect, reflecting the change in participation from the change in tax. The proof of this is intuitive. An incremental increase in the tax on w_i directly transfers an amount of revenue $n_i dt_i$ to the government, and this transfer has a social value of $(1 - W'(c_i))n_i dt_i$. In addition there is an induced reduction in labor supply of $dn_i = -n_i \eta_i dt_i / (c_i - c_0)$, leading to a change of tax revenue of $-(t_i - t_0)n_i \eta_i dt_i / (c_i - c_0)$. This change in revenue is the social value arising from the change in labor supply dn_i since those marginal persons exiting the labor force are just indifferent. (Labor supply of other types is unaffected since their reward from working is unchanged.) The sum of these two effects will be zero when the above condition is satisfied.

This expression (3.4) for the optimal tax structure has the following implications. First, suppose that $W'(c_i) > 0$ for all persons. Then, since the average value of $W'(c_i)$ is unity, it will generally be the case that $W'(c_1) > 1$. In that case, $t_1 < t_0$, implying that the marginal tax rate applying at the bottom of the earnings distribution is *negative*. This will also be the case for other skill levels near the bottom. This is contrary to the standard model in which labor supply varies by hours worked—the intensive margin labor response. We saw above that marginal tax rates must be nonnegative in that case, and in fact are likely to be highly positive near the bottom. Note that this result will be strengthened if $W'(c_0) < W'(c_1)$, which implies that the government gives less social weight to consumption by those who choose not to work compared with all those who do. That may be regarded by some as a reasonable assumption given that many persons who choose not to work may be high skilled persons with a strong preference for leisure. Note further that since $W'(c_i) < 1$ for persons at the top of the income distribution, there should be a tax on participation for the high-skilled persons. This result, which occurs because all persons who choose not to work are given the same social weight, might be regarded as anomalous to the extent that one thinks that persons of a given skill level who choose not to work should not receive a higher transfer than those who do work. In fact the issue of how the government should treat persons with different preferences is a vexing one, and one that we return to in chapter 5.

Next consider how taxes change as one goes up the earnings scale. Rewrite (3.4) as follows:

$$t_i = \frac{c_i - c_0}{\eta_i}(1 - W'(c_i)) + t_0.$$

Then, t_i will rise with income, so the marginal tax rate on income is positive, if the right-hand side of this expression rises with income. Given that both c_i and $1 - W'(c_i)$ rise with income, so will t_i as long as the participation elasticity η_i is nonincreasing in income (Jacquet, Lehmann, and Van der Linden 2010). Evidence is limited on that question, although the results reported in Meghir and Phillips (2010) support the suggestion that η_i declines with income. If that is the case, the optimal income tax structure (3.4) could be implemented by an income tax system with positive marginal tax rates combined with a refundable employment tax credit targeted at low-income workers, a system that is in place in some OECD countries. How progressive the rate structure should be is another matter that we return to briefly below.

This argument for negative marginal tax rates at the bottom has been derived from a fairly special model. Changing the assumptions will restore the standard results. For one thing, if the government objective function is highly egalitarian, the result will not apply. Consider the extreme case of a maximin social welfare function. Suppose also that the unemployed group earning $w_0 = 0$ includes those who are judged to be the worst off. In this case the government gives no weight to persons with earnings $w_i > 0$, so $W'(c_i) = 0$ for $i \geqslant 0$. It follows from the optimal tax formula (3.4) that $t_i > t_0$ for all i, so marginal tax rates are positive at the bottom.[35] In fact for all wage groups there is positive tax associated with choosing to work. The change in tax liabilities in going from w_i to w_{i+1} will still be positive if η_i is nonincreasing, as above.

For another thing, as soon as we assume that labor supply involves more than a participation decision, negative marginal tax rates at the bottom become less likely. Saez (2002b) considered one such case. Suppose that individuals can choose among three options: work in the

---

35. Saez (2002b) notes that marginal tax rates will also be positive if the government has no redistributive motive, so $W'(c_i)$ is the same for all income levels, and thus less than unity.

occupation suited to their skill, work in the occupation of the next lowest skill (which requires less effort), or not participate in the labor market. Thus jobs at any skill level i can include both type-i and type-$(i+1)$ persons. Maintaining the quasi-linear-in-consumption utility function so only relative rewards affect labor choice, the supply function of workers to jobs requiring skill level i can be written $n_i(c_i - c_0, c_i - c_{i-1}, c_{i+1} - c_i)$. The first argument represents the reward from participation, the second is the reward a type-i person obtains from choosing job i rather than a less skilled job, and the third the reward of a type $i+1$ choosing occupation i. Define the elasticity of occupational choice for type-i workers as

$$\varepsilon_i(\cdot) = \frac{c_i - c_{i-1}}{n_i} \frac{\partial n_i(\cdot)}{\partial(c_i - c_{i-1})},$$

the presumption being that it takes more effort to do a higher skilled job, so consumption c_i must be rising in i. Then Saez (2002b) shows, using similar techniques as above, that the optimal tax schedule satisfies

$$\frac{t_i - t_{i-1}}{c_i - c_{i-1}} = \frac{1}{\varepsilon_i n_i} \sum_{j=i}^{I} n_j \left[1 - W'(c_j) - \eta_j \frac{t_j - t_0}{c_j - c_0} \right] \qquad \text{for } i \geqslant 1. \tag{3.5}$$

This tax function now includes two tax margins: the participation margin, $t_j - t_0$, and the occupational choice margin, $t_i - t_{i-1}$. Whether marginal tax rates are positive or negative depends on the relative magnitudes of the participation elasticity η_j and the job choice elasticity, ε_i. To see this, note that in the extreme case where $\eta_j = 0$, optimal taxes now satisfy

$$\frac{t_i - t_{i-1}}{c_i - c_{i-1}} = \frac{1}{\varepsilon_i n_i} \sum_{j=i}^{I} n_j (1 - W'(c_j)) \qquad \text{for } i \geqslant 1. \tag{3.6}$$

It follows that if $W'(c_i)$ is decreasing in i for all $i \geqslant 0$, the marginal tax rate across occupations must be positive, $t_i > t_{i-1}$.[36] This includes those at the lowest skill level, so $t_1 > t_0$. At the other extreme where $\varepsilon_i = 0$, the general formula (3.5) reduces to (3.4), where as we have seen marginal tax rates at the bottom will be negative. When both participation and job choice elasticities are positive, the sign of marginal tax rates will

---

36. This is because $\sum_{i=0}^{I} n_i = 1$ and $\sum_{i=0}^{I} n_i W'(c_i) = 1$. Then, assuming $W'(c_0) > W'(c_1)$, we must have the case that $\sum_{j=i}^{I} n_j (1 - W'(c_j)) > 0$ for all $i > 0$.

depend on the relative magnitude of the two elasticities, so we can no longer be sure that marginal tax rates at the bottom from choosing to participate in the labor market should be zero.

Jacquet, Lehmann, and Van der Linden (2010) have studied the case where instead of choosing among occupations, labor market participants choose intensity of effort. There is a fixed cost of labor market participation that varies among individuals, and given that, individuals must choose first whether to work, and then if so, how many hours. They show remarkably that in this more general context, as in the simple extensive-margin context, as long as the participation elasticity η_i is increasing in skills, the marginal income tax rate on earnings will be positive throughout the income distribution. Of course, there can still be a positive subsidy to participation. They calibrate their model to US data and find that the pattern of marginal tax rates takes an inverted U-shape, but is otherwise fairly flat regardless of the aversion to inequality in the social welfare function. In other words, the tax structure appears to exhibit limited progressivity. Figure 3.3 depicts the qualitative pattern of marginal tax rates reported by Jacquet, Lehmann, and Van der Linden when there are both intensive and extensive labor market responses.

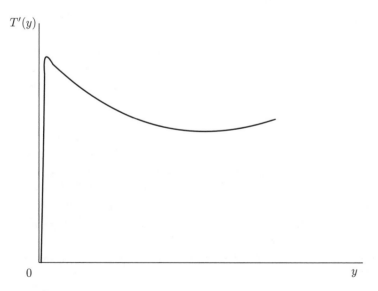

Figure 3.3
Marginal tax rates with intensive and extensive margins (Jacquet, Lehmann, and Van der Linden 2010)

It is worth re-emphasizing an important element of extensive-margin approach of Diamond (1980) and Saez (2002b): decisions about participation and occupational choice are partly driven by heterogeneous individual preferences for work. As we will see later, it is not entirely obvious how persons with different tastes for work or leisure should be treated for social welfare purposes. One can imagine giving more weight to those who have a distaste for work to the extent that work genuinely makes them worse off than their peers without the same distaste. One can also imagine the opposite, treating those with a distaste for work as leisure lovers who are more of a burden on society than they should be.[37] Which view one takes will partly determine how redistributive the tax-transfer system should be. One might even attribute different national approaches to redistribution as reflecting different views about preferences for leisure. Some societies might be more tolerant of low-income persons, regarding their lot as simply bad luck. Other societies might regard low income as a sign of laziness and prefer not to reward it. An alternative approach is to be neutral with respect to preferences, and neither reward nor penalize persons according to their preferences. This is in keeping with the Principle of Responsibility that was mentioned earlier, according to which persons ought not to be compensated for outcomes for which they are regarded as being responsible, one of which might be their preferred choices. We return to this concept again later.

The results mentioned so far are mainly for the pattern of marginal tax rates. Analytical results on average tax rates are scarcer. One suggestive finding that is based on algebraic analysis rather than simulation is by Boadway and Jacquet (2008) for the Mirrleesian case where labor varies according to hours worked or effort rather than participation. They show that for a maximin social welfare function, the pattern of average tax rates (taxes per unit of income) will be single peaked under the same reasonably weak assumptions mentioned above. Of course, total tax liabilities will rise throughout the skill distribution. These results reinforce those obtained from simulation analysis. Even with a highly egalitarian social welfare function, there are significant limits to redistribution arising from the information constraint that the government faces. Figure 3.2 depicts both average and marginal tax rate for the maximin case.

---

37. This distinction is stressed in Cuff (2000) and Marchand, Pestieau, and Racionero (2003).

These constraints to redistribution are even more apparent when less information is available to the government. As Marhuenda and Ortuño-Ortin (1997) and Chander and Wilde (1998) show, if the government cannot observe income and must rely on a system of self-reporting subject to auditing and penalties, redistribution is severely constrained. Chander and Wilde show that even if incomes are fixed, so there is no labor–leisure distortion, the optimal income tax might even be regressive under tax evasion (and given some reasonable restrictions on penalties for evasion). If auditing is subject to errors, redistribution is constrained even more, and the revelation principle may no longer apply (Boadway and Sato 2000). In particular, if there are no rewards for honest reporting (i.e., for persons who have been audited and found to be reporting truthfully), intentional evasion will not be deterred, unlike in standard optimal tax models with evasion, including Cremer and Gahvari (1996), Marhuenda and Ortuño-Ortin (1997), and Chander and Wilde (1998).

In fact tax evasion can be incorporated into the efficiency cost of redistribution by interpreting the elasticity of earnings e, used in the derivation earlier of the optimal tax formula from the income distribution, to be the elasticity of taxable income, as suggested by Feldstein (1999). Following Chetty (2009), consider linear progressive taxation for simplicity and assume preferences are quasi-linear in consumption. Assume also that households can shelter an amount of income s at a cost $\phi(s)$, where $\phi(s)$ is strictly convex. For now, sheltering can be interpreted as being tax avoidance or evasion. The household with wage rate w maximizes $c - d(y/w) - \phi(s)$ subject to a budget constraint $c = m + (1 - t)(y - s) + s$, where $y - s$ is taxable income and m is the lump-sum component of the tax system. This results in an indirect utility function $v(t,m)$ with $v_t = -(y - s)$ and $v_m = 1$. Suppose that the government increases the tax rate and returns the extra revenues back to the household as a lump-sum transfer, so $dm = y - s + td(y - s)/dt$. The change in the utility of the household, which here is the change in social utility if we assume a utilitarian social welfare function, is $dv/dt = v_t + v_m dm/dt = td(y - s)/dt$.

This suggests that it is the elasticity of taxable or reported income that is relevant for the elasticity e in the optimal marginal income tax rate formula. Empirical estimates suggest that the elasticity of taxable income can be relatively high at high-income levels compared with low-income levels, leading to an argument for limiting the progressivity at the upper end of the income distribution.[38] However, as Chetty (2009) points out, this ignores the fact that not all costs of sheltering constitute resource costs. Some represent a transfer to another agent, including the government through a fine. As well, taxpayers may overestimate the expected cost of evasion (auditing and penalties). Taking both of these into account would reduce the efficiency cost of sheltering below that obtained by using the elasticity of taxable income.

Progressivity is also affected by human capital accumulation. In the next chapter I consider the question of whether education policy aimed at reducing the skill distribution is as effective a device for redistribution as the income tax system. Perhaps surprisingly, it seems not to be. However, the existence of education can itself affect the optimal progressivity of the income tax. Bovenberg and Jacobs (2005) show that since progressive earnings taxation discourages human capital accumulation, endogeneity of human capital reduces optimal progressivity. However, this can be mitigated by subsidizing human capital accumulation in tandem with progressive taxation.

One final and potentially important effect on progressivity concerns uncertainty. In the standard Mirrlees model of optimal income taxation, there is no uncertainty. Alternatively, one could interpret the model as assuming all uncertainty (about skills) has been resolved ex ante. This naturally leads to interpreting redistributive taxation as a form of social insurance against the possible bad fortune of being endowed with low skills. Extensions of the Mirrlees model to dynamic settings, as in Golosov, Kocherlakota, and Tsyvinski (2003), allow for the stochastic evolution of skills but retain the property that redistributive labor income taxation is implemented after wage uncertainty is resolved (see also Golosov, Tsyvinski, and Werning 2007; Diamond 2007). As we have seen, in these models there is still uncertainty involved with savings decisions, which occur before future wage uncertainty is resolved. But the policy implications of this form of uncertainty lead to an argument for capital income taxation rather than progressivity of the labor income tax (see also Varian 1980 for the seminal argument for the income tax as an insurance instrument against uncertain savings).

---

38. Recent estimates for Canada in Department of Finance (2010) report elasticities of the order of 0.62 to 0.72 in the top percentile of the skill distribution compared with about 0.2 in the top decile. These are comparable to findings in the United States (Gruber and Saez 2002).

From the point of view of income tax progressivity, the more interesting case is where labor supply decisions are taken before uncertainty about outcomes is resolved. Early analyses of this case are found in Eaton and Rosen (1980) and Tuomala (1984). The analysis is complicated by the fact that both uncertainty and the income tax affect labor supply in sometimes confounding ways. For example, uncertainty can alone increase labor supply as individuals attempt to self-insure themselves by precautionary means. In these circumstances there is a trade-off in choosing the degree of progressivity. More progressivity enhances insurance but at the same time induces possibly adverse incentive effects via reduced labor supply as individuals reduce self-insurance. Given the difficulties of obtaining analytical results, Eaton and Rosen use simulation analysis to illustrate how the progressivity of a linear progressive tax system is affected by uncertainty about ex post outcomes. They consider a simple economy in which there are two classes of persons, each with different ex post wage distributions but with different expected wages. They compute how the marginal tax rate of the linear progressive tax varies with different parameters. Not surprisingly, the tax rate increases with the degree of risk aversion of individuals. They also show that increased revenue requirements increase the marginal tax rate. Interestingly they show that progressivity is not unambiguously higher when individuals take their labor supply decisions ex ante than when they take them ex post, but this finding depends on the extent of risk aversion. Presumably, progressivity would also depend on the extent of inequality aversion in the social welfare function, which Eaton and Rosen take to be zero by assuming a utilitarian social welfare function.

Low and Maldoom (2004) have recently greatly clarified the trade-offs involved in the choice of progressivity. Their analysis focuses on ex ante identical individuals who choose the same labor supplies but achieve different outcomes ex post because of idiosyncratic uncertainty. The two key determinants of ex post progressivity are the coefficient of prudence—which determines the extent of precautionary labor supply induced by uncertainty—and the degree of risk aversion—which determines the insurance benefit of progressivity. Formally, the progressivity of the income tax depends on the following ratio involving the utility of consumption $u(x)$:

$$P(x) = -\frac{u'''(x)/u''(x)}{u''(x)/u'(x)},$$

where the numerator represents the degree of prudence and the denominator the extent of risk aversion. For sufficiently large positive values of $P(x)$, the incentive effect dominates the insurance effect and the marginal tax rate declines with income, and vice versa.

This is based on a relatively simple model of redistribution and uncertainty, and other elements have been added by other authors. An important extension is that of Sinn (1996), who takes account of the fact that social insurance broadly conceived may induce an increase in socially beneficial risk-taking by individuals. This serves to mute the moral hazard effect of insurance, and seemingly enhances the case for progressivity. Indeed social insurance may even result in more pre-tax inequality in this context, which presumably cannot be seen as a bad thing. Cremer and Pestieau (1996), following Rochet (1991), have considered the consequences of the fact that at least some risk faced by individuals may be insurable. The more such insurance is available, the less needs to be done through the income tax system.

3.5   Asymmetric Information and Market Failure

Much of the optimal tax literature has focused on asymmetric information between the government and the private sector and the implications that might have for policy. At the same time asymmetric information can occur within the private sector as well, resulting in inefficient outcomes (relative to the first-best outcome). In some cases, even though the government may be no better informed than the least-informed agents in the private sector, it may still be able to improve outcomes by fiscal policy intervention. Although it is beyond the scope of our approach to do justice to this literature, some lessons might nonetheless be summarized.

Consider labor markets first. For the purposes of optimal tax analysis, firms are assumed to be fully informed about their employees, both their productivity and their work effort. Realistically, neither of these apply in practice. Firms may not be able to observe fully how much effort workers are exerting, in which case they must resort to various means to learn something. The classic paper by Shapiro and Stiglitz (1984) supposes that firms' supervisors can monitor workers randomly to determine whether they are shirking, and in the event that they are found shirking, they can be fired. In such a setting the equilibrium wage must be such that enough involuntary unemployment is created so that the cost of being fired induces workers not to shirk. The model is a very simple one incorporating a number of stark assumptions: costless and errorless monitoring, the inability of the government to observe whether workers have been fired or laid off, the absence of performance bonds, and so on. Nonetheless, the intuition is compelling and gives rise to unambiguous policy advice. Welfare can be improved by a wage subsidy, though worsened by unemployment benefits that do not distinguish between those laid off for shirking and those laid off involuntarily (in equilibrium, however, there is no shirking in the simple Shapiro–Stiglitz model).[39]

In Shapiro and Stiglitz, asymmetric information takes the form of hidden action by the workers: all workers are of identical potential productivity. Alternatively, workers may differ in ability, and that may not be observable by firms. Weiss (1980) constructs a simple model with workers drawn from a continuum of skills who may be employed in one of two sectors. In one sector, skills are observable and rewarded accordingly. In the other, skills cannot be observed, perhaps because workers work in teams. All workers receive the same wage rate despite differing in productivity, so all workers with a skill level greater than the wage paid in the uninformed sector go to the other sector. Uninformed firms hire workers (randomly from the pool) such that the expected marginal product equals the wage rate. Given that the marginal worker produces more than the expected (or average) wage, too few workers are hired by the uninformed sector. That is, the market-clearing wage is below the optimal wage. In these circumstances, an employment subsidy will be efficiency improving even though the government is no better informed about worker quality.

Moreover Weiss shows that there may be involuntary unemployment in this two-sector model: the market wage offered in the uninformed sector may be above the market clearing level. The reason is that there is an adverse selection effect at work. If the wage is above the market-clearing level, firms may be reluctant to reduce it because, despite reducing labor costs, a lower wage attracts lower quality workers into the sector. So the optimal policy response still calls for an employment subsidy.

---

39. Boadway, Cuff, and Marceau (2003) study optimal policy in an efficiency-wage model in which the government can observe the reason for layoffs, and in which there is voluntary unemployment arising from a participation decision among workers with different values of leisure, as in Saez (2002b). In this context, there may or may not be involuntary unemployment in a second-best optimum, and the optimal employment or wage tax can be positive or negative.

In the hidden information setting of Weiss, high-ability workers will have an incentive to reveal their types to the firms, and firms will have an incentive to learn worker types. Both will devote resources to obtaining this information. Firms may, for example, engage in pre-screening of potential employees using tests or other devices. Workers may engage in costly signaling activities, such as performing well in education or training programs (Spence 1973). These kinds of activities tend to mitigate the asymmetric information problem and also the case for fiscal intervention.

Imperfect information about worker types can also lead to costly search and matching procedures that are also inefficient. Diamond (1982) develops a simple search or matching model in which the chance of a suitable match between a job applicant and a firm depends on the aggregate number of vacancies posted and the number of job applicants. In these circumstances the firm's decision to post vacancies involves a negative externality on other firms in the labor market. A tax on employment can then be efficiency improving.

More recently Hungerbühler et al. (2006) study optimal income taxes in a Mirrlees-type setting but with frictional unemployment induced by costly matching.[40] In their context, matching occurs for every skill level, and each wage rate is determined by Nash bargaining between workers and firms. Taxes affect the bargaining process by affecting the surplus to be bargained for and the marginal gains from bargaining. In particular, an increase in the marginal tax rate reduces the incentive for workers to bargain, causing a fall in the wage rate and an increase in labor demand. Unemployment falls below the most efficient level. In contrast, an increase in average tax rates has the opposite effect: wage rates increase, reducing labor demand. Governments are induced to increase marginal tax rates both to compensate for the effect of average tax rates on labor demand and to raise revenue. The result is that marginal tax rates exceed average tax rates, implying increasing average tax rates (contrary to the standard results). Moreover the marginal tax rate at the top will be positive. Their simulations show that with ability-specific matching and wages determined by Nash bargaining, taxes are much more redistributive than in the Mirrlees (1971) setting. This is an interesting finding, and serves to temper the agnostic

---

40. Boone and Bovenberg (2002) and Boadway, Cuff, and Marceau (2003) also study redistribution policy when frictional unemployment exists in the labor market. Their models are somewhat simpler in design.

progressivity results of the standard model, especially with tax evasion added. However, it remains to be seen to what extent the results would survive more realistic wage determination mechanisms.

Parallel considerations apply in other markets. Consider the case of credit markets. Stiglitz and Weiss (1981) develop a simple model of entrepreneurs who are endowed with projects characterized by different values of the probability of success p and the return if successful R. Each project requires a given amount of capital, and is financed entirely by a bank loan of size B, assumed to be the same for all projects. Competitive banks know the distribution of projects by (p, R), and although they do not know the characteristics of any given project, they do know a project's expected return pR. They offer an interest rate r for projects of a given expected return and rely on entrepreneurs to decide whether to demand a loan. An entrepreneur will request a loan if the expected profit of the project, $p(R - (1 - r)B)$, exceeds the return the entrepreneur can obtain elsewhere. Those that turn out to be successful are able to repay the loan, while the others declare bankruptcy and the bank receives nothing.

Two main results fall out of the Stiglitz–Weiss setup. First, too few projects will be undertaken relative to the social optimum. In particular, entrepreneurs with higher risk (lower p) projects choose to take a loan (given that losses on unsuccessful projects are borne entirely by the banks, while the entrepreneurs retain the profit of successful projects), while those with lower risk (higher p) projects do not. In equilibrium too few low-risk projects are undertaken from an efficiency point of view. Second, there is a possibility of credit rationing whereby the market interest rate is set below the market-clearing level, creating an excess demand for loans. Banks are reluctant to raise the interest rate because doing so screens out more low-risk projects and reduces the probability of success of those remaining in the pool.[41] Regardless of whether credit rationing occurs, efficiency can be improved by the government offering a subsidy on loans, even though it is no better informed than the banks.

The results of Stiglitz and Weiss are model specific. De Meza and Webb (1987) show that if banks are assumed to be able to observe the return on projects if successful, R, instead of the expected return, pR, too many projects are undertaken and those that are will be the lower

---

41. In the extreme this kind of adverse selection in the credit market can cause the market to fail completely and not provide any loans. See Mankiw (1986) for an example of this.

risk (higher p) ones. Moreover no credit rationing can occur since an increase in the interest rate will screen out low-p projects and increase the average probability of success of projects undertaken. In this scenario, taxing entrepreneurs will increase efficiency.

Boadway and Keen (2006) generalize the Stiglitz–Weiss and de Meza–Webb cases to allow the banks to know only the general two-dimensional distribution from which p and R are drawn. In this general case, too few low-risk, low-return (high-p, low-R) projects will be undertaken and too many high-risk, high-return (low-p, high-R). (And credit rationing also remains a possibility.) A progressive tax on entrepreneurs would be welfare improving if it can be implemented. This would entail subsidizing projects with a low return and taxing those with a high return. Of course, since the government does not know R, it cannot impose such a tax without acquiring further information. In practice, it would have to rely on self-reporting by entrepreneurs, backed up by an effective audit and penalty system as in the standard income tax system.

As these examples indicate, much rides on what the banks are assumed to know. It can be argued that the de Meza–Webb assumption is more reasonable, at least in the context of these simple models. It seems less onerous to know the return that a project will yield if it is successful than its expected return, which involves knowing how project returns are related to probabilities of success. Once we allow for equity rather than debt finance, there is another reason to suppose that knowledge of R is reasonable. The payment to creditors for holding equity in the entrepreneur's project depends on R and must be verified. This can be done by a system of ex post monitoring.[42] Given that, one can assume that the terms of the equity finance are contingent on the project's return if successful R. Boadway and Keen (2006) show that if entrepreneurs are financed entirely by equity, overinvestment will unambiguously occur, as in the case of debt finance when R is known. Note that this is in sharp contrast with the classic result of Myers and Majluf (1984) for the case of new equity-financed investments by existing firms. They argued that there would be underinvestment in such projects. Because potential shareholders will not be perfectly informed,

---

42. Ex post monitoring of projects declared bankrupt must also be done in the case of debt finance. Boadway and Keen (2006) allow for such monitoring and find that it makes little qualitative difference to the results. Williamson (1987) considers some of the broader consequences of ex post monitoring. Crucially, he assumes that monitoring is error free in the sense that once a project is monitored at a cost, the true return is learned.

they cannot observe either the true value of new projects or the true value of existing capital in the firm. They will both undervalue high-quality projects and obtain a share of high-value existing capital at the expense of existing shareholders.[43]

More generally, if firms have a choice between debt and equity finance, high-R, low-p projects will opt for debt finance, while low-R, high-p projects (i.e., safer projects) will opt for equity (Hellmann and Stiglitz 2000; Boadway and Keen 2006). Intuitively the residual return of a high-R project goes to the entrepreneur in the case of debt. There will be overinvestment in both debt- and equity-financed investments, calling for a tax on all new projects. Moreover equity projects are the source of an additional form of inefficiency because all such projects must be monitored ex post, and not just unsuccessful ones as in the case of debt finance.

These simple models emanating from Stiglitz and Weiss (1982) and de Meza and Webb (1987) can be extended in some other directions to incorporate other assumptions about asymmetric information. Suppose that entrepreneurs have some initial wealth, and differ only in the probability of success. Entrepreneurs with a higher p would be more willing to offer collateral than low-p types. A set of separating contracts can be offered such that all entrepreneurs receive their actuarially fair interest rate, and higher p entrepreneurs pledge collateral. Assuming such an equilibrium exists (i.e., setting aside existence problems raised by Rothschild and Stiglitz 1976), entry of entrepreneurs will be efficient since marginal entrepreneurs—those with the lowest p—are not distorted.

A slightly more complicated case is that in which entrepreneurs can vary the size of their project, and therefore the amount of finance they require (Boadway et al. 1998; Boadway and Keen 2006). Consider again the case where p is not known. Also let entrepreneurs vary by an ability parameter that influences the amount of capital they will demand. In particular, revenues if successful are given by $aR(K)$, where a is ability and K the amount of capital chosen. Given p, higher ability entrepreneurs will demand more capital. To make things as simple as possible, suppose that p and a are perfectly correlated, although the correlation

---

43. New equity finance may also be provided by venture capitalists, who provide not only finance but also advice to entrepreneurs. Asymmetric information between venture capitalists will give rise to both adverse selection and two-sided moral hazard. For an analysis of some of the tax policy consequences of this, see Keuschnigg and Nielsen (2003, 2004).

can be positive or negative. In the case where a rises with p, higher ability entrepreneurs will demand more capital and in a first-best setting would pay a lower interest rate. The first best will not be incentive compatible unless differences in the demand for capital are relatively high compared with differences in actuarial interest rates. To achieve incentive compatibility, high-ability entrepreneurs must be offered a contract that forces high-ability types to use more capital than in the first best. A separating outcome will be inefficient since too much capital is being used. However, the number of entrepreneurs who choose to enter is efficient since decisions of the marginal entrepreneur are not distorted. Interestingly the inefficiency associated with overuse of capital can be mitigated by a tax on low-interest loans. The argument extends also to the case where the low-ability entrepreneurs have the higher probability of success. A tax on low-interest loans improves efficiency in this case as well.

Another extension involves new entrepreneurs facing adverse selection in both credit and labor markets. This case, which combines the models of de Meza and Webb (1987) and Weiss (1980), has been studied by Boadway and Sato (2011). Entrepreneurs differ in their probability of success, or ability, reflected in p. They hire a number of workers from a pool of workers of differing quality, and the return if successful depends on the average quality of workers hired. Since worker quality cannot be observed, a common wage must be offered to each one in the entrepreneurial sector, with the result that the lowest quality workers opt for this sector and the others go elsewhere to receive a wage equal to their true ability. However, higher ability entrepreneurs will undertake projects. There are three sources of inefficiency in this setup. As in de Meza and Webb, adverse selection in the credit market will tend to cause too many low-p entrepreneurs to enter. In the labor market, workers of too low a quality will be attracted to the entrepreneurial sector, and those that are attracted will generally be mismatched with entrepreneurs of different abilities. It turns out that multiple equilibria can occur, of which stable ones can either be in the interior with some entrepreneurs entering or at the corner where none enter. Those equilibria in the interior may involve involuntary unemployment, as in Weiss. As well, they may involve credit rationing contrary to de Meza and Webb. If the interior stable equilibrium involves involuntary unemployment, too few entrepreneurs will enter, while if the interior involves full employment, there may be too many or two few entrepreneurs: de Meza–Webb arguments encourage too many entrepreneurs, while the desire to increase the number of higher quality workers that enter induces too few. In addition to taxes or subsidies on entrepreneurs, it may be efficient to impose a tax or subsidy on employment or on wages. It may even be necessary to deploy a "big push" policy—that is, a temporary subsidy substantial enough to encourage enough entry of entrepreneurs to take the economy past the unstable equilibrium—if the initial equilibrium is a corner solution.

One final interesting case to consider involves nonrenewable natural resources, like oil and gas or minerals. A number of features of these, along with asymmetric information, make them unique and worthy of study. In most countries natural resource wealth is the property of the government, so the government is necessarily involved both in the commercial exploitation of the resources and the diversion of rents from the resources to the public sector. Natural resource exploration tends to be very uncertain, investment can be large, and eventual extraction can last for decades. On top of that, the government is likely to be much less informed than the firms that are exploiting the resource about the costs of extraction and perhaps even of revenues. Arrangements made by governments to contract with private firms to exploit natural resources must take account of all these circumstances. The large initial investment gives rise to commitment problems that can be particularly severe given the changes in market prices than can occur after the contract has been negotiated. The uncertainty about the size and value of deposits means that risk-sharing between the government and private firms is relevant. Moreover methods for obtaining revenues from natural resources can lead to inefficiencies in exploitation to the extent that policy instruments do not mimic resource rents.

These issues have been addressed in detail elsewhere (Boadway and Keen 2010), but a few brief comments are in order. It is first useful to note that there are a variety of different policy instruments for extracting rents from natural resources, and they vary mainly by the timing of rent extraction. Rents can be obtained up front by auctioning the rights to discover, extract, and develop natural resources. To the extent that auctions are competitive and that bidders are fully informed, the winning bid should be the present value of future rents discounted by risk. There are a number of issues that arise in designing an auction to ensure adequate participation and competitive bids, including the form of the auction, its scope with respect to the size of properties, the bundling of properties, and any future charges or obligations associated with resource development. Of particular importance is the need to ensure that the bidding encompasses the full rents of the resource to account for all initial costs that have been incurred in discovering the resource property so that exploration activity is rewarded and not discouraged.

Alternatively, rent taxes can be designed that are neutral and therefore capture economic rents over the lifetime of the project. Various forms of rent taxes can be applied, ranging from a cash-flow tax or R-based tax of the Meade Report (1978) to the various cash-flow equivalent taxes that I mentioned earlier, such as the allowance for corporate equity (ACE) tax that has been used in some European countries (Klemm 2007) and has been recommended for the Australian nonrenewable resource sector by Australian Treasury (2010) (the Henry Review), the resource rent tax (RRT) proposed by Garnaut and Clunies Ross (1975), and more generally the class of neutral taxes analyzed by Boadway and Bruce (1984b). Rent taxes differ from auctions not only in the timing of their revenues but also in the proportion of total rents raised. In principle, auctions will divert 100 percent of expected risk-adjusted rents, whereas rent taxes will typically be at rates much less that 100 percent. Rent taxes might also be progressive in the sense of applying a higher tax rate to higher rent outcomes. Of course, auction prices will discount any future taxes the government might impose, including those that reflect commitment failure, that is, political risk.

The choice among resource tax regimes, including combinations of tax instruments, hinges on a number of considerations. One is the matter of commitment. Given the long time horizon and the large initial investments in natural resource projects, it is very tempting for even benevolent governments to tax quasi-rents obtained in the future once investment is in place, and this is especially true when natural resource prices are relatively high. While it is difficult to undo this temptation completely, some measures may mitigate the problem. Up-front investment incentives can offset some of the discouragement of investment that is a natural consequence of the holdup problem. As well, tax structures that postpone tax liabilities until the future and that are progressive with respect to rents can reduce the political desire to increase taxes when rents are high.

The optimal timing of resource tax revenues will also depend on the discount rate of the government relative to the resource firms. On the one hand, given the political risk faced by the firms, their discount rate might be relatively high, and this would suggest postponing tax revenues to the future. As well, governments may be better able to shed risk, and some in developing countries might also have access to loans at concessionary rates. On the other hand, the social discount rates might be especially high in developing countries owing to the expectation that future generations will have much higher levels of per capita consumption.

Finally, asymmetric information considerations might lead to combining tax instruments to alleviate the problem, and can account for the observed use of seemingly distortionary policies. Suppose, for example, that the government cannot observe the rents earned by resource firms but relies on them to self-report. It may be much easier for them to overreport their costs than to underreport their revenues, especially since they are typically large corporations operating internationally and able to take advantage of international cost-shifting opportunities. In these circumstances the government might be able to tax more efficiently by combining a tax on revenues (i.e., a royalty or severance charge) with a profit tax. In principle, this combination ought to undo the consequences of overreporting of costs. Other imaginative tax combinations might also be used to overcome other sorts of asymmetric information problems. For example, if firms differ in their costs in ways that are unobserved by the government, it might be possible for the government to separate them by contract offers that involve different combinations of royalty and lump-sum or rent components.

These are but a sample of the manner in which asymmetric information constrains the choice of optimal policies. Other well-known examples include goods markets (Akerlof 1970) and insurance markets (Rothschild and Stiglitz 1976; Dahlby 1981), but these lead to no new issues of principle. Information and other constraints to redistribution naturally invite us to consider whether there are policy instruments that can be used to relax those constraints. There has been a substantial literature on this, to which we turn in the next chapter. First, it is useful to review briefly the main message for tax design that the normative analysis reviewed in the chapter suggest.

3.6 Policy Lessons from Normative Analysis

Normative tax-transfer analysis continually evolves. In recent years alone, we have seen new directions of inquiry that have contributed to the way we think about tax policy. Examples include dynamic optimal tax analysis, the relevance of extensive versus intensive labor supply responses to taxation, the role of commitment, and alternative information assumptions. The tax reform process itself has been informed both by empirical work, which the Mirrlees Review has relied on extensively, and the explosion of political economy research. Recent research has also highlighted some challenges whose resolution will undoubtedly influence policy perspectives. We return to these later.

It is worth taking stock of the main messages for policy that we might take away from the normative literature as it now stands. Not all the results point in a common direction, and that is not surprising given the diverse number of model variants. Nonetheless, one can distill from the rich body of optimal tax literature some broad tax policy implications that the theory both suggests and supports. What follows is a list of such implications that seem to us to be warranted. No doubt others will disagree or compile different lists, but given the complexity of the subject and the value judgments involved, that should not be surprising.

3.6.1   Uniform Broad-Based Commodity Taxation

The theoretical argument for taxing commodities at uniform rates is based on the Atkinson–Stiglitz theorem and its antecedents, including the Corlett–Hague theorem. An optimal tax system should tax goods (and services) at uniform rates if preferences are weakly separable in goods and leisure. I have recounted well-known caveats to the Atkinson–Stiglitz theorem, such as: preferences may be nonseparable, and if so, higher tax rates should be placed on goods that are more complementary with leisure; goods that take more time to consume should bear a higher rate; the income tax may not be set optimally; and there may be a sizable informal (nontaxpaying) sector. While these caveats are well taken, it is not clear that their force is such as to warrant deviating from uniformity. For example, identifying which goods are more complementary with leisure is not a simple task. Such goods will almost certainly not be those goods that are typically taxed preferentially in VAT system, on the ground that they are relied on relatively more by the poor. There are much better ways to address the tax consequences for the poor, such as through refundable tax credits and in-kind transfers. Similar difficulties exist with drawing policy inferences from the other caveats. Moreover administrative arguments favor tax uniformity. Differential tax rates increase collection and compliance costs, and inevitably lead to arbitrary classification decisions given that there are an extremely large number of goods that must be divided into groups for tax purposes. There are some cogent arguments for the differential taxation of present versus future consumption—the taxation of asset returns in their various forms—but they rely on arguments other than complementarity relations with leisure.

3.6.2 Production Efficient Taxation

The case for production efficiency in taxation is much less contentious than uniformity since it relies mainly on efficiency considerations. It is based on the production efficiency theorem of Diamond and Mirrlees (1971), which argues that an optimal tax system should satisfy production efficiency. Similar caveats apply as in the Atkinson–Stiglitz theorem: the tax system may not be optimal, pure profits may go untaxed, and the existence of an informal sector undermines the case for production efficiency. Despite the validity of these caveats, the case for deviating from production efficiency is weak. Put simply, it is not clear in what direction deviations should apply. Perhaps the strongest case for adopting an inefficient tax system applies in developing countries with large informal sectors. The argument is that a system of trade taxes provides an indirect way of taxing both the informal sector and profits in the formal sector. However, that argument relies on there being strict constraints on tax policy instruments available to governments in developing countries, constraints that might be relaxed by a wholesale reform of the tax system. Together with uniformity, production efficiency favors a broad-based VAT with uniform rates as part of the tax mix. Reforms of tax systems in that direction have been one of the main features of recent tax reforms internationally.

3.6.3 Taxation of Asset Income

The design of a direct tax system involves two separate issues: the choice of a base and of a rate structure.[44] The optimal tax literature contributes to both. The choice of a direct tax base is largely concerned with the treatment of capital income, which in principle can include financial income, imputed income from consumer durables, and the return on human capital investment. A standard extension of the Corlett–Hague and Atkinson–Stiglitz theorems would suggest that capital income should be taxed only if future consumption were more complementary with leisure than current consumption. On these

---

44. The choice of a taxpaying unit (e.g., family versus individual) is also important, though one we do not address here.

grounds, one could not reasonably argue for a differential tax on future consumption, which is what a capital income tax is. The dynamic optimal tax literature has instead emphasized other arguments for taxing capital income. Capital income taxation serves as a useful adjunct to redistribution when higher skilled persons have higher savings rates, when future earnings are uncertain and cannot be insured, when earnings tax rates cannot vary over the life cycle, and when inheritances are not fully observable. While these arguments are reasonably convincing, an equally strong case can be made for not taxing capital income at the same rate as earnings. Capital income tax revenues are likely more elastic with respect to tax rates than earnings. Some forms of capital income are difficult to tax, such as the imputed income of human capital investment, or are taxed preferentially for reasons of principle, such as saving for retirement or consumer durables. In these circumstances limiting the tax rate on ordinary capital income reduces inter-asset distortions and tax planning. These suggestions tend to support a schedular approach to taxation whereby capital income and earnings are taxed at different rates. This is an approach that is gaining traction after having been pioneered by the Nordic countries. A final related issue concerns the treatment of inheritances. On grounds of social welfare as well as of equality of opportunity, a case for taxing inheritances either as part of the direct tax base or as a separate tax is strong, despite the tendency for countries to reduce their reliance on inheritance taxation.

3.6.4 Progressivity

The message of the optimal income tax literature about progressivity has been fairly consistent and has survived innovations in the analysis, although with some important recent nuances. The basic message of the standard model is that the optimal rate structure is, perhaps surprisingly, not that progressive. Apart from close to the bottom and close to the top, marginal tax rates are relatively flat for a wide range of aversions to inequality, and this translates into modest amounts of progressivity over most of the range of skills or income. This finding of limited progressivity is exacerbated by more restrictive information assumptions, such as those that lead to evasion or avoidance activities. It also survives alternative modeling assumptions, such as allowing labor variability along the extensive (participation) and job choice margin, and letting individuals vary in their preferences or needs for leisure. The one dimension where progressivity is particularly relevant is at the bottom of the skill distribution. Social welfare functions that exhibit high aversion to inequality—maximin being the limiting case—lead to a high degree of progressivity over lower ranges of income. As well, the treatment of those who do not participate in the labor force, so earn zero income, is relevant. The recent extensive-margin literature shows when participation is a matter of choice, the "participation tax" for low-skilled workers should be negative unless the social welfare function is highly risk averse. This provides considerable support for refundable tax credits for low-income workers (contingent on participation in the workforce), while leaving the qualitative nature of the tax structure among workers of different incomes intact. The strength of this argument is, however, reduced to the extent that nonparticipants in the workforce are unable to work and the government cannot identify them as such. In practice, such nonparticipants are dealt with by stand-alone transfer or welfare systems. The integrity of such systems depends on the government being able identify nonparticipants who are employable versus those who are not. This raises the general issue of how the government can improve the information it has available to itself, a topic that will be discussed further in the next chapter. Also discussed in the next chapter are other policy instruments that the government might find helpful to relax the information constraints it faces.

3.6.5   Business Taxation

The discussion of this chapter covered relatively briefly some of the consequences of normative tax policy analysis for business taxation, though not enough to do the subject justice. The literature on business taxation is large and rich, and this chapter only touched on a few limited aspects. I briefly discussed some ways in which asymmetric information in the private sector can motivate some government intervention, even if the government is no better informed than the least informed private agents. The examples I gave were purely illustrative. Thus asymmetric information between banks (or other creditors) and entrepreneurs seeking finance for risky projects gives rise to adverse selection effects that a tax or subsidy on entrepreneurs can mitigate. In the reasonable case in which asymmetric information involves the probability of a project being successful, a tax on new projects is warranted. Similarly, to the extent that firms face asymmetric information problems in the hiring of labor, too few workers will be hired, calling for a subsidy on employment. The literature has also been instructive in guiding the design of business tax systems that tax any rents generated by firms in an efficient way. This is especially useful in industries that generate significant rents, such as natural resource industries. But governments in various countries have adopted cash-flow taxes or their equivalent, such as ACE corporate taxation, not only to tax natural resource industries, but also as part of their basic business tax system.

4   Relaxing the Second-Best Constraints

The "new new welfare economics," as Stiglitz (1987) has labeled the modern approach to normative policy analysis, emphasizes information as the main constraint facing a benevolent government that precludes it from achieving first-best outcomes. The particular way in which information constraints are imposed in optimal fiscal policy analysis is in itself somewhat demanding and unrealistic. In the standard optimal income tax analysis, as we have noted, the government is assumed to be unable to observe the one characteristic—ability or productivity—that differs among households, which seems a reasonable simplification. However, what government can observe is equally relevant. It can observe individual incomes, and it does know the distribution of skills among the population. These are both heroic assumptions that give the government much more information than it likely has in the real world. Even so, the constraints imposed on policy choices by even this generous interpretation of what the government knows are considerable. As I noted in chapter 3, there has been some consideration in the literature of supposing that the government cannot observe incomes but must rely on self-reporting enforced by a combination of random auditing and penalties for misreporting. There has been relatively little consideration of the government not knowing the distribution of skills. There has also been limited analysis of the consequences for policy of individuals having more than one unobservable characteristic.[1]

Despite the fact that these informational assumptions of the standard model are demanding, the model is nonetheless instructive as a

---

1. Some examples are Besley and Coate (1995), Cremer, Pestieau, and Rochet (2001), Brett and Weymark (2003), Boadway et al. (2006), Brett (2007), and Beaudry, Blackorby, and Szalay (2009).

reference point. It illustrates in an intuitive way both the constraints on normative policy and how policies must be adapted to mitigate the consequences of information constraints. In particular, it is these constraints that provide the rationale for tax distortions in the first place. Distorting the behavior of low-skilled persons through taxes makes it more difficult for the high-skilled to mimic them, so more redistribution can be achieved.

It is worth dwelling on this for the two-type case, although the logic applies more generally. In the absence of incentive constraints, the government can achieve any point on the first-best utility possibilities frontier (UPF) tracing out feasible combinations of utility levels for the two types, given technological and resource constraints. When the government does not know individual types, it can nonetheless achieve a limited number of first-best allocations around the laissez faire by offering consumption–income bundles to the two types that are non-distorting. These allocations are those for which the incentive constraints are slack. However, they do not include any allocations along the first-best UPF that would be chosen by a government with non-negative aversion to inequality. These allocations entail that the low-wage types are at least as well off as the high-wage types, and such outcomes are not incentive compatible.

To achieve more redistribution than incentive-compatible first-best allocations will allow, the bundles offered must introduce distortions on at least one type. In particular, the incentive constraint applying to the high-wage type will be binding. To redistribute more to the low-wage types, their consumption–income bundle must be distorted to preclude high-wage types from selecting the bundle intended for the low-wage types, thereby relaxing the incentive constraint. This is done by exploiting the fact that the amount of extra consumption required to compensate the low-wage types for earning additional income is greater than that required by the high-wage types (the single-crossing or Mirrlees–Spence condition). Equivalently, inducing the low-wage types to earn less income, and reducing their consumption by an amount required to compensate them for that, will deter the high-wage types from mimicking (since their consumption would have to be reduced by a lesser amount to compensate them for the reduction in their income). The result is that the incentive constraint is relaxed by imposing a positive marginal income tax rate on the low-ability types. More redistribution is achieved, though at the cost of moving inside the first-best UPF.

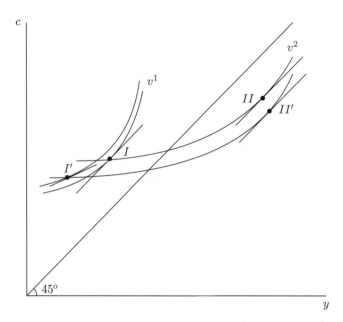

Figure 4.1

The point can be illustrated using figure 4.1. The figure shows indifference curves for high-wage (type-2) and low-wage (type-1) individuals in consumption–income (c, y) space, where the utility of a person with wage w in terms of c and y is given by $v(c, y, w) = u(c, y/w)$. In choosing a redistributive tax structure, the government effectively offers bundles (c_1, y_1) and (c_2, y_2) such that each type will choose the bundle intended for them and the government's budget is balanced. In the absence of government intervention, both types choose points along the 45° line where $c = y$ and tax payments are zero. Redistributive taxation shifts results in type-2's being on a lower indifference curve, and type-1's on a higher one. As long as the incentive constraint is not binding, the government can offer bundles that are nondistorting in the sense that the marginal rates of substitution between c and y for the two types are unity. The figure depicts two alternative allocations. In the first, labeled I and II, the tax payment by type-2's and the transfer to type-1's are both nondistorting. Moreover the incentive constraints on both types are satisfied, and just binding in the case of type 2's $(v(c_2, y_2, w_2) = v(c_1, y_1, w_2))$. However, it is clear that any attempt to redistribute further using non-distorting taxes and transfers will not be incentive compatible: type-2's will prefer the bundle of the type-1's.

Further redistribution starting from *I* and *II* can only be achieved if the allocation of the type-1's is distorted. One such allocation is shown as *I'* and *II'*, where type-1's consumption–income bundle has been distorted. Effectively, a tax is imposed on type-1's income. This principle extends to more than two types. In order to facilitate redistribution from higher to lower skilled types, the income of all but the highest skilled must be distorted downward.

The logic of this intuition invites us to consider other ways in which the incentive constraints can be relaxed. What follows is a catalog of various ways that this can be done, all of which might be seen as ways of expanding utility possibilities beyond those that can be achieved by a nonlinear income tax on its own. Some of these involve using supplementary policy instruments of the sort whose use could not be easily rationalized except as ways of relaxing the incentive constraints. We also consider ways in which the incentive constraints can be relaxed by having the government acquire more information.

In pursuing these policy extensions, some caveats should be emphasized that will serve to temper the direct policy implications that can be drawn. The extensions rely on the fact that incentive or information constraints are relevant. In the real world incentive constraints cannot literally be taken to be binding. Unless there is a continuum of skills, the income tax schedule would have to have discontinuous marginal tax rates at all bundles chosen by individuals, and that is clearly not the case.[2] For example, linear or piecewise linear income tax schedules that are typically used would not induce binding incentive constraints.

More generally, the real world is much more complicated than the models used in the extensions we are about to consider. Individuals have more than one characteristic, their labor supply decisions involve more than the choice of work effort, production is likely to be nonlinear, and so on. As well, the government may face constraints other than behavioral ones. They may have commitment problems. They may face political constraints arising from a lack of consensus among the population about social values, or asymmetric information between the voters and the politicians, or the politicians and the bureaucracy. Individual decisions may also respond to behavioral patterns that call

---

2. In terms of figure 4.1, the budget line facing the two types would be of the form $c = y - t(y)$, where $t(y)$ is the income tax function. To induce type-1's to choose point I' and type-2's to choose II', the budget line would have to have a kink at I', implying a discontinuity in $t'(y)$.

into question the individualistic approach to economic policy implied by welfarism.

I return to these various problems later. In the meantime we would argue that the policy suggestions we obtain by extending the standard second-best normative policy model are nonetheless useful despite these caveats. They are derived under somewhat demanding circumstances, that is, under the assumption that the government is able to exploit its ability to impose a nonlinear income tax to the fullest extent possible given only information constraints. We might presume that to the extent that the government is not exploiting these advantages to the fullest, perhaps because of the sheer complications required to implement a second-best incentive compatible fiscal system or because it is not as well informed as we supposed, the supplementary policies we are suggesting that do exploit other avenues of relaxing information constraints would carry even more force. However, more certainty in this regard requires further development of the literature.

I begin with a discussion of the use of policy instruments in addition to the nonlinear income tax that would not be used in a first-best world of lump-sum taxes and transfers. These include not only the strategic use of commodity taxes and public goods, but also the public provision of private goods and various forms of quantity or price controls. I then briefly consider ways of enhancing the information available to government, some of which the government now makes extensive use of, others that it does not.

4.1   The Use of Supplementary Policy Instruments

Once we move away from the first-best world of personal lump-sum taxes and transfers with full information and no distortions, there are a number of reasons why governments might deploy policies that economists have traditionally thought of as inefficient and unnecessary, or might use standard policies in nonstandard ways. Three reasons that I have already made reference to stand out in particular, and each of them is associated with a seminal contribution. The first is that in a distorted economy, prices no longer convey information about social values. Not only is there then no presumption that piecemeal policy rules should be followed as the theory of second best taught us (Lipsey and Lancaster 1956–57), but also quantity rationing might be welfare improving. Guesnerie and Roberts (1984) showed this to be the case even for an economy with optimal commodity and nonlinear income taxation. See also the discussion in Mirrlees (1986), where the potential role for quantity controls and restrictions in a more general optimal tax world was contemplated.

Second, when governments are limited in the amount of information they have about taxpayers or intended transfer recipients, incentive constraints become important. In these circumstances, Nichols and Zeckhauser (1982) showed that redistribution can be enhanced by distorting the behavior of those who are the government's intended targets of redistribution. These distortions could take the form of either price or quantity controls.

Third, in an intertemporal context governments may not be able to commit to future tax policies. In a second-best setting in which individuals or firms make long-run decisions, optimal policies are generally time inconsistent, as we have seen. Second-best optimal policies that are announced before agents' long-run decisions are taken will no longer be optimal after the decisions have been made, even for benevolent governments. Time-consistent fiscal policies will result in suboptimal saving and investment decisions, and inferior outcomes will result (Fischer 1982; Hillier and Malcomson 1984; Calvo and Obstfeld 1988). In these circumstances governments may choose to mitigate these adverse consequences by using policy instruments that would not be used in a first-best world (where commitment is not an issue).

What follows are some examples of the use of policy instruments motivated by one or more of these factors. The first example is one that we have already encountered and spent considerable time discussing.

4.1.1 Differential Commodity Taxes

In a first-best world with no externalities, commodity taxes would not be used, only direct lump-sum taxes on individuals. Once information becomes a constraint on government, distorting income taxation becomes optimal, and by the same token, so may differential commodity taxes. In an optimal nonlinear tax setting, commodity taxes assume a role to the extent that they relax the incentive constraints applying to the income tax. The result reported in Atkinson and Stiglitz (1976) for the continuous-wage case, and in Edwards, Keen, and Tuomala (1994) and Nava, Schroyen, and Marchand (1996) for the discrete case, illustrate this clearly. Higher commodity tax rates should be imposed on those goods that are more complementary with leisure. The relevant analysis was presented in chapter 3.

The intuition is clear. Suppose that we start with only the optimal nonlinear tax in place. The optimal nonlinear tax is Pareto efficient, and satisfies the government's revenue constraint and the incentive constraints, where the latter apply downward from higher wage persons to the next lowest wage persons. A tax reform that imposes a small tax on a good complementary with leisure and at the same time adjusts the income tax to compensate all individuals for the commodity tax will leave utilities unchanged, will be revenue neutral (since the amount each person has to be compensated for a small increase in commodity tax is the increment in tax revenue itself by the envelope theorem[3]), and will relax the incentive constraints. The reason for the latter is that persons mimicking the consumption–income bundle of a lower wage person will take more leisure (since they require less labor to earn the given income) and therefore will consume more of the taxed good. The reduction in the income tax will not be sufficient to compensate them for the excise tax increase, so their utility will fall. This relaxes the incentive constraint and allows the government to adjust the nonlinear income tax system to improve social welfare.

It is apparent that the same logic does not apply if goods and leisure are separable, since then mimickers would consume the same bundle of goods from their disposable income as those they are mimicking. The implication is that, if a nonlinear income tax is accompanied by differential commodity taxes in an Atkinson–Stiglitz world of weak separability, welfare can be improved by eliminating the differential commodity taxes and adjusting the nonlinear income tax.

As a mentioned earlier, Konishi (1995), Laroque (2005), Kaplow (2006), and Gauthier and Laroque (2009) have proposed that the same logic suggests that differential commodity taxes ought to be eliminated even if the income tax is not set optimally, as long as preferences are weakly separable. Their analysis shows that, starting with differential commodity taxes and a nonoptimal income tax, eliminating the former and adjusting the individual tax liabilities under the income tax can lead to a social welfare improvement without violating the revenue or incentive constraints. However, that requires that the nonoptimal tax

---

3. By the envelope theorem, $\partial v(\mathbf{q}) / \partial q_i = \partial v(\mathbf{q}) / \partial t_i = -\alpha x_i$. Therefore $dv / \alpha |_{dt_j=0, j\neq i} = -x_i dt_i$, which is the change in revenue.

in place to begin with can be adjusted arbitrarily as part of the tax reform. If that is the case, there should be nothing to prevent the income tax from being set optimally to begin with. If there are some restrictions that preclude the government from moving to the optimal nonlinear tax, the exercise will not apply. For example, if the income tax is for some reason restricted to be linear, the welfare improving tax reform cannot be done. Indeed we know that under optimal linear progressive taxation, the conditions for uniformity of commodity taxes are more restrictive than is the case for a nonlinear tax.

4.1.2 Public Goods and the Marginal Cost of Public Funds

Somewhat parallel considerations apply to the choice of the level of public goods. The analogue of the Atkinson–Stiglitz theorem in this context has been provided by Christiansen (1981). In the standard optimal nonlinear income tax setting where utility functions in consumption c and labor ℓ are expanded to $u(c, g, \ell)$, with g being a pure public good, the Samuelson rule for public goods applies if the utility function takes the weakly separable form, $u(f(c, g), \ell)$, and a nonlinear income tax is in place. Here the Samuelson condition is $\sum_i u_g(c_i, g, \ell_i)/u_c(c_i, g, \ell_i) = p_g$, where i indexes individuals and p_g is the producer price of the public good in terms of the private good.[4] In the event that the utility function is not separable, choosing g to deviate from the Samuelson condition can improve welfare by relaxing the incentive constraints. For example, if g is more complementary with leisure than is c, the provision of g should be restricted such that

$$\sum_i \frac{u_g(c_i, g, \ell_i)}{u_c(c_i, g, \ell_i)} > p_g.$$

Formally, write the utility function of a person with wage rate w_i as $v^i(c, g, y) = u(c, g, y/w_i)$. In the two-type case, the government chooses g and bundles of (c_i, y_i) to maximize $\rho_1 v^1(c_1, g, y_1) + \rho_2 v^2(c_2, g, y_2)$ subject to a revenue constraint $n_1(y_1 - c_1) + n_2(y_2 - c_2) = p_g g$ and an incentive constraint $v^2(c_2, g, y_2) \geqslant v^2(c_1, g, y_1)$, where p_g is the cost of the public good and ρ_1, ρ_2 are the weights that the government puts on the utility

---

4. Tuomala (1980) derives a related result using effective labor supply, $y = w\ell$, as the numéraire. Boadway and Keen (1993) show that the Samuelson condition using y as the numéraire will be satisfied if the utility function takes the following form $u(c, \ell / (h(c, g)))$, which is different from the case in the text where c is the numéraire. This is one of those reasonably rare cases where the choice of numéraire makes a difference.

of the type-1's and type-2's. From the first-order conditions, one obtains, using the fact that $v_g^i / v_x^i = u_g(c_i, g, \ell_i) / u_c(c_i, g, \ell_i)$:

$$n_1 \frac{u_g(c_1, g, \ell_1)}{u_c(c_1, g, \ell_1)} + n_2 \frac{u_g(c_2, g, \ell_2)}{u_c(c_2, g, \ell_2)} = p_g + \frac{\gamma \hat{v}_c^2}{\lambda} \left[\frac{\hat{v}_g^2}{\hat{v}_c^2} - \frac{v_g^1}{v_c^1} \right].$$

where $\hat{v}^2$ refers to the utility of a mimicking type-2. The mimickers obtain the same levels of the private good c_1 and the public good g as the type-1's, but supply less labor to obtain y_1. Therefore $\hat{v}_g^2 / \hat{v}_c^2 > v_g^1 / v_c^1$ if g is more complementary with leisure than is c. In this case the sum of the marginal rates of substitution should be greater than p_g in an optimum. Only if preferences are weakly separable in c, g will the Samuelson condition apply.

Intuitively, since a person who is mimicking a lower wage person will consume more leisure, they will also place a higher marginal value on the public good if it is complementary with leisure. Starting in an allocation in which the Samuelson condition is satisfied, a small reduction in g accompanied by a reduction is tax liabilities for all persons by their marginal valuations of g will leave all nonmimicking persons equally well off and maintain budget balance, but will make mimickers worse off. The incentive constraints are weakened, so social welfare can be improved.

Kaplow (2008) has argued that this line of reasoning implies that the Samuelson condition should be satisfied even if the income tax is not set optimally, as long as preferences are weakly separable as above (see also Gauthier and Laroque 2009). His argument relies on the same intuition as for the differential commodity tax case. Regardless of the income tax in place, if the Samuelson condition is violated, it will be possible to change g and adjust individual tax liabilities such that the Samuelson condition is satisfied, the incentive constraints are not violated, and the government has additional tax revenue to make everyone better off. However, the same objection applies here as in the commodity tax case just considered. For the policy change to be welfare improving, the government must be able to change individual tax liabilities at will. If they are not choosing the optimal nonlinear income tax to begin with, there might be a presumption that there is some restriction that prevents them from choosing individual taxes without restriction.

Indeed we know from the literature on the marginal cost of public funds (MCPF) emanating from Atkinson and Stern (1974) that if the government uses only linear taxes, the Samuelson conditions will generally be violated even if the above-noted separability conditions are satisfied.[5] The point of this literature is that raising a euro of incremental tax revenue has an opportunity cost of more than one euro. It includes both the euro of resources taken from the private sector and the marginal deadweight loss of increasing the tax rate (which can be substantial if the tax base is fairly elastic).[6] A marginal increase in the public good g has two, possibly offsetting, effects. On the one hand, any additional tax revenue required carries with it the MCPF, which is greater than unity. On the other hand, an increase in g can have indirect effects on tax revenues, to the extent that changes in g affect the demand for taxed commodities. In principle, the latter can be positive or negative, so the overall effect on the Samuelson rule is ambiguous.[7] If g is separable in the utility function, the indirect effect disappears, and the optimality condition for public goods becomes the qualified Samuelson rule:

$$\sum_i \frac{u_g(c_i, g, \ell_i)}{u_c(c_i, g, \ell_i)} = \text{MCPF} \cdot p_g > p_g.$$

4.1.3 Quantity Controls: In-kind Transfers

The use of differential commodity taxation and variations in public goods supply to relax the incentive constraints involve otherwise conventional policy instruments. However, it may be useful to deploy policy instruments that are typically viewed as being inefficient simply in order to relax the incentive constraints. In-kind transfers is a case in point. The traditional argument against in-kind transfers is that from the point of view of the recipient, they are inferior to cash transfers:

---

5. The MCPF is the social cost of raising an increment of tax revenue in a distorted economy. The literature on the MCPF is large, including Browning (1976), Stuart (1984), King (1986), Wildasin (1984), Usher (1986), Sandmo (1998), Gahvari (2006), and Christiansen (2007). The concept has been used in a variety of settings, such as evaluating tax reform (Ahmad and Stern 1991), fiscal federalism (Dahlby 2008), regulation (Laffont and Tirole 1993), and development (Laffont 2005). Laffont argues that the MCPF is of the order of 1.3 in developed economies, implying that it costs the citizens 1.3 euros every time the government raises one euro. Dahlby (2008) has provided a careful survey of the literature with its many applications.
6. The deadweight loss element is avoided in the Kaplow exercise since the government is presumed to be able to raise marginal revenues by lump-sum individual-specific adjustments to the income tax.
7. Lau, Sheshinski, and Stiglitz (1978) and Besley and Jewitt (1991) have developed conditions on preferences such that the Samuelson conditions will be satisfied when linear taxes are used.

recipients are at least as well off with cash transfers since they can use them as they see fit, rather than having their preferences potentially distorted by being forced to consume more of a particular good than they would have chosen. If a given value of resources could be transferred to recipients, they would be better off with the transfer as cash rather than as an in-kind transfer of a particular good. That suggests that for in-kind transfers to be beneficial they must enable more resources to be transferred.

In-kind transfers are common. Indeed it could be argued that more redistribution takes place through the provision of goods and services than through the tax-transfer system. Examples include public housing, food stamps, school lunches, and public transportation. Indeed widespread in-kind transfers such as public education and some forms of health care are some of the more important categories of public expenditure. Private charities also typically provide in-kind transfers to their clientele, such as food and clothing banks, as well as shelter. Even where in-kind transfers are not given, indirect subsidies on particular goods are sometimes used as an alternative (although they benefit all purchasers of the good and not just the needy). A subsidy might be a particularly useful substitute if the good in question is retradable, in which case the in-kind transfer is equivalent to a cash transfer since it can always be converted to cash by trading.

There are various reasons why in-kind transfers might be the chosen form of redistribution. To the extent that transfers are motivated by altruism, donors might prefer to give in-kind transfers, or to have the government provide them on their behalf, if their altruistic preferences are paternalistic. From a social welfare point of view, if such altruistic preferences "count"—as they would under a strict welfarist approach to social welfare maximization (Kaplow 2008)—optimal policy would reflect a bias in favor of donors preferences. Of course, under strict welfarism, benefits that transfers yield to both donors and recipients should count, and this would enhance the value of transfers overall.[8]

---

8. In the case of voluntary transfers, the fact that both donors and recipients benefit leads to a case for a Pigouvian subsidy on voluntary transfers under the strict welfarist approach, as Kaplow (2008) argues. This is an efficiency argument. The transfer also affects redistribution based on equity considerations, given that it leads to benefits for both donors and recipients. Note, however, the argument of Schall (1972) and Archibald and Donaldson (1976) that if altruism is nonpaternalistic, competitive markets are efficient (i.e., the first theorem of welfare economics applies) unless there is scope for Pareto-improving transfers in the sense of Hochman and Rodgers (1969).

A second argument for in-kind transfers is that they might be useful as ways of targeting those most in need. Thus public housing or transportation, food banks, secondhand clothing, and so on will tend to be used by those most in need and shunned by the more affluent. Of course, for this to be the case, the good must be perceived to be inferior, which perhaps reduces its attractiveness for redistributive purposes, given the stigma that might be attached to its use. The use of in-kind transfers might also be useful on behavioral grounds as a means of encouraging needy persons to resist the temptation to spend cash on goods that might have detrimental effects on them in the future, such as those that can result in addiction, undernourishment, and ill health. Of course, some may object that this amounts to unwarranted paternalism by the government, an issue that will be discussed further in the next chapter.

A closely related, but somewhat more rigorous normative argument for in-kind transfers is that while they are not the preferred policy instrument and would not be used in a first-best world, they can serve to relax the incentive constraint in a second-best world of optimal income taxation. The idea that in-kind transfers can be useful in this way was first noted informally by Nichols and Zeckhauser (1982), and was formally developed in a series of papers by, inter alia, Blackorby and Donaldson (1988), Munro (1991), Blomquist and Christiansen (1995, 1998a, b), Boadway and Marchand (1995), Gahvari (1995), Cremer and Gahvari (1997), Boadway, Marchand, and Sato (1998), and Currie and Gahvari (2008). The basic intuition is similar to the case of differential commodity taxes when used alongside an optimal nonlinear income tax. In the latter case, imposing a relatively high tax on goods that are complementary with leisure will be welfare improving. Equivalently, and more to the point here, imposing a subsidy on goods that are more substitutable for leisure will be welfare improving. The subsidy will be of more value to persons being mimicked than to those mimicking their income, given that the former have lower wage rates and consume less leisure, so consume more of the good in question. By the same token, if a good that is not retradable is relatively more substitutable for leisure than other goods, an in-kind transfer that is binding on low-wage persons will be welfare improving since it will weaken the incentive constraint: it will force mimickers to consume more of the good than they otherwise would voluntarily choose.

The method of analysis leading to the case for public provision can be illustrated by an example drawn from Boadway and Marchand

(1995). Let the utility of a type-i person ($i = 1, 2$) be written $u(x_1, x_2 + g, y/w_i)$, where x_1 and x_2 are private goods, $y = w_i \ell$ is income, and g is public provision of good x_2, provided in equal amounts to all persons. Suppose that the producer prices of all goods are unity, and $x_2, g \geqslant 0$, reflecting the inability of persons to retrade x_2. The government can observe income y, and can infer disposable income $c = x_1 + x_2$, but cannot see how c is divided between x_1 and x_2. We proceed as we did when we analyzed the differential taxation of x_1 and x_2 by disaggregating the individual's problem artificially into two stages: the choice of income and therefore disposable income, and the choice of x_1 and x_2. Begin with the latter for a type-i person. Given y^i, c^i, and g, and using the budget constraint $c^i = x_1^i + x_2^i$, the household chooses $x_1^i \geqslant 0$ to maximize $u(c^i - x_2^i, x_i^2 + g, y^i/w_i)$. This yields a demand function $x_2^i(c^i, y^i, g)$, and a value function $v^i(c^i, y^i, g)$ for $i = 1, 2$. Similarly, for a type-2 mimicking a type-1 person, the demand for x_2 is $\hat{x}_2^2(c^1, y^1, g)$ and the value function is $\hat{v}^2(c^1, y^1, g)$. Note that as g increases, x_2^i falls (provided that x_2 is normal). Denote by g^i the value of g at which a type-i person's demand for x_2 just gets crowded out, and similarly $\hat{g}^2$ for the mimicker.

In the first stage, the government chooses consumption-income bundles for the two types. Taking g as given and assuming the government is utilitarian, the government problem is to choose c^i, y^i for $i = 1, 2$ to maximize $n_1 v^1(c^1, y^1, g) + n_2 v^2(c^2, y^2, g)$ subject to a resource constraint, $n_1(y^1 - c^1) + n_2(y^2 - c^2) = (n_1 + n_2)g$, and an incentive constraint, $v^2(c^2, y^2, g) \geqslant \hat{v}^2(c^1, y^1, g)$. The first-order conditions give the standard optimal income tax structure and a social value function, $\Omega(g)$. By the envelope theorem, the change in the social value function Ω with a change in g is just the partial derivative of the Lagrange function for the government's optimal income tax problem. The results, using the first-order conditions for the government problem, is

$$\frac{d\Omega(g)}{dg} = n_1(v_g^1 - v_x^1) + n_2 + \mu(v_g^2 - v_x^2) - \mu(\hat{v}_g^2 - \hat{v}_x^2),$$

where $\mu > 0$ is the Lagrange multiplier on the incentive constraint. From this we can infer that if and only if $\hat{g}^2 < \min(g^1, g^2)$, public provision of $g > \hat{g}^2$ will be welfare improving up to some amount strictly above $\min(g^1, g^2)$. Intuitively, increasing g beyond the point where type-1's or type-2's get crowded out makes them worse off. But increasing g beyond the point where the mimicker gets crowded out relaxes the incentive constraint. A necessary and sufficient condition for $\hat{g}^2 < \min(g^1, g^2)$ is that x_2 be *less* complementary with leisure than x_1 (since the mimicker enjoys more leisure than either the type-1 or the type-2 person).

This analysis is for a special case. More generally, two design issues naturally arise. The first concerns the manner in which the in-kind transfer is provided. Two broad options studied are the supplement model and the opt-out model. The supplement case is the one considered in the analysis above, and used, for example, by Boadway and Marchand (1995). In it, the government provides a given amount of a good that all individuals consume, and they may supplement the amount provided with further purchases on the market. In the opt-out model, studied, for example, by Blackorby and Donaldson (1988) and Blomquist and Christiansen (1995), the government provides a given quantity of a nonretradable good, and individuals may choose to take it or not.[9] The government observes who opts in, and can condition the income tax on that information. Those who opt out may be able to purchase the good on the private market. Both of these can serve as a device for relaxing the incentive constraint, but which one might be preferred depends on the circumstances.

Blomquist and Christiansen (1998a) show that the in-kind transfer scheme with supplementary purchases allowed will be best if the non-traded good being provided by the government is a substitute for leisure (complement with labor). The opposite applies when the good is a complement with leisure: providing the in-kind transfer with opting out and with no supplementation allowed is the optimal scheme. The intuition is as follows. The optimal design aims to deter high-wage individuals from mimicking low-wage individuals. Suppose that the private good provided publicly is complementary with leisure. A high-wage individual who is mimicking will be consuming more leisure than the low-wage person, and therefore has a higher preference for the private good. By prohibiting topping-up, the government makes mimicking undesirable. Conversely, if the private good and leisure are substitutes, low-wage individuals have a higher willingness to pay for the private good so prohibiting topping-up can only make them worse off (or indifferent at best). Thus topping-up or supplementary purchases should be allowed.

---

9. In principle, different quantities could be provided to different income groups in a multi-type model. Similar intuition applies in this case.

The second design issue arises because of the similarity between the conditions required for in-kind transfers to be welfare improving and those required for differential taxes. In the case with supplementary purchases allowed, in-kind transfers are welfare improving if the good is a substitute for leisure. In this case a subsidy on the good is also welfare improving, as we have noted. The question then becomes: Is a subsidy or an in-kind transfer or some mix of both optimal? Boadway, Marchand, and Sato (1998) show that there should always be public provision in an optimum, whether or not a subsidy is also used. Moreover it may or may not be optimal to have a subsidy along with public provision, though relying on public provision alone is optimal under reasonable circumstances. Finally, if the use of a subsidy and public provision are mutually exclusive for some reason, public provision will be welfare superior under reasonable assumptions. The main point is simply that public provision may well be part of the optimal policy mix, and this applies in the opt-out version of the model as well.

While much of the literature on in-kind transfers puts them in the context of a second-best world where the government has access to a nonlinear income tax, Blackorby and Donaldson (1998) focus on a relatively more parsimonious world where there is no labor-leisure choice. In their setting, individuals simply differ in their preferences for two goods, one a numéraire consumption good and the other a good, say, medical care, that is needed by only one of the two types of persons. Assuming the latter good is nonretradable and that the government can choose to monopolize its supply, the government can exploit this difference in preferences by making transfers of the numéraire good to the two persons conditional on the amount of the other good they choose to consume. Blackorby and Donaldson show remarkably that such a scheme is Pareto-superior to a scheme in which the nonretradable good is taxed or subsidized, what they call a market solution.

4.1.4 Price Controls

Governments also engage in direct control of prices through regulation of minimum or maximum prices. These might be seen as potentially attractive policy instruments because they have no direct budgetary implications. A prime example of a minimum price is the minimum wage, while rent controls exemplify a maximum price. Both minimum and maximum price controls are devices for redistribution, and both are typically discredited as interfering with market equilibrium because they create excess supply or demand, as the case may be. As with quantity controls there is a literature on the use of price controls in a second-best setting with imperfect information, although the manner in which price controls alleviate information constraints is somewhat different. The discussion of this section focuses mainly on minimum wages for illustrative purposes. It also is restricted to settings comparable with those used in the optimal tax literature, including the assumption of competitive product and labor markets and second-best restrictions on taxes. Minimum wages can have some role in other settings, such as monopsonistic labor markets or labor markets characterized by other imperfections such as efficiency wages or frictional search, as discussed in the survey material contained in the longer paper by Lee and Saez (2009).

Guesnerie and Roberts (1987), exploiting their earlier findings on quantity controls (Guesnerie and Roberts 1984), showed that a minimum wage might be welfare improving when the government uses only a linear progressive income tax. However, this no longer generally applied when the government was able to use nonlinear income taxation, and Allen (1987) showed that this was the case even if relative wages were endogenous. The models used by Guesnerie and Roberts and by Allen were restricted by the assumption that minimum wages reduce employment along the intensive margin (hours of work per person) rather than creating a loss of jobs (the extensive margin). In this setting, they are unable to relax the incentive constraint on redistribution. Marceau and Boadway (1994) instead assumed the minimum wage induced firms to lay off some workers. The labor supply of low-skilled workers satisfied a binding participation constraint. In these circumstances, the minimum wage becomes unambiguously welfare improving, and it becomes more so if accompanied by unemployment insurance. Interestingly, this beneficial effect of the minimum wage applies even though it tightens the incentive constraint, since the higher wage makes mimicking more attractive. The ability of the minimum wage to target low-wage workers more than overcomes that. Of course, it is assumed that the minimum wage can be enforced at the firm level, even though the government cannot observe workers' wage rates, an assumption shared with Guesnerie and Roberts (1987).

Boadway and Cuff (2000) take a rather different approach to relaxing the information constraint. They work in the context of a continuous-type Mirrlees optimal nonlinear income tax model where there is bunching at the bottom. An increase in the minimum wage pushes everyone below the minimum wage into unemployment. They make the important assumption that even though the government cannot in general observe wage rates while firms can, it can enforce a minimum wage by monitoring and legal sanctions (since hiring workers at below the minimum wage is illegal). They show that precluding hiring at a wage below the minimum wage combined with rules that oblige low-income workers to accept jobs that are offered to them—which is a feature of low-income transfer systems in the real world—will not only relax the incentive constraint and increase social welfare, but might also increase employment. Their results depend crucially on the ability of the government to enforce a legislated minimum wage in a world where it cannot otherwise observe wage rates. This does not seem unreasonable, although there is no doubt a cost of enforcement.

More recently Lee and Saez (2009) take on this seeming informational inconsistency more directly. They adopt the fixed hours of work model of Diamond (1980) and Saez (2002b), which assumes that governments can observe all persons' wage rates, thereby avoiding the supposed inconsistency inherent in previous models. Being able to observe all wage rates is arguably a much stronger assumption that simply being able to observe those earning the minimum wage via legally sanctioned self-reporting. In their model, workers are of two different skill levels (for simplicity), and these are imperfect substitutes in production so wages are endogenous. Workers have different tastes for work or leisure, and in a competitive equilibrium, those with the least taste for leisure are employed and the rest voluntarily unemployed. A minimum wage at a level above the wage of the low-skilled persons creates involuntary unemployment. Crucially, they assume that those laid off are the ones with the highest value of leisure, that is, employment rationing is efficient. Given these assumptions, they show that a minimum wage improves social welfare under reasonable assumptions.[10] Note that social welfare is evaluated using an additive social welfare function in the utility of all workers, where the disutility of work is treated as a source of social disutility. As we will see later, this manner of treating different preferences for social welfare purposes is not innocuous, although how it affects the results here is not obvious.

---

10. These include that the elasticity of supply of low-skill workers is positive, while the elasticity of demand for them is finite (hence the requirement for skills to be imperfect substitutes). As well, the government must value redistribution from the high- to the low-skill workers.

Finally, Boadway and Cuff (1999) show that a minimum wage can be welfare improving in a model in which both voluntary and involuntary unemployment exist. Involuntary unemployment is frictional and arises from a simple imperfect matching process, while voluntary unemployment will occur if individuals choose not to participate in the labor market, that is, choose not to search for jobs or accept job offers. Thus, like Saez (2002b), labor market decisions are entirely at the extensive margin. The government cannot observe who is voluntarily unemployed as opposed to involuntarily unemployed, although as discussed below it may be able to obtain imperfect information by monitoring job search activities. Therefore it cannot offer full unemployment insurance since to do so would induce voluntary unemployment: consumption of low-income workers must exceed that of the involuntarily unemployed. A minimum wage will increase the level of unemployment above the frictional level and will increase the wage paid to those employed. It will be welfare improving (on utilitarian grounds) if the government transfer to the unemployed is small enough relative to the transfer to the low-income employed, that is, if unemployment insurance is sufficiently inadequate. We return to this case below when we discuss the Boadway–Cuff model slightly more formally.

It is thus possible to construct a reasonable case for minimum wages if one is willing to adopt certain informational assumptions. Which of the sets of alternative assumptions, if any, is the most reasonable is a matter of judgment. The Marceau–Boadway–Cuff approach assumes that the government is able to monitor minimum wage enforcement, which seems to accord with the way minimum wages are enforced in practice. Alternatively, the Lee–Saez approach assumes that the government can observe all wage rates but cannot observe the taste for leisure. In addition they require that involuntary unemployment be allocated efficiently according to the taste for work, without which their minimum wage results fail to hold, as they explicitly recognize.

Minimum wages are but one example of price controls used by the government, and suffice to illustrate how price controls can be welfare improving in an information-constrained environment.[11] There are issues that affect the use of price controls other than those on which we have focused. One that is of some importance at the moment concerns the pricing of environmental externalities, of which the use of

---

11. For a recent analysis of rent controls under asymmetric information, see Cuff and Marceau (2009).

carbon pricing is an example. Suppose one accepts, in principle, that the government ought to impose a price on carbon dioxide emissions into the atmosphere, along the lines discussed in Stern (2007) and Sinn (2008). This begs the question of why governments should do this in a world in which the externality is global, and free-riding at the national level is tempting. But, our concern is rather with the difficulties of implementing optimal policies, given normative government behavior. Even such governments will face daunting problems of information in implementing such a scheme.

4.1.5 Workfare

Requiring low-income persons to devote a given amount of time to some public work project as a condition for receiving a transfer is a form of quantity control, not unlike in-kind transfers. The intuition behind the effectiveness of workfare parallels that of in-kind transfers, so we can be relatively brief. There are, however, some additional conceptual issues that arise.

There might be various rationales for workfare. It might be viewed as providing labor market experience or changing one's attitude to work. It might serve to break the cycle of poverty passed on from parents to children in the family. Workfare might also be simply regarded as a way for transfer recipients to pay something back to society. In the normative redistribution literature, workfare is treated solely as a screening device, that is, as a device for targeting transfers to the most deserving or needy. The basic idea is simply that workfare might be beneficial as a screening device if the opportunity cost of taking up workfare is less for intended transfer recipients than for potential mimickers. If so, the incentive constraint can be relaxed. Whether such a workfare scheme is welfare improving then depends on the cost of operating the scheme, and that partly depends on the assumed features of the model.

In the seminal contribution of Besley and Coate (1992), some key assumptions are made. Utility is assumed to be quasi-linear in consumption. As well, labor supplied to the market and to a workfare program are perfect substitutes in utility. This implies that labor supplied to a workfare program crowds out market work on a one-for-one basis. That being the case, the opportunity cost to participants in workfare per unit of labor supplied to the program is simply the wage rate (as long as positive work continues to be supplied to the market), implying that workfare is more costly for high-wage workers so will make it more difficult for them to mimic low-wage ones. At the same time there is a social cost to workfare since workfare is assumed to be nonproductive, while the crowding out of labor supplied to the private market reduces output. Besley and Coate adopt a nonwelfarist objective function that attaches social value only to the consumption of the low-wage transfer recipients and not to their leisure time.[12] This biases the argument in favor of workfare, but even so, workfare may or may not be beneficial depending on the value of screening out high-wage persons from obtaining a transfer versus the cost of screening.

Subsequent models have adopted somewhat different assumptions. Cuff (2000) takes a welfarist approach and considers second-best Pareto optimal policies when the government can use workfare in addition to a nonlinear income tax. See also Brett (1998). Following Cuff, suppose that workfare can be productive and yield revenue to the government. In such a setting, and again assuming quasi-linear preferences and two wage-types as in Besley and Coate (1992), the following results can be obtained. Unlike in Besley and Coate, nonproductive workfare is never welfare improving. There will, however, be some minimal level of productivity of workfare such that it is welfare improving. In these circumstances it is always optimal for workfare to crowd out low-wage labor supply completely.

To see this, consider the following simple model. Individuals supply labor ℓ to the market, and consume c, but they may also be required to supply labor d to a public workfare program, where d is perfectly substitutable for ℓ in utility, but may produce less output. Let $\bar{w}$ be the output produced per unit of d, assumed to be the same for all persons. The utility function is quasi-linear in consumption, so $u(c, \ell, d) = c - g(\ell + d)$, where $g(\ell + d)$, the disutility of labor, is increasing and strictly convex. The total supply of labor $\ell + d$ therefore depends only on the wage rate w, so an increase in the workfare requirement d crowds out ℓ on a one-for-one basis. As usual, we can rewrite the utility function in terms of consumption and income as $v^i(c, y, d) \equiv c - g(y/w_i + d)$.

There are two wage-types with wages rates $w_2 > w_1$. The government redistributes from type-2's to type-1's using a nonlinear income tax. In

---

12. More precisely, the objective of the government is to minimize the cost of providing a given level of consumption to low-wage persons. This is equivalent to maximizing their consumption, given a budget constraint.

addition it can set a workfare requirement d on one or both types contingent on their (c, y) bundle. A workfare requirement would in fact never be imposed on the high-ability persons since that simply tightens the self-selection constraint by making it more attractive for them to mimic. So we concentrate on the case where d is imposed only on the low-ability types. We proceed in two stages, first obtaining the optimal nonlinear tax structure given d, and then considering the effects of changing d.

The government problem is taken to be a Pareto-optimizing one. Given d, the government chooses c_i and y_i for the two types to maximize the utility of type-1's, $c_1 - g(y_1 / w_1 + d)$, subject to $c_2 - g(y_2 / w_2 + d) \geqslant \bar{v}^2$, a revenue constraint, $n_1(y_1 - c_1 + \bar{w}d) + n_2(y_2 - c_2) = R$, and an incentive constraint, $c_2 - g(y_2 / w_2) \geqslant c_1 - g(y_1 / w_1 + d)$. The solution to this problem gives the standard optimal nonlinear income tax structure and a value function $\Omega(d)$.

The effect of changes in d can be obtained by applying the envelope theorem: $\Omega'(d)$ is the partial derivative of the Lagrange expression for the optimal tax problem with respect to d. We obtain, after using the first-order conditions for the optimal tax problem:

$$\Omega'(d) = -(1-\gamma)g'\left(\frac{y_1}{w_1} + d\right) - \gamma\left(g'\left(\frac{y_1}{w_1} + d\right) - g'\left(\frac{y_2}{w_1} + d\right)\right) + \lambda n_1 \bar{w},$$

where $\gamma > 0$ is the Lagrange multiplier on the incentive constraint and $\lambda > 0$ is the Lagrange multiplier on the revenue constraint. As well, $1 - \gamma > 0$ by the first-order condition on c_1, and $g'(y_1 / w_1 + d) > g'(y_2 / w_1 + d)$ since $g''(\cdot) > 0$. Therefore the first two terms of $\Omega'(d)$ are negative.

From this expression for $\Omega'(d)$, we can infer the following. First, nonproductive workfare will be welfare decreasing ($\Omega'(d) < 0$ if $\bar{w} = 0$) (Cuff 2000). Second, there will be a value of $\bar{w}$ such that for any productivity of workfare above that, workfare will be welfare improving. Finally, if workfare is optimal, it will fully crowd out the low-ability person in this model (since $g'(\cdot)$ is constant until $\ell_1 = 0$). Intuitively, workfare has a cost and a benefit. Its benefit is that it weakens the incentive constraint applying to the high-ability types. For them, mimicking is more costly with workfare since the opportunity cost of devoting more of their time to workfare is valued at their market wage rate, which is higher than for the low-ability types. The cost of workfare is the fact that the productivity in workfare is less than the productivity of working in the market.

The Besley and Coate (1992) case can be seen as a special case of the above in which the objective function of the government is c_1 rather than $c_1 - g(y_1 / w_1 + d)$. The idea is that the members of the public who are contributing to the transfers to low-income persons value only the consumption of the poor and not their leisure. (In the Pareto-optimizing problem, the minimum utility of the type-2's is still taken as given.) In that sense they are paternalistic, and the leisure cost of imposing d on the low-ability persons is not treated as a cost. Proceeding as above, we obtain by the envelope theorem:

$$\Omega'(d) = \gamma g'\left(\frac{y_1}{w_2} + d\right) + \lambda n_1 \bar{w} > 0.$$

Thus the fact that the disutility of labor of workfare is not being counted implies that workfare is welfare improving, even if nonproductive ($\bar{w} = 0$). The market supply of labor for the types 1's will again be fully crowded out.

Cuff (2000) extended the analysis of the base case to allow for heterogeneous preferences for leisure (distaste for work). Let there be two preference-types: those with high disutility for labor, denoted h, and those with low disutility of labor, l, where $g_h(\ell + d) > g_l(\ell + d)$, $g_h'(\ell + d) > g_l'(\ell + d)$, for the two types. Assume that all high-ability persons are type l, whereas low-ability persons can be either h or l, so there are three categories of persons: $1h, 1l, 2l$.

Household preferences are now given by $v^{ij}(c, y, d) = c - g_j(y / w_i + d)$, $i = 1, 2, j = h, l$. The slopes of indifference curves in c, y–space are given by

$$-\frac{v_y^{ij}}{v_c^{ij}} = \frac{g_j'(y/w_i + d)}{w_i} > 0.$$

The single-crossing property applies, so for common values of c and y (see figure 4.2):

$$-\frac{v_y^{1h}}{v_c^{1h}} > -\frac{v_y^{1l}}{v_c^{1l}} > -\frac{v_y^{2l}}{v_c^{2l}}.$$

The nature of the optimal redistribution plan depends upon the weights the government gives to the welfare of the high- and low-disutility-of-labor types, and that may depend on whether the difference in disutility of labor reflects a disability beyond the control of the households as opposed to the household's preferences. On the one

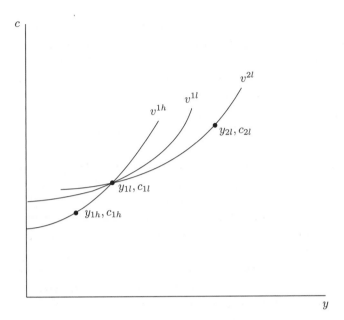

Figure 4.2

hand, type-h persons may be regarded as disabled, and therefore the government may wish to redistribute toward them from all the type-l's. Alternatively, type-h's may be regarded as lazy, and the government may want to redistribute toward the low-ability type-l's from the other two. In these two cases, the incentive constraint binds in different directions. We revert to the assumption that the objective of government is Paretian in the utility of the low-ability person, rather than their consumption as in the previous case.

In the case where the types h's are regarded as disabled, the incentive constraints bind from $2l$ on $1l$ and from $1l$ on $1h$. In this case nonproductive workfare ($\bar{w} = 0$) is never welfare improving. The analysis is directly parallel to the earlier two-type case, though with one additional consideration. Workfare would never be imposed on the type-h low-ability households since it is more costly for them that it is for the type-$1l$'s who might mimic them. As well, following the analysis in the basic case, workfare would not be imposed on the type-$1l$'s when it is nonproductive.

When the government intends redistribution to go toward the low-ability type-l's (e.g., because they are less lazy), incentive constraints apply for both type-$1h$'s and type-$2l$'s with respect to the type-$1l$'s as in figure 4.2. In this case Cuff (2000) shows that nonproductive work-fare may be welfare improving. The intuition is that workfare weakens the incentive constraint on both type-1h's and type-2l's. Type-h's incur more disutility from supplying labor to workfare, while as before high-ability types have a higher opportunity cost of supplying labor to workfare relative to the market. The combination of these two benefits may be enough to compensate for the fact that the workfare is nonproductive.

In the case of heterogeneous preferences for leisure, other possibili-ties can arise. It may be, for example, that some of the type-1h's have special needs, and others simply have different preferences. Given that they are observationally equivalent, this complicates the optimal policy of government: it must decide whether to redistribute toward the type-1h's as a group or toward the type-1l's. Presumably that depends on the relative numbers of "needy" versus "lazy" types. Workfare could exacerbate matters because it screens out the most deserving types.

More generally, government attitudes to different preferences for leisure are not clear-cut and can make a qualitative difference to out-comes. As Boadway et al. (2002) show, if households differ in both wage rates and preferences for leisure, it may be impossible to distin-guish persons with high wages and high preferences for leisure from those with low wage rates and low preferences for leisure. Not only does this make the problem of redistribution more difficult, it also confounds the direction of redistribution depending on the weight that the government places on persons with different preferences for leisure. Indeed the government may prefer not to give any weight to different preferences for leisure, regarding preferences as something for which individuals themselves are responsible and not warranting any special treatment one way or the other (Roemer 1998). We return to this issue later.

4.1.6 Other Issues Affecting Instrument Choice

So far we have focused on the adoption of nonstandard policy instru-ments motivated by their ability to relax the incentive constraints and thereby facilitate further social-welfare-improving redistribution. The choice of policy instruments to supplement the tax-transfer system may reflect other considerations that might arise in a second-best setting. We briefly outline some of them here.

Some policies might be used as devices to counter the adverse con-sequences that can arise when agents are unable to commit to future choices. As we have mentioned, the agent might be the government. If the long-run decisions of individuals depend on future government fiscal policies and if the government is unable to commit to those future policies, the policies it chooses in the future will take individuals' long-run decisions as irrevocable and will therefore not take into account how its ex post policies will affect ex ante individual choices. A time-consistent equilibrium in which individuals correctly anticipate future government decisions can be vastly inferior to a second-best one in which government policies are announced ex ante and carried out. Some individuals will undersave, underinvest in skills, or underinsure for their future well-being if they anticipate that the government will either tax away some of the fruits of their choices or will come to their rescue in the event of an adverse future outcome. In these circumstances the government might introduce measures up front that undo at least some of the adverse consequences of its own future behavior. These can include tax incentives for individuals to save or acquire skills, or for firms to invest (Vigneault 1996, 1997) or underinvestment in resources to combat tax evasion (Boadway and Keen 1998). They can also include measures that mandate forms of individual behavior, such as forced saving for retirement, training by potential welfare recipients (Bruce and Waldman 1991) or compulsory education (Boadway, Marceau and Marchand 1998). The government might intervene in the market provision of some goods or services to overcome commitment issues, such as unemployment insurance to preclude the government's macroeconomic policies from exploiting unemployment insurance providers (Boadway and Marceau 1994) or participation in natural resource exploitation (Boadway and Keen 2010).

Some factors may actually exacerbate the commitment problem. The constitution of a nation may stipulate obligations of the government that require it to come to the aid of disadvantaged persons regardless of how they came to be disadvantaged. Decentralization can also lead to commitment issues. Subnational governments will face a soft budget constraint to the extent that the national government cannot commit to a set of ex ante intergovernmental transfers (Goodspeed 2002; Rodden, Eskeland, and Litvack 2002; Wildasin 2004; Boadway and Tremblay 2006; Vigneault 2007). In these circumstances the subnational governments' own ability to commit will be compromised. The national government may attempt to control the soft budget constraint problem by implementing balanced-budget regulations or restrictions on subnational borrowing.

It is worth re-emphasizing that commitment issues apply to benevolent governments as well as those driven by special interests. This
makes the problem a particularly challenging one. Indeed the problem
of commitment may apply more to the former than to the latter, given
that self-serving governments may have the interest in building a repu-
tation and the opportunity to do so.

Commitment problems can also compromise the behavior of agents
other than the government. Coate (1995) argues that even if the government is able to commit not to coming to the aid of persons who have
brought misfortune on themselves in anticipation of support, similar
consequences can arise if private donors ("good Samaritans") cannot
commit. This too can provide a rationale for the government to mandate
forms of self-insurance or self-improvement if the Samaritan's dilemma
is severe enough. However, given that the altruism of good Samaritans
will be compromised by a free-rider problem that will preclude optimal
(fully efficient) redistribution, the problem is bound to be less severe
than that facing a benevolent government that cannot commit.

Individuals themselves may be the agents facing commitment problems. As the behavioral economics literature has stressed, preferences
may exhibit time inconsistency to the extent that individuals at any
given time discount the entire future excessively (i.e., over and above
the standard discount rate that applies in a compound fashion from
period to period). The result is that they take decisions at any given
time that provide more current gratification than would be the case if
their decisions were taken from a longer run perspective. Thus they
overestimate current benefits and underestimate current costs, resulting in too little saving, too much consumption of products that have
long-run costs, procrastination, and so on.[13] If governments take it on
themselves to attempt to correct individual behavior—bearing in mind
that so doing will contradict the sovereignty of consumer choice and
therefore arguably a premise of welfarism—this will also lead to a
number of nonstandard policy prescriptions. Examples include mandatory saving for retirement (Diamond and Kőszegi 2003), mandatory
education, excise taxes on goods that are tempting but lead to future

13. The literature on behavioral economics is vast. The idea of time-inconsistent prefer-
ences goes back to Strotz (1955), and was resurrected by, among others, Laibson (1997).
Some key references and surveys include Rabin (1998), Gul and Pesendorfer (2001),
Mullainathan and Thaler (2001), Frederick, Loewenstein, and O'Donoghue (2002),
Diamond and Vartiainen (2007), Diamond (2008), Thaler and Sunstein (2008), and Della
Vigna (2009).

problems, including addiction (Gruber and Köszegi 2004; O'Donoghue and Rabin 2006), and providing individuals with an opt-out rather than an opt-in option for contributory pensions (Thaler and Sunstein 2008).

Related to this is the fact that individuals may systematically err in the expectation of the happiness or enjoyment that their choices or their situations may yield (Besley and Layard 2008). This may lead them, for example, to work excessively to earn income that is used to purchase commodities that turn out not to be of lasting value. The effect is similar to overconsumption of goods that generate future costs that are discounted by the individual, although in the case of happiness overestimation, these costs are not anticipated. This will reduce the efficiency cost of income taxation and presumably lead to more redistribution and government provision of goods and services to the extent that the government chooses to correct this misperception. Along the same lines, individual satisfaction may be highly influenced by their outcome relative to others. For example, if relative income is a determinant of individual welfare, the government might choose a more redistributive tax policy on that account. Boskin and Sheshinski (1978), in a linear income tax model, and Oswald (1983), assuming nonlinear income taxation, show that if individual utility functions depend negatively on the incomes or consumption of others (Oswald's case of jealousy), optimal marginal tax rates will be higher (and correspondingly lower in the opposite case of altruism).

Individuals may also take decisions on the basis of social or ethical values rather than in their own self-interest. Indeed it is almost axiomatic that ethical behavior will make a person worse off in the standard sense. Ethical or fair behavior seems to be the norm in experimental and anonymous settings (Fehr 2001; Andreoni 2001; Fehr and Schmidt 2002), which is quite gratifying when one thinks of what the world would be like if that were not the case. One could even think of the government as being the collective will of the ethical preferences of the voters (Brennan and Hamlin 1998). Given that voting is apparently not in the voters' own self-interest, it might be reasonable to assume that voters vote according to social rather than individual preferences. The prevalence of ethical behavior could temper the responsiveness of individuals to taxation (Bordignon 1993; Boadway, Marceau, and Mongrain 2007), to minimum wages (Falk, Fehr, and Zehnder 2006), or to environmental policies (Nyborg, Howarth, and Brekke 2006). The policy implications of moral behavior can be contentious. If persons voluntarily transfer resources to others for moral reasons (rather than for altruistic reasons that presumably make them feel better off), how should this affect their welfare for social welfare purposes? Should they be treated as being worse off? We return to a consideration of these issues later.

As a final observation on other motives for government intervention, we return to the standard optimal nonlinear income tax setting. In the Mirrleesian model, individual wages rates are taken as given, and are the ultimate source of differences in welfare. If government were able to affect wage rates, that might be a useful policy instrument to complement nonlinear income taxation. The obvious way for this to happen is through education policy, and there has been a limited amount of literature investigating this idea. The presumption of the literature, following Arrow (1971), is that high-skilled persons are also more adept at improving their skills through educational resources: the increment of skill increase per unit of resources is increasing in the original skill level. The question that arises then is what should be the extent to which the government should use educational policy as a redistributive instrument alongside nonlinear income taxation, or whether education should instead be based on efficiency goals of maximizing potential output. On the one hand, total output is maximized when educational resources are relatively concentrated on high-skilled persons. On the other, concentrating educational resources on high-skilled persons creates more inequality to begin with, and also violates nonwelfaristic norms of equality of opportunity that would suggest making wages more equal as an objective in itself.

Perhaps surprisingly, the welfarist literature tends to favor not using education as a redistributive device, but relying largely on the nonlinear income tax system instead. In particular, redistributing via education so as to reduce inequality in wage rates is inefficient for two main reasons. First, devoting educational resources to low-skill persons achieves less aggregate productivity than devoting them to high-skill persons, so the size of the pie available for redistribution is smaller (Bruno 1976; Ulph 1977; Hare and Ulph 1979). Second, as wage rates become more equal, it becomes more difficult to separate types. The incentive constraints become tighter, and the distortionary cost of taxation increases (Krause 2006; Stephens 2009; Cremer, Pestieau, and Racionero 2009). This tips the balance in favor of relying on the income tax for redistribution, and focusing educational resources on enhancing aggregate productivity, even though this entails increasing wage rate inequality. Fleurbaey, Gary-Bobo, and Maguain (2002) add educational effort to the optimal choice of educational resources and optimal income taxation, and find that as long as effort and educational assistance are complements, education assistance should be regressive. The presumption then is that at least on social welfare grounds, the case for using education to reduce skill differences is not well founded. These studies do abstract from some considerations that might provide more of a role for the public education policy, such as peer group effects, externalities of education, and the role of education as a device for relaxing incentive constraints or as a pre-commitment device discussed above.

Studies of the effect of changing the wage distribution on optimal redistributive policy are in fact scarce. Brett and Weymark (2003) characterize the optimal nonlinear tax system in the presence of productivity-augmenting education. Individuals are distinguished in two respects: by their innate labor productivity and by their ability to generate productivity through education. In the model both characteristics can be summarized by a single variable (a type aggregator) that reduces the problem to a single dimension. Individuals choose consumption, labor supply, and education, taking the tax system as given, while the government maximizes a utilitarian social welfare function, using the tax system subject to individual's decisions and the economywide resource constraint. The problem is distinguished from the standard Mirrlees analysis by the presence of a nonlinear term for the cost of education in the resource constraint. Thus the solution to the problem differs from that of the standard model in a number of respects. First the marginal tax rate at the top of the distribution (individuals with the highest innate productivity and highest ability to generate skills through education) may not necessarily be zero, and will be strictly positive if there is bunching at that point. Second, if there is bunching at the bottom of the skill distribution, there may be a negative tax rate. The subsidy increases these individuals' demands for education through a higher net wage, which translates into higher incomes. Finally, if there is no bunching at the bottom of the distribution, then all individuals face a positive marginal tax rate, except perhaps at the endpoints.

A recent paper by Brett and Weymark (2008a) considered the effect of an increase in one wage rate in an optimal nonlinear income tax model with a discrete number of wage rates and quasi-linear-in-leisure preferences. The persons whose wage rate increases will benefit from an increase in consumption, as do all those with higher wage rates, while the consumption level of those with lower wage rates will fall. However, it proves to be difficult even in this simple case to obtain more general results about the effect on social welfare. The literature on tagging, which we consider next, studies among other things how optimal nonlinear taxes vary between groups with different distributions of a given set of wages.

4.2   Making Use of, and Acquiring, More Information

As we have emphasized, asymmetric information is at the heart of second-best normative policy problems. Much of the literature on optimal nonlinear tax analysis has adopted the assumptions of Mirrlees (1971), augmented to allow for multiple consumer goods by Atkinson and Stiglitz (1976) and Guesnerie (1995). The government cannot observe the one characteristic that is assumed to differentiate individuals—their ability or skill level, reflected in their wage rate—nor can it observe the commodities they consume, including leisure. It can observe individual income and levy an individual income tax, and therefore infer aggregate consumption or disposable income. Although the government cannot observe how an individual divides disposable income among various commodities, it can observe anonymous transactions and impose linear commodity taxes on them. If individuals reveal their types by their choice of income, the government can infer how they spend their disposable income since it knows their preferences.

In a two-period (or, more generally, multi-period) setting, the government still observes income in each period. Some analysts (Golosov, Tsyvinski, and Werning 2007; Diamond 2007) also assume that savings can be observed, or equivalently aggregate consumption in each period (which is different from disposable income in the presence of saving). This can be interpreted as a pedagogical device used to determine the optimal nonlinear taxation of capital income in ideal conditions: if capital income should not be taxed when saving can be fully observed, it presumably should not be if it cannot be fully observed and only a linear tax on capital income is feasible.

These informational assumptions are not necessarily regarded as the most realistic, but they do offer a useful benchmark case for obtaining reasonable qualitative results. There are a number of obvious ways of varying these assumptions, and some literature explores that. As mentioned above, the income tax evasion literature recognizes that government information on individual incomes comes in the first instance from the individuals themselves (or their employers) when they file tax returns. Depending on the efficacy of the tax administration and the willingness of taxpayers to abide by tax-reporting laws, to the extent that underreporting of income for tax purposes responds to marginal and average tax rates, redistribution options can be significantly constrained (Marhuenda and Ortuño-Ortin 1997; Chander and Wilde 1998). The government can influence income reporting through its ex post monitoring or auditing efforts. We return below to the use of monitoring to enhance incomes and other sorts of information that might be useful to the government in pursuing its redistribution objectives.

The informational context can be made more complicated by assuming individuals possess more than one characteristic. If none of these characteristics is directly observable, the government faces a multidimensional screening problem. Unless characteristics are highly correlated, little of a general nature can typically be said, owing mainly to ambiguity about the pattern of binding incentive constraints (e.g., Besley and Coate 1995; Boadway et al. 2000; Cremer, Pestieau, and Rochet 2001; Boadway et al. 2006; Beaudry, Blackorby, and Szalay 2009; Choné and Laroque 2009). Multi-characteristic problems become much more tractable if some of the characteristics are observable. A particularly interesting case is that where individuals possess two characteristics, only one of which is observable. This gives rise to the possibility of tagging as a way of enhancing the information available to the government.

In what follows, we focus attention on two sources of additional information to the government that can serve to relax the incentive constraints. The first is tagging, where the government makes use of some signal that is correlated with unobserved ability. The other is the use of monitoring to address situations in which the government must otherwise rely on self-reporting to inform itself about relevant individual information.

4.2.1 Tagging

Tagging, a concept attributable to Akerlof (1978), involves the use of an observable signal that is correlated with some characteristic that is relevant for policy purposes. Tagging is widely used as an aid to target transfers to needy or deserving recipients, such as in welfare or social

insurance programs in industrialized economies or in poverty allevia-
tion programs in developing countries. The analogue of tagging is also
used in the private sector as a way of designing prices or contracts
under asymmetric information. For example, statistical discrimination,
such as the setting of different insurance premiums for persons of different age or gender, is a form of tagging. The fact that some forms of
statistical discrimination are ruled out by legislation or constitutional
fiat has its parallels in the reluctance to use tagging for public policy
purposes.

Some of the key features of tagging in a second-best policy setting
have been set out by Parsons (1996).[14] He studies the simple case where
persons may either be able to work or are disabled. If they are able,
they can choose whether to participate in work or remain idle; that is,
they can vary their work along the extensive margin. The government
relies on some unspecified signal or tag to divide persons between two
categories: the tagged and the untagged. The tag might be a medical
certificate indicating some disability, for example. In general, both the
tagged and the untagged categories can include both able and disabled
persons, with the proportions differing in the two categories for the tag
to be informative. The government has a given amount of income to
transfer and, using a utilitarian social welfare function, would like to
make the marginal utility of consumption as equal as possible among
individuals. In the absence of tagging, redistribution is hampered by
an incentive constraint, according to which the able must be at least as
well off working as not working and receiving the transfer intended
for the disabled. If tagging is used, two forms of redistribution apply:
within each group and between the tagged and untagged groups.
Within both the tagged and untagged groups, transfers are made
preferentially to the disabled to the extent allowed by the incentive
constraints.[15] As well, lump-sum transfers are implicitly made between
the two groups as a whole. Not surprisingly, assuming the tag is
correlated with disability, optimal transfers go from the untagged
to the tagged group so as to equalize the average marginal utility of
consumption between groups. Aggregate utility will be higher with
tagging than without, and the gain will be higher the more accurate is
the tag.

---

14. See also Keen (1992), Blackorby and Donaldson (1994), and Salanié (2002) (who
allows individual incomes to vary).
15. As Parsons shows, it may be optimal not to induce the able in the tagged group to
work.

A number of observations on the applicability of the Parsons tagging model in more general contexts are relevant. Tagging will generally involve two types of errors: type I errors whereby some of the disabled do not get tagged, and type II errors whereby some able persons are mistakenly tagged. In the Parsons framework where the only decision is work participation, the untagged disabled will be worse off than without tagging, while the tagged able will be better off. Thus, even though expected utility is higher, so is inequality. The more aversion to inequality there is in the social welfare function, the lower will be the value of tagging. Indeed tagging will reduce social welfare if aversion to inequality is high enough. This will certainly be the case for a maximin social welfare function since the least-well-off persons, the untagged disabled, are made worse off by tagging.

In addition to the inequality created by tagging, there are problems that detract from its efficacy as an aid to redistribution. There may be a stigma attached to being tagged (Moffitt 1983). The stigma might arise from either a loss in self-esteem in being labeled as disabled and in need of a transfer, or it may arise because of resentment one might feel from the rest of the community. Such stigmatization not only directly reduces the value of tagging as a device for enhancing aggregate utility, but also might deter persons from applying for a transfer in the first place, thus reducing the take-up and effectively increasing type I errors (Jacquet and Van der Linden 2006). Stigmatization is also used as one of the arguments, along with political economy arguments, against targeting and in favor of universality of social insurance programs (Atkinson 1999; Van Parijs 1995). Take-up might also be affected by costs of application, which can be significant in a developing country context. Potential applicants might not be well enough informed to realize that they are entitled to transfer programs, or it may simply be costly to apply at an office that may not be close to their place of residence.

Tagging might also be costly. The tag may involve obtaining new information, such as a medical certificate, that involves some payment to the providers of the information. Perhaps as important, there may be agency costs. Tagging is typically administered by government workers, such as social workers in the case of welfare and disability transfers, and there is no reason to believe that their interests are aligned with that of the government. Social workers may be more or less sympathetic to welfare applicants than is the government. Moreover the accuracy of tagging by social workers may depend on the effort they exert, which is not observable by the government. Boadway, Marceau, and Sato (1999) study the consequences of these agency problems for the design of a welfare system, including whether the welfare system should separate those able to work from those unable. Both the severity of the social worker incentive constraint and the cost of inducing participation in work by able welfare recipients (the extensive margin) are relevant. Moreover it may be optimal to have a negative marginal tax rate at the bottom to induce participation by able, but low-skilled, welfare recipients, anticipating the findings of Saez (2002b).

The importance of errors and administrative costs in tagging leads some governments to consider alternatives to tagging as a means of improving targeting. One possibility is to use some form of community tagging, that is, to condition the transfer of funds on the average income level of entire communities rather than on individual incomes. Another is to target the needy by in-kind transfers, such as basic food assistance, which are disproportionately taken up by the poorest. We have discussed this case above.

The mechanism of tagging highlights once again the importance of commitment, or the lack thereof. In the Parsons model, individuals reveal their type—at least if untagged and possibly if tagged as well—by their decision to work. This immediately reveals whether a person is able or disabled. To the extent that disability is a permanent characteristic, if the government could not commit to a transfer, the incentive constraint could be binding for at most one period. This has obvious implications for the usefulness not just of tagging, but of transfer programs more generally.

Finally, while most of the policy literature on tagging has focused on its role in transfer programs, it is potentially applicable to the more general setting of nonlinear income taxation. Suppose that there is an observable signal that is imperfectly correlated with the wage rate (as opposed to being unobservable as in the multi-characteristic optimal income tax problem). In principle, a separate optimal income tax system could apply to tagged and untagged groups, with an implicit lump-sum transfer between them. More generally, the population could be divided into more than two observable groups, though little additional insight is obtained by considering this case. As well, the observable characteristic could be welfare relevant rather than simply a useful signal. An example might be family circumstances (Brett 2007; Apps and Rees 1988) or needs for particular consumption goods (Rowe and

Woolley 1999; Boadway and Pestieau 2003). We restrict attention to pure signals here.

There have been relatively few analyses of the use of tagging in optimal nonlinear income taxation.[16] An early paper by Immonen et al. (1998) introduced tagging into the Mirrlees (1971) model of nonlinear income taxation. Simulation techniques were used to determine patterns of marginal tax rates in each of two tagged groups, one with a higher average skills and income than the other. Their findings were intriguing. Marginal tax rates tended to decline with skills in the higher-income group, but increased in the lower wage group. Not surprisingly, the latter was a recipient of transfers from the former. They also found that calculated welfare gains (the sum of utilities) were significantly higher when tagging was used compared with when it was not.

Analytical results were obtained by Boadway and Pestieau (2006) in a setting consisting of a discrete number of wage-types whose utility functions exhibited quasi-linearity in consumption, following Diamond (1998); see also Cremer, Gahvari, and Lozachmeur (2010). They showed that when the social welfare function had constant absolute aversion to inequality, tagging would always be welfare improving, contrary to the case with only an extensive labor supply margin discussed above. Moreover the tax would be more progressive in the group with the higher proportion of high-wage individuals. Of course, there is no guarantee that these results would hold with other forms of the social welfare function or other preferences. Nonetheless, taken together with the results of Immonen et al., they are suggestive.

Although the scope for tagging to improve social welfare by enhancing the information available to government is inviting, actual income tax systems apparently make little use of them. There may be many reasons for that, apart from the administrative costs and stigmatization discussed above. Tagging will only be useful if observable characteristics of individuals are systematically correlated with skills, and the skill distributions are known. There may be relatively few observable tags

---

16. Viard (2001) studied the case of linear progressive income taxation where a common marginal tax rate is used, but a different lump-sum component applies to different tagged groups. Interestingly, this corresponds with the form of the income tax obtained in a political economy setting by Dixit and Londregan (1998). Using a Downsian party competition model in which both the voters and the political parties put some weight on ideology, they find that in a Nash equilibrium, parties offer tax systems that have a common constant marginal tax rate, but different lump-sum components for various income groups that depend on their political clout.

for which that is the case. In a federal economy there may be different distributions of skills across regions. A system of decentralized income tax setting combined with redistributive interregional transfers might be optimal, although that might be compromised if individuals are mobile across regions (Hamilton and Pestieau 2005). Perhaps one weighty argument against tagging is that it leads to horizontal inequities: otherwise identical individuals who are in different tagged groups will generally be treated differently. Conflicts between horizontal equity and social welfare have been observed in other contexts (Mirrlees 1972a), but these might not be viewed to be as egregious as in the tagging context. Examples of signals that might, in theory, be suitable bases for tagging include physical characteristics such as gender (Alesina, Ichino, and Karabarbounis 2007) and height (Mankiw and Weinzierl 2010) for which some evidence might exist about relative wages rates. Whether it would be socially (or constitutionally) acceptable to impose systematically different tax structures based on these characteristics is dubious.

4.2.2 Monitoring

Governments also enhance their information by various forms of monitoring. Monitoring individuals ex ante to determine relevant personal characteristics is comparable to tagging, albeit with endogenous cost and accuracy (Jacobsen Kleven, and Kopczuk 2011). More common is monitoring ex post to verify information that has been self-reported or reported on an individual's behalf.

Ex post monitoring is a necessary complement to the self-reporting of tax liabilities by both individuals and firms in the income tax system. The usual assumption, following the early tax evasion literature starting with Allingham and Sandmo (1972), is that the tax authorities monitor a selection of taxpayers, either purely randomly or conditioned on some feature of their reported income. True incomes are revealed for those that are audited, and some penalty is imposed for those who report untruthfully. Taxpayers choose how much income to report based on an expected utility calculation where they weigh the chance of being caught and the resulting penalties against the chance of not being caught and avoiding some tax liabilities.

This approach to modeling tax evasion has a number of well-known drawbacks. It apparently predicts much more tax evasion than is observed in practice, perhaps because it does not capture the fact that citizens might have more aversion to breaking the law than the theory assumes. It also has difficulty explaining the comparative-static effects of changes in the tax rate on evasion, and the tendency for penalties imposed for evasion to be relatively low. The assumption that there are no errors in auditing is also important and leads to some fairly strong assumptions. For example, when combined with the standard Mirrlees approach to optimal redistribution using mechanism design techniques, it leads to truthful revelation of incomes by all taxpayers (Cremer and Gahvari 1996; Marhuenda and Ortuño-Ortin 1997; Chander and Wilde 1998), which too is counterfactual. Even so, as mentioned earlier, simply adding tax evasion to the standard Mirrlees model results in a significant further constraint to redistribution as a price to be paid for inducing truthful revelation of incomes. Once errors of administration or unintentional reporting errors are admitted, the revelation principle no longer necessarily applies and seemingly unattractive features of optimal redistribution and tax administration can result (Boadway and Sato 2000). Innocent taxpayers might end up being punished, and the penalties the government might want to apply are thereby significantly limited. Optimal redistribution is further constrained.

Ex post monitoring using audit-and-penalty techniques can apply in settings other than the self-reporting of taxable income. One example concerns the enforcement of regulations imposed on firms when the government has limited information on firm choices. Firms are expected, for example, to abide by environmental regulations, health and safety regulations, minimum wages and pay or employment equity conditions. Just as in the case of law enforcement, government agencies must rely on investigation backed up by the possibility of penalties to enforce such regulations. If the penalties were high enough, all firms would fully comply with the regulations, and we would observe no prosecutions for breaking the law. Of course, such is not the case. Penalties are apparently less than required to ensure full compliance.

The fact that full compliance is not the norm does not imply that analyses that rely on truthful or lawful behavior are not useful. On the contrary, by focusing on the limiting case of full compliance, they serve to illustrate the constraints imposed on second-best policies in an otherwise ideal world. An example applying to redistribution is useful here. Boadway and Cuff (1999) consider the case of monitoring job market search activities in unemployment insurance programs for the temporarily unemployed, and in welfare systems for employable but long-term unemployed workers. These programs often have as a criterion for support that recipients be actively looking for employment and accepting any employment offer that they receive. The government cannot observe these activities, but can rely on administrators to monitor job search and acceptance by transfer recipients. Boadway and Cuff assume that monitoring is random and reveals job market activity perfectly. In these circumstances the government can design monitoring intensities and reward structures to ensure that all recipients do comply. The result is that monitoring provides information to the program administrators that improves the level of unemployment insurance provided and transfers targeted to the intended recipients relative to the no-monitoring optimum. Nonetheless, the costs of monitoring restrict the extent of redistribution that can be achieved, and the technique of constraining policies to force compliant behavior serves to emphasize this.

More formally, consider a population of persons normalized to unity of which a proportion θ are type-A's who are able to work, and $1 - \theta$ are type-D's, unable to work. A given proportion p of the A's are employed and the remaining $1 - p$ are involuntarily unemployed for some unspecified reason.[17] To obtain one of the jobs, able persons must engage in a job search comprising two sequential steps. In step s, they search and apply for jobs they discover. In step o, they accept job offers. Both steps are necessary to obtain work. For simplicity, the government knows who is type A and D, but job applications and job offer acceptances are not observable. However, the government can monitor job search activities. A proportion q^s of unemployed type-A's are randomly monitored to see if they searched for a job. For those monitored, the truth is revealed, so there are no monitoring errors. Similarly a proportion q^o of unemployed type-A's are randomly monitored to see if they refused a job offer. For those monitored, the truth is again revealed. The cost of monitoring is assumed to be $m(q^s, q^o)$, which is increasing in both arguments and convex.

Those working produce an output of w, and obtain consumption c_w and utility $u(c_w) - d$, where d is the disutility of work. For those not working and not found to have refused or not applied for a job, consumption is c_n and utility is $u(c_n)$. The consumption of the type-D's is

---

17. Boadway and Cuff allow p to be endogenous using a simple matching model of employment search. That does not affect the main result, but it does allow for other policy options, as discussed below.

c_d, and this is taken to be an index of their utility as well. For those who are monitored and found either not to have applied for a job or refused a job offer, zero consumption is given (the maximum monetary penalty). Their utility is $u(0)$. In equilibrium all incentive constraints will be satisfied, so no one will actually be punished. (In a more general setting, errors in monitoring can lead to some punishment in equilibrium.)

The government problem is taken to be a Pareto-optimizing one. It maximizes the utility of the type-D's, subject to a minimum level of expected utility of the type-A's denoted $\bar{v}^a$, a resource constraint and relevant incentive constraints. In the first-best (full-information) benchmark, the government chooses consumption levels (equivalently, an unemployment insurance system) to maximize c_d subject to $p(u(c_w)-d)+(1-p)u(c_n) \geqslant \bar{v}^a$ and $\theta(p(c_w - w) + (1 - p)c_n) + (1 - \theta)c_d = R$, where R is a given amount of revenue that is available to the government to transfer to this subset of the population. It is straightforward to see that in the first best, $u'(c_w) = u'(c_n)$, so there is full consumption smoothing, or full unemployment insurance. This results in $u(c_n) > u(c_w) - d$, so is not incentive compatible if the government is not able to observe who is involuntarily versus voluntarily unemployed. In the absence of monitoring, the best the government could do would be to set c_w and c_n such that the type-A's do not choose to be unemployed, or $u(c_w) - d = u(c_n)$. This involves less than full insurance. As such, the resources required to achieve the minimum expected utility for the type-A's would be greater than in the first best since they would have to be compensated for the consumption risk they face. Less would be left for the D's.

The ability to monitor the unemployed type-A's enhances the amount of unemployment insurance that can be provided, so reduces the risk faced by the type-A's. The problem of the government is now to choose the consumption levels as well as the intensity of the two types of monitoring q^s and q^o to maximize c_d subject to $p(u(c_w)-d)+(1-p)u(c_n) \geqslant \bar{v}^a$, $\theta(p(c_w - w) + (1 - p)c_n) + (1 - \theta)c_d + m(q^s, q^o) = R$ and the following two incentive constraints. Type A's will choose to accept job offers if $u(c_w)-d \geqslant q^o u(0)+(1-q^o)u(c_n)$, and will choose to search and apply for jobs if $p(u(c_w)-d)+(1-p)u(c_n) \geqslant q^s u(0)+(1-q^s)u(c_n)$. All constraints will be binding in the optimum.

To interpret the solution to this problem, note that the idea is to choose c_w and c_n along with q^o and q^s so as to achieve $\bar{v}^a$ in the least costly way without violating the incentive constraints. That will maximize the amount left for the type-D's. The two incentive constraints and the minimum expected utility constraint for the type-A's constitute three equations in four unknowns: c_w, c_n, q^o, q^s. Differentiating the constraints, we obtain the changes in, say, c_w, c_n, and q^o as q^s changes:

$$\frac{\partial q^o}{\partial q^s} = \frac{1-pq^o}{p(1-q^s)} > 0,$$

$$\frac{\partial c_w}{\partial q^s} = -\frac{(1-p)(u(c_n)-u(0))}{p(1-q^a)u'(c_w)} < 0,$$

$$\frac{\partial c_n}{\partial q^s} = \frac{u(c_n)-u(0)}{(1-q^s)u'(c_n)} > 0.$$

These relations indicate, first, that q^o and q^s are complementary: an increase in one form of monitoring must be accompanied by an increase in the other if the constraints are to be satisfied. It can also be shown that if one of q^o or q^a is zero, the other will be of no use. Second, as monitoring intensity increases, the differential $(c_w - c_n)$ falls, that is, unemployment insurance increases. Moreover consider the net amount of resources transferred to the able: $\theta[p(c_w-w)+(1-p)c_n]$. Differentiating this with respect to q^s, we obtain

$$\theta\left[p\frac{\partial c_w}{\partial q^s}+(1-p)\frac{\partial c_n}{\partial q^s}\right] = \frac{\theta(1-p)[u(c_n)-u(0)]}{1-q^s}\left[\frac{1}{u'(c_n)} - \frac{1}{u'(c_w)}\right] < 0.$$

This represents the benefit of monitoring. The greater the monitoring, the more unemployment insurance can be provided, and the less resources must be transferred to the able to meet the $\bar{v}^a$ constraint. In the optimum the marginal benefit of the additional monitoring—an increase in q^s accompanied by the required increase in q^o—must just equal the additional cost, which is $dm(q^s, q^o(q^a))/dq^a$.

Boadway and Cuff (1999) extend this model in a number of ways, one of which is to consider the efficacy of a minimum wage, as mentioned earlier. An abridged version of their analysis is as follows. They construct a simple matching model where firms post vacancies and wage offers and the probability of a match depends on the number of unemployed workers and vacancies. The upshot of this model is that the probability of employment is a function of the wage, $p(w)$, with $p'(w) < 0$, where the wage is endogenously determined. When the government imposes a minimum wage $\bar{w}$ above the market-clearing level, the probability of employment becomes $p(\bar{w})$. To determine the effect of the minimum wage, consider the Lagrange expression for the problem above of the government:

$$L = c_d + \mu(p(u(c_w)-d)+(1-p)u(c_n)-\overline{v}^a)$$

$$-\lambda(\theta(p(c_w - w)+(1-p)c_n)+(1-\theta)c_d + m(\cdot)-R)+$$

$$\phi^o(u(c_w)-d-q^o u(0)-(1-q^o)u(c_n))$$

$$+\phi^s(p(u(c_w)-d)+(1-p)u(c_n)-q^s u(0)-(1-q^s)u(c_n)) ,$$

where the probability of employment is given by $p(w)$. The effect of a minimum wage is obtained by applying the envelope theorem with $p = p(\overline{w})$:

$$\frac{\partial L}{\partial \overline{w}} = (\mu + \phi^s)(p'(\overline{w})(u(c_w)-d-u(c_n)))-\lambda\theta p'(\overline{w})(c_w - w - c_n)+\lambda\theta p(\overline{w})$$

$$> 0 \text{ if } c_w - w > c_n.$$

That is, the minimum wage will improve welfare if the transfer to the employed type-A's is large enough relative to the unemployment insurance benefit c_n. In a more general model, where there are multiple skill-types this condition applies for the bottom skill-type and is not implausible.

Monitoring can also be applied ex ante at the stage of application for government programs. Ex ante monitoring is common in social insurance and transfer programs that are administered separately from the income tax system. Unlike the latter, which rely on self-reporting and enforcement by auditing and penalties, eligibility for these programs is usually done by application and investigation by program administrators. These programs typically determine eligibility by criteria other than income, such as health or disability status, number and type of dependents, employability, and asset ownership. The benefits provided by these programs can take various forms, including cash transfers, in-kind transfers and services such as training or counseling. (Of course, continued eligibility might require that recipients fulfill certain criteria, e.g., search for employment, and this requires ongoing monitoring as just discussed.) These programs serve as a useful complement to transfers delivered through the income tax system because they can be targeted using more detailed criteria of need and desert, and because they can be more responsive to short-term changes in circumstances. Given the difficulty than needy persons might have in self-insuring (Chetty and Looney 2006), timeliness is an important property.

These programs are, however, more costly to administer since they require program administrators or caseworkers who must determine the eligibility of applicant by ex ante investigation. Effectively the caseworkers are involved in tagging applicants, and this can give rise to various potential problems. As in the case of costless tagging discussed earlier, there can be errors, especially given the complexity of the criteria and the difficulty in observing whether the criteria are satisfied. Some eligible persons might inadvertently be rule ineligible by caseworkers (type I errors), while some ineligible applicants are incorrectly ruled eligible (type II errors). The latter add to the cost of the program while the former compromise its coverage.

The size of both of these types of errors is to some extent endogenous. Type I errors will reflect the number of eligible persons who apply. Application may be deterred by costs of application, information about the program, or stigma associated with being a recipient. The latter can depend on the number of type II errors: the more ineligible applicants are deemed eligible, the more resentment all recipients might feel from members of the general public. However, applicants might feel stigmatized simply as a result of the perceived intrusiveness of caseworker investigation and the fact that they are labeled as needy. The level of errors will also presumably reflect the resources than have gone into the program as well as the complexity of the program itself. As Jacobsen Kleven and Kopczuk (2011) argue, increased complexity helps reduce type II errors, but it also deters application.

There can also be agency problems between the government and the caseworkers that affects the accuracy of monitoring for eligibility. Boadway, Marceau, and Sato (1999) consider the case where caseworkers can vary the amount of effort they provide in investigating applicants, for simplicity, whether they shirk. The government problem is to design a tax-transfer system to apply to three types of persons: high- and low-wage employable persons and the disabled. Two broad schemes are available: (1) an optimal nonlinear income tax scheme in which the types are separated by self-selecting into income–consumption choices, with the low-skilled and disabled types assumed to be transfer recipients; or (2) an income tax applied to the high-skilled combined with a separate welfare-disability transfer system administered by caseworkers. If option 2 is chosen, the high-skilled self-select into the income tax system, while the low-skilled and disabled apply for the separate transfer system. A tagging system is then applied by caseworkers to separate the low-skilled and disabled persons. The tagging technology generates type I and II errors whose sizes are determined by whether the caseworkers exert effort or shirk. Finally, the government must decide whether under option 2, the untagged low-skilled and disabled are separated by inducing the former to work.

The government cannot observe whether caseworkers shirk but can obtain information on that in one of two ways. If untagged low-skilled workers are induced to work to separate them from the disabled, their number will be revealed and therefore so will the accuracy of tagging. In this case the effort of caseworkers is revealed, albeit at the cost of offering a generous enough transfer to the untagged unskilled workers to induce them to separate from the disabled. Alternatively, if the government chooses not to separate the types, it can monitor caseworkers randomly and penalize those found shirking. As in the ex post monitoring schemes discussed above, there are no errors of monitoring. The choice among these regimes then turns on comparing the costs of separating the untagged low-skilled and disabled versus the costs of monitoring the caseworkers. Moreover the choice between option 1) (an optimal nonlinear tax system) and option 2 (an income tax combined with a separate disability-cum-welfare system) depends on the cost of the caseworker managed tagging system.[18]

The Boadway–Marceau–Sato analysis of agency problems in administering stand-alone welfare programs assumes caseworkers are identical, so shirking is the only relevant form of agency problem. (Of course, such agency problems might also apply to those who administer the income tax system, which would add a further degree of complexity.) However, social workers might also vary by unobserved type, so there is a selection problem as well. Prendergast (2007) has studied the case where case-workers—or bureaucrats more generally in his analysis—differ in their "intrinsic motivation" in their job. This motivation influences the extent of effort they exert as well as the biases they might have toward those in the public with whom they are dealing (their "clients"). For example, potential caseworkers may be motivated in varying degrees by their empathy or identification with the needs of the deserving recipients of transfers. Those who are more sympathetic will have an intrinsic interest in ensuring that transfers are targeted

---

18. It also depends on whether a nonnegative income constraint on the low-skilled types is binding. If it is, labor supply for those persons is effectively at the extensive margin, and a negative marginal tax rate must be used. This increases the cost of the income tax system since it entails subsidizing the low-skilled workers to induce participation.

to the truly needy, or that type-I errors are minimized. They will presumably exert more effort and err in favor of tagging. Other potential caseworkers who may be inclined to be indifferent to the interests of the disabled will exert less effort and err against tagging. To the extent that the government prefers to make the disabled as well off as possible, it would prefer to hire caseworkers whose intrinsic motivation aligns with that of the government, since they will be more inclined to supply effort. For other jobs in the bureaucracy, the government might prefer those whose sympathies lie much less with the clients. Tax administrators or law enforcement officers might present similar instances of agency problems.

Prendergast argues that self-selection of potential bureaucrats to jobs does not necessarily result in the correct matching of persons with the government's desired bias. In his model, persons selecting a given job will include a mix of those most preferred by the government and those least preferred, and none between.

4.3 Conclusions

The various examples in this chapter show the potential importance and richness of the information approach to the design of normative policy. Many of the phenomena discussed have their counterparts in real-world policies. Indeed some policies would hardly exist if it were not for informational problems. To that extent, the normative approach based on information constraints may be vindicated and useful.

To summarize the theme of the chapter, a useful benchmark is the first-best, or full-information, setting. A benevolent government that has full information about individuals and firms can rely on personalized lump-sum taxes and transfers to raise revenues and achieve redistributive goals. The exception to that is the use of Pigouvian taxes and subsidies to internalize externalities or possibly to satisfy paternalistic altruism to the extent that redistribution is motivated by the preferences of the donor population. Once we are in the second best where imperfect information is the norm, lump-sum taxes and transfers, although feasible to the extent that they are conditioned on observables, can only achieve limited amounts of redistribution: the existence of incentive constraints sees to that. In a second-best setting where there are incentive constraints, governments are justified in using policy instruments that would be considered anathema in a full-information setting.

The primary example of this is the nonlinear income tax. In the classical optimal tax literature from Ramsey (1927) to Diamond and Mirrlees (1971), it was simply assumed that the government was restricted to distorting taxes, typically linear income and commodity taxes. Once information constraints were recognized as being the key second-best restriction on government policy, the use of distorting taxes becomes a matter of choice, as the optimal nonlinear income tax literature's has emphasized. Distorting the labor supply of lower wage persons downward relaxes the incentive constraint by making it more difficult for higher wage persons to mimic those with lower wages. This applies whether labor supply varies along the intensive or extensive margin.

Even when nonlinear income taxes are set optimally, incentive constraints continue to bind. Other policy instruments then become useful to the extent that they can relax these constraints further. The argument for differential commodity taxes can be seen in this light. Imposing a higher tax on goods that are relatively more complementary with leisure makes it more difficult for higher wage workers to mimic lower wage workers, since in doing so they would take more leisure and therefore consume more of the taxed good than those being mimicked. The same principle applies to the provision of public goods. If public goods are relatively more complementary with leisure than are private goods, restricting the supply of public goods below the level dictated by the Samuelson condition will make it more difficult for high-wage worker to mimic low-wage worker, assuming that an optimal nonlinear income tax is in place.

Even more nonconventional policy instruments might be useful as ways of relaxing incentive constraints. These could include in-kind transfers as well as price controls such as minimum wages and rent controls. They could also include self-selection schemes like workfare under which the receipt of transfers is contingent on participation in a public work or training program, or unemployment insurance where the receipt of a transfer is contingent on the unemployed person being both involuntarily unemployed and actively searching for a job. The circumstances under which these devices are useful are similar to the case of differential commodity taxes in that they involve complement-substitution relation with leisure.

Finally, the strategic importance of information as a constraint on government invites us to both consider other information assumptions than is the standard case and to seek ways to improve the government's access to information. We saw some implications of both. Thus, if the government cannot observe even the incomes of individuals and must rely on self-reporting, optimal policy is even more constrained. Alternatively, the government might be able to use information that is correlated with characteristics of individuals—that is, signals or tags—that are relevant for redistribution.

There are many caveats to the results reported in this chapter. An important one is that governments for whatever reason might not implement fully optimal policies that exploit the incentive constraints to the fullest. As was argued in this chapter, this does not vitiate the general results of the normative approach. More important, however, are a series of caveats to which we turn in the next chapter.

5   Challenges for Second-Best Analysis

As the preceding discussion indicates, tremendous advances have been made in second-best optimal policy analysis since the seminal contributions of Corlett and Hague (1953), Lipsey and Lancaster (1956–57), Harberger (1964, 1971), and especially Diamond and Mirrlees (1971), and Mirrlees (1971). Many of the findings from this vast literature have informed policy analysis and prescription. However, given that this theory is necessarily based on abstract models that focus on particular aspects of the policy problem, and that this theory is continuously evolving, it is inevitable that at any given point of time, shortcomings and caveats can be identified that require us to temper our prescriptions or change their focus. In this final chapter I identify some of the more pressing challenges that normative second-best theory faces. These challenges are largely unresolved, and my intent is not to resolve them. It is rather to identify the nature of the challenges and review some of the preliminary approaches that have been used to address them.

Let us begin by reminding ourselves of some of the fundamental underpinnings that characterize the standard theory, especially the assumptions that are embedded into it. This will serve as a starting point for a discussion of some of the more radical critiques of the standard theory and some suggestions for approaches to addressing them.

5.1   Fundamentals of the Standard Approach

The standard approach to optimal second-best policy is based on a number of premises, some of which we now better understand as a result of recent advances in economic analysis. The second-best policy problem is taken to be principal-agent in form, where the government is the principal and the taxpayers are agents. The government is

imperfectly informed about aspects of the taxpayers' characteristics or
their behavior, or both. The government has as its objective a social
welfare function that embeds a number of normative principles. It is
worth elaborating on those principles.

First and foremost is the principle of welfarism, which roughly
speaking says that policy options should be evaluated solely based on
how they affect the welfare or utility of individuals in society (Sen
1977). Welfarism respects individualism. That is, the welfare of individuals is based on their own preferences as opposed to some paternalistic judgment of what is good for them. The government is assumed
to know individual preferences, though it is rarely specified how it
comes by this knowledge, and it is often assumed for simplicity that
all individuals have the same preferences.

Aggregating individual preferences into a social welfare function
involves important value judgments. Perhaps the least controversial is
the Pareto principle according to which changes in the allocation of
resources that make at least one person better off without making
anyone worse off are always socially beneficial. Technically speaking,
this is the so-called strong Pareto principle. For some purposes, only
the weak Pareto principle is assumed. It says that if all individuals
strictly prefer one economic state to another, so should social preferences. Some of the implications of this distinction are discussed in
Boadway and Bruce (1984a). We need not be concerned too much with
such subtleties here.

Very few policy changes lead to Pareto improvements, and social
preferences must include ways of comparing allocations in which some
persons are made better off while others are made worse off. That is,
they must be prepared to make interpersonal welfare comparisons. In
principle, this requires that welfare or utility be to some extent measurable and/or comparable among persons.[1] If utility is neither measurable nor comparable, the only information the government might have
is the preference orderings of individuals. In this case, as Arrow (1951)
famously showed, the only social preference ordering that satisfies
some reasonable axioms, such as welfarism, the weak Pareto principle,
and no restrictions on the domain of preferences, is a dictatorship,

1. Attempts to appeal to hypothetical compensation tests to avoid interpersonal welfare
comparisons have been largely discredited. The normative standing of such criteria is
weak, given that the compensation is only hypothetical. Moreover compensation tests
only give partial rankings, and some versions violate transitivity. See, for example, the
discussion in Boadway and Bruce (1984a) and Blackorby and Donaldson (1990).

whereby some person's preferences determine social preferences regardless of the preferences of others. This is obviously an unsatisfactory outcome for normative policy purposes. While there are various ways out of the Arrow paradox, the way that second-best analysis has adopted is to assume the government has more information than simply preference orderings of individuals, that is, by allowing at least some comparability of utility among individuals and possibly measurability as well. Where this information comes from is very much an open question, especially given the value judgments involved. Presumably one hopes for sufficient societal consensus. This issue will come up in our subsequent discussion.

Conceptually there are various assumptions that can be made about both the measurability of individual utility and the comparability of utility or welfare among persons.[2] Perhaps the least restrictive is to eschew measurability so that only preference orderings are known, and to rely solely on comparability of levels of utility across persons. In this case the normative policy analyst must be prepared to judge whether, between any two persons, one is better off or worse off than the other, or whether they are equally well off in any given social situation. If one makes the further judgment that it is socially preferable to redistribute from better-off to less-well-off persons, one is left with a leximin social preference ordering. According to this, policies that make the worst-off persons better off are socially preferred. Those that leave the worst-off persons' welfare unaffected but make the next worse-off person better off are socially preferred, and so on up the line. (The identity of the worst-off person can change from one social situation to another but that does not affect the principle.) A more extreme form of social ordering that relies only on comparisons of welfare levels is maximin according to which only the welfare of the worst-off person counts. The difference with leximin is that under maximin, if the worst-off persons in two allocations are equally well off, society should be indifferent between the allocations even though the next worse-off persons are not indifferent. For many second-best applications the distinction between leximin and maximin is not relevant. For example, in the standard optimal nonlinear income tax model, there is a unique maximin

---

2. A simple summary of the implications of various assumptions about measurability and comparability for the form of the social welfare function can be found in Boadway and Bruce (1984a). Again, the details of this are not especially relevant for our general discussion.

allocation of resources so the issue of comparing second-best optimal
allocations where the worst-off person is indifferent does not arise.

The attraction of leximin and maximin social orderings is that their
informational requirements, or equivalently the extent of their value
judgments, are minimal. Only levels of utility need be compared. At
the same time they lead to more extreme forms of egalitarianism when
compared with other social orderings that require more information.
Indeed, it is common in second-best policy analysis to assume a more
general social welfare function that allows for a trade-off among the
utilities of individuals. The most common general form of such a social
welfare function takes the following additive form:

$$W(u^1(y^1), \ldots, u^j(y^j), \ldots, u^J(y^J)) = \sum_{j=1}^{J} G(u^j(y^j)), \tag{5.1}$$

where y^j is some money metric measure of the welfare level of individual j such as real income measured at some reference prices, $u^j(y^j)$
is the individual's utility as a function of real income, and $G(u^j(y^j))$ is
the social utility attributable to person j as a function of that person's
utility level.[3] This form of utility function assumes that the same function $G(\cdot)$ applies to all persons' utilities so that all persons are treated
alike (the so-called principle of anonymity).

Depending on the measurability assumption used, different forms
of the social welfare function apply. For example, if utility can be measured on a cardinal scale (i.e., up to an affine transformation), changes
in utility between two allocations can be compared across individuals.
In this case, in addition to leximin and maximin social welfare orderings, generalized utilitarianism (the weighted sum of utilities) is permissible as well (Deschamps and Gevers 1978; Blackorby, Bossert, and
Donaldson 2002). If utility can be measured on a ratio scale, proportional changes in utility can be compared across persons. In this
case, if one assumes that the social preference ordering is anonymous
so all persons are treated alike, the commonly used constant elasticity
version of the social welfare function taking the following form is
permissible:

3. Technically speaking, the money metric used to measure real income will generally
not be unique. The usual money metric is the expenditure function indicating the amount
of income needed to achieve different utility levels. This will generally depend on the
set of relative prices used to measure the expenditure function. The choice of reference
relative prices is a detail that need not detain us since it does not affect the general principles involved.

$$W(u^1(y^1), \ldots, u^j(y^j), \ldots, u^J(y^J)) = \sum_{j=1}^{J} \frac{(u^j(y^j))^{1-\rho}}{1-\rho}. \qquad (5.2)$$

The parameter ρ, which is the elasticity of marginal social utility (i.e., the elasticity of $\partial W(\cdot)/\partial u^j$), can be interpreted as the coefficient of aversion to inequality. (It is analogous to the coefficient of relative risk aversion.) This utility function nests the utilitarian case for which $\rho = 0$ and the limiting maximin case which is approached as $\rho \rightarrow \infty$. Finally, if utility can be measured on an absolute scale, a unique number can be attached to each indifference level of an individual. In this case fully general forms of the social welfare function (5.1) are possible.[4] Provided that that society has a nonnegative aversion to inequality in utilities, the social welfare function $W(\cdot)$ is quasi-concave in utilities.

The next leading question is: Where does the information come from that leads to these measurability and comparability assumptions, and therefore leads to actual social welfare functions? Since the answer to this is relevant for our subsequent discussion, some elaboration is in order. The raw material for social preferences that satisfy welfarism is the preference orderings of individual allocations. In the standard theory, individualism is respected so individual preferences are used. Although individualism is widely regarded as reasonable, it is not a given. It is possible to build normative theories based on preference orderings that are not individualistic (Adler, forthcoming), although it is not clear where such preference orderings come from and how they might come to be agreed on as ingredients in the social ordering. As we will see later, there may be circumstances in which individual preferences are overridden in social preferences, such as when the former are based on irrationality or limited information.

Given individual preference orderings, aggregating these into a social welfare function can in principle involve two separate steps, corresponding to the two functions appearing in (5.1), namely obtaining individual utility functions $u^j(y^j)$ and obtaining the social utility function $G(u^j)$ (Kaplow 2010). With respect to the former, one might take various views. Some might argue that in principle $u^j(y^j)$ is objectively measurable; that is, one's level of satisfaction or welfare can be measured, whether on an absolute scale or a cardinal scale. This view harks back to Bentham (1791) and seems to be the one adopted by Kaplow

---

4. Technically speaking, an additional separability assumption is required in order that the social welfare function be additive as shown. See Boadway and Bruce (1984a).

(2008).[5] Related to this view is the idea that cardinal measures of individual utility can be uncovered by observing the individual's preferences over lotteries, and in that sense individual preferences reveal not only rankings of alternatives but also cardinal measures of those alternatives, or von Neumann–Morgenstern utilities (von Neumann and Morgenstern 1944). Finally, some persons might take a much more restrictive line, following Arrow (1951), and suppose that the only objective information available is ordinal preferences. In this case the individual utility functions $u^j(y^j)$ are a matter of social evaluation or value judgment about how utility varies with real income, perhaps in some absolute sense. This view corresponds with that taken by cost–benefit manuals used to evaluate public projects in developing countries, such as Dasgupta, Margin, and Sen (1972) or Little and Mirrlees (1974). More recently this approach has been used to obtain a notional social discount rate for evaluating the costs and benefits of policies for addressing global warming (Stern 2007). Of course, this begs the question of who decides on individual utility functions or how such a consensus might be formed. This does not preclude normative analysis from being done, but it does mean that such analysis must be regarded as contingent on whatever social evaluation (or range of social evaluations) about individual utility functions is used.

The choice of a social utility function $G(\cdot)$ is related to how individual utility functions are chosen. If the only objective information is taken to be individual preference orderings, the distinction between the social evaluation of individual utilities—the choice of utility functions $u^j(y^j)$— and the choice of a social utility function $G(\cdot)$ is somewhat arbitrary. Both involve value judgments and nothing is lost by collapsing these into a single step. That is, one might as well just write the social welfare function in the simple additive utilitarian form

$$W(u^1(y^1), \ldots, u^j(y^j), \ldots, u^J(y^J)) = \sum_{j=1}^{J} u^j(y^j), \qquad (5.3)$$

where the choice of individual utility functions $u^j(y^j)$ incorporates the complete social evaluation of individual outcomes. However, if one treats individual utility functions as reflecting objective measures of individual utility, the value judgment involves how to aggregate

---

5. Kaplow (2008, p. 377) suggests that "advances in brain science may ultimately provide a scientific basis for measuring individuals' utility in an interpersonally comparable fashion."

individual utilities into a social welfare function, that is, how to choose $G(\cdot)$ in the additive case. While, in principle, different value judgments lead to different degrees of concavity of the social utility function $G(\cdot)$, Harsanyi (1955, 1977) famously argued that applying the same rationality principles to social choice as one applies to individual choice under uncertainty, and assuming welfarism with equal weighting for all individuals, lead one to utilitarianism.

In the standard second-best approach, these distinctions about the meaning of individual utility functions—whether they reflect scientifically measurable utilities or value judgments—are relatively inconsequential. Everyone is assumed to have the same preferences and utility function. The formal analysis and interpretation of results is not affected by one's view about what the individual utility function represents. However, once we move from that simple realm, more is at stake, as I will argue.

Besides the principle of welfarism and its implications for social preferences, some other important premises of the standard approach should be highlighted. Individuals, in addition to having identical utility functions, are all assumed to be fully informed about the options facing them, and to behave rationally in pursuing their own interests (as defined by their utility function). The government is assumed to be benevolent and to make decisions that achieve the highest social welfare level unconstrained by political objectives or by nonwelfarist objectives. Although the government is not perfectly informed, it is nonetheless well informed. It cannot observe the only characteristic that distinguishes individuals (their productivity in models with intensive labor supply, and their preferences for leisure in extensive-margin models), but it can observe their incomes. And, the government is assumed to be able to commit to carrying through its announced policy, even if the response to that policy reveals individual characteristics. This is so not just in multi-period versions of the theory but also in one-period versions where government announces policies before individuals make their decisions.

In what follows we focus on some of these key assumptions. There are, of course, many challenges in using the standard theory for policy analysis even given the assumptions it adopts. Within the standard framework, the choice of an economic model can have qualitative effects on results, as some examples will remind us. The form of the optimal income tax schedule, especially at the bottom end, depends on the nature of labor supply variation, whether it be variability of hours of work, occupational choice or participation. The qualitative features of the rate structure are also affected by the form of the social welfare function (e.g., maximin versus utilitarian), the individual utility function (e.g., quasi-linear, separable), the distribution of skills (e.g., bounded versus unbounded, discrete versus continuous), and the production technology (e.g., fixed versus variable producer prices). For example, the marginal tax rate at the bottom is zero if the distribution of skills is continuous and the aversion to inequality in the social welfare function is finite. However, if the distribution is finite or the social welfare function is maximin, the marginal tax rate at the bottom is positive, and this can affect the shape of the marginal tax rate schedule. Whether or not the Diamond–Mirrlees production efficiency theorem applies depends on whether full lump-sum profit taxation is available, as well as whether producer prices are fixed. Moreover the role of indirect commodity taxation is affected by the form of the utility function (separable or not) and on the possibility of household or non-market production.

The optimal income tax is also critically dependent on the informational assumptions adopted, such as the assumption that the government can observe individual incomes, as well as on when information is revealed to individuals, that is whether they face uncertainty about their wage rate that is not resolved until after some decisions have been made. Optimal policies also depend on whether there are restrictions imposed on policy instruments, such as linearity of income taxes, restriction to annual income taxes, or limitations on the subsets of goods on which differential commodity taxes can be imposed.

Finally, virtually all results are derived from simple models that of necessity abstract from complications in order to focus on the problem at hand. For example, as soon as one moves away from the Mirrleesian assumption of a single characteristic, technical problems can arise that not only obscure the analysis but can affect the qualitative results. Moreover, once the models used become more complicated, the interpretation of the results in terms of actual income tax systems becomes difficult. This is particularly apparent in dynamic versions of the Mirrlees analysis. In these models one derives various wedges between relative consumer values and producer costs, including both labor wedges and intertemporal wedges. As Kocherlakota (2004) shows, implementing these wedges using taxes on labor and capital income is not straightforward. For example, positive intertemporal wedges do not necessary imply positive capital income taxes because of interdependencies that arise between the two wedges.

These and other extensions of the standard model have already been discussed. On top of this, there are more practical issues, such as costs of administration and compliance that might restrict the extent of complexity of the tax system. These are all matters that we know how to deal with in principle. Instead, we turn our attention to some more fundamental issues.

5.2   The Commitment Issue

The order of decision-making can have a profound effect on policy outcomes. The discussion above has alluded to several examples of this. In the dynamic version of the Ramsey optimal tax problem, if a benevolent government cannot commit to future taxes on capital or capital income, the time-consistent outcome can be significantly inferior to the full-commitment (second-best) case. Private agents who anticipate that the government will unavoidably choose excessively high capital tax rates will restrict their asset accumulation to levels far below the optimum (Fischer 1980). This incentive to tax previously accumulated assets arguably has wide-ranging consequences. It applies particularly to capital accumulated by firms, and perhaps accounts for the high taxes borne by capital in such forms as corporation income tax rates, taxes on firms' capital, and high taxes on natural resource properties, particularly those that have seen large price increases. Governments might engage in ex ante policies to mitigate the problem, for example, by offering subsidies or tax holidays on asset accumulation, applying lax enforcement on capital income tax avoidance or evasion, and designing business tax structures ex ante that are explicitly progressive, notably in the natural resource sector where taxes might depend on cumulated rents (Garnaut and Clunies Ross 1975; Boadway and Keen 2010).

In a redistributive context, governments face the classical problem of the Samaritan's dilemma. Ex post redistribution can induce various forms of behavior that take advantage of the anticipated redistribution. Persons of lower skill levels might exploit government social insurance or welfare transfer systems by choosing not to better themselves or by engaging in risky behavior. Governments might in turn respond by introducing programs of public insurance or mandating training or other self-betterment programs (Bruce and Waldman 1991). Households might be discouraged from accumulating human capital if they expect that governments will impose excessive taxes on the returns to human capital investment. This can again lead to suboptimal equilibria, in some cases even worse than the laissez-faire outcome, and can motivate education subsidies or mandatory education (Boadway, Marceau, and Marchand 1996; Konrad 2001; Pereira 2009a, b).

In a federalism context there are more than two levels of decision-making and the possibilities multiply. The usual approach to the normative study of federalism is to suppose that the federal government moves first, followed by the subnational governments, followed by private agents. Assuming that the federal government adopts a welfaristic approach and takes account of the welfare of all national residents, the optimal policy outcome is the second-best one (Sato 2000). Once the order of decisions changes, socially inferior outcomes result. There are two interesting ways in which such deviations can occur, both of which have some plausibility. First, one can imagine subnational governments choosing their policies before the federal government. In these circumstances an outcome analogous to the Samaritan's dilemma can arise. Subnational governments correctly anticipating financial relief from the federal government overextend themselves by spending too much or taking on excessive debt (Wildasin 2004; Boadway and Tremblay 2006; Vigneault 2007).

Second, the decisions of economic agents might be taken before those of governments, some of whose consequences we have discussed. In the federalism context the case that gives additional insight is that in which individuals are free to migrate from one region to another. In the standard approach a social welfare maximizing federal government implements a set of redistributive (equalization) transfers to subnational governments that, in part, addresses well-known inefficiencies of subsequent migration that arise in local public goods economies (Buchanan and Goetz 1972; Flatters, Henderson, and Mieszkowski 1974; Boadway and Flatters 1982; Albouy 2009). If migration occurs before the federal and subnational governments choose their fiscal policies, the subgame perfect equilibrium outcome generally involves migrants concentrating excessively in one region (Mitsui and Sato 2001).

The intuition is as follows. Consider the simple case where utility is additively separable between a subnational pure public good and a numéraire private good. A utilitarian federal government that cannot commit will choose policies that equalize the marginal utility of consumption across regions ex post. If utility functions are the same for all, this implies equalizing private consumption for all individuals regardless of where they reside and how much income they earn. At the same time there are economies of scale in consuming the public good, and the subnational public good provision will be increasing in population. In these circumstances it will be in the interest of individuals to move to the most populous region in order to have access to the highest level of public good. In equilibrium individuals will allocate themselves disproportionately to one or more of the most populated regions. This will be inefficient if there are diminishing marginal products of labor in each region, perhaps because of some fixed factor of production. The inability of the federal government to commit to the second-best system of redistributive inter-regional transfers will therefore lead to an inferior time-consistent equilibrium.

In the standard optimal nonlinear income tax setting, a further troublesome potential source of commitment problem arises. Recall that the only constraint put on the planner is an informational constraint that precludes knowing the skill of each person. The problem is solved using the revelation principle, which entails all persons revealing their type to the planner. In order to induce revelation, the planner's policy choices—which in the direct mechanism used in the analysis involves a menu of consumption–income bundles offered to individuals—must satisfy a set of incentive constraints. It is the incentive constraints that account for the qualitative properties of the optimal nonlinear income tax, in particular the positive marginal tax rates that apply for most of the skill distribution.

The potential problem with the revelation principle is apparent. Once individuals reveal their types, what is to preclude the planner from using that information to revise the policy choice, especially since doing so would seem to open up the possibility of achieving a first-best outcome using type-dependent lump-sum transfers? There seems to be no natural way to assume that the planner can commit not to doing that, given that the order in which decisions are actually made involves policies being implemented after individuals have made their labor supply decisions. Knowing that, individuals will change their first-period behavior in ways that reduce the social value of the outcome overall. However, this presumes that the government can easily change policies from those announced on the basis of individual behavior. In the real world, policies must be legislated, and since the act of legislation is a long-run decision, that in itself might mitigate the commitment problem to a great extent. It might account for the fact that we seem to observe relatively few instances of government policies systematically deviating from what might be thought of as those chosen before the private sector acts. The exception are cases where private decisions are very long run in nature, for example, major long-run investments by firms, such as in the natural resource sector, or wealth accumulated by individuals either for retirement or for passing on to their heirs.

Much of the attention in the literature has been to the case where there is more than one time period, and information gained from one period reveals something useful about individuals that can be used in the next period. One of the first contributions to study this was by Brito et al. (1991), but as we noted in chapter 4, various authors have studied optimal nonlinear income taxation in multi-period models without commitment, including Roberts (1984), Apps and Rees (2006), Acemoglu, Golosov, and Tsyvinski (2010), Brett and Weymark (2008b), Krause (2009), and Pereira (2009a, b). In these cases skills are constant over time, or they may vary but be subject to some correlation over time (possibly perfect). These models typically assume that commitment is possible within each period, but information revealed in one period can be used in subsequent ones. However, the problem is more serious than that since even within a single taxpaying period, once skills are revealed that information could be used instantaneously.

To take an example, consider the basic tagging model of Parsons (1996) consisting of able and disabled persons who are being considered for a transfer program. Tagging is imperfect so the tagged group consists of both able and disabled persons. They must be separated by offering them a transfer that varies according to whether they accept work or not. Once the able tagged persons choose to work, they reveal that they are able and the government has an incentive to renege on the promised transfer. A similar problem exists within the untagged group if some disabled persons mistakenly go untagged. The same principle applies to any redistributive scheme that relies on voluntary revelation. Indeed it even applies to cases where the government is even less well informed than we normally assume. Thus, in the analysis of optimal redistribution when households can misreport their incomes, the revelation principle is often assumed to apply to the audit and penalty mechanism that the government deploys (Cremer and

Gahvari 1996; Marhuenda and Ortuño-Ortin 1997; Chander and Wilde 1998).[6]

Moreover, even if the incentive constraint is not binding, persons typically implicitly reveal their types. This is so for the case of linear income taxes. If individuals have the same preferences and differ only in skills, they will pick different points on the tax schedule. In principle, their types can be recovered by a planner that knows their preferences. The planner could then use that information to implement lump-sum redistributive transfers. At least from a theoretical point of view, the problem of commitment would seem to be potentially very serious.

With the relatively few exceptions mentioned above, normative optimal income tax analysis generally simply assumes that the government can commit. This is certainly the case in static models, and is also true in many dynamic models, including those of the new dynamic public finance (e.g., Cremer and Gahvari 1995; Kocherlakota 2004, 2005; Golosov, Kocherlakota, and Tsyvinski 2003; Golosov, Tsyvinski, and Werning 2007; Diamond 2007). A recent paper by Acemoglu, Golosov, and Tsyvinski (2010) provides a novel theoretical rationale for assuming commitment based on political economy considerations. They construct a dynamic optimal nonlinear income tax model in which heterogeneous taxpayers with stochastically evolving skills live forever, as do potential politicians and voters. The retrospective voting model of Barro (1973) and Ferejohn (1986) is used to make politicians accountable to the voters (who have identical policy preferences). A politician who is defeated can be replaced by another otherwise identical politician. Acemoglu, Golosov, and Tsyvinski show that politicians are induced to behave as if they were fully committed so that they can be re-elected and obtain the perks of office. While this is an ingenious story, one drawback is that to achieve commitment by politicians, it effectively assumes that voters can commit to voting on the basis of the past performance of politicians. Given that defeated politicians will be replaced by politicians of exactly the same type, it is not obvious why voters would carry out their threat to vote a nonperforming politician out of office.

While the issue of commitment remains a serious one for the theoretical analysis of optimal taxation using the revelation principle, what

---

6. However, the revelation principle may not be applicable in other assumed tax evasion settings. For example, if there are errors in auditing or tax reporting, the revelation principle may well be violated. See Boadway and Sato (2000).

does it imply for the policy implications that we can learn from the theory? The first thing to note is that commitment seems not to be a widespread issue in practice. Income taxes typically tax earnings on an annual basis. An exception is where income averaging applies, but even here past information about a taxpayer is not exploited to determine current liabilities. No doubt this is partly a reflection of the fact that income tax systems are not designed on the basis of the revelation principle of our theories. Incentive constraints are not binding in the typical piecewise linear tax systems used in practice. Moreover, direct mechanisms are not used by governments to set their taxes. Instead, tax schedules are applied directly without reference to the revelation principle. Of course, as mentioned, it may still be possible to recover individuals' types by their choices from the tax schedule provided, but given that governments restrict themselves to tax schedules that are not tailored to individual taxpayers, they cannot be used to exploit particular individuals. Perhaps more important, the fact that governments do not exploit their apparent ability to re-optimize when they obtain more information may simply be explained by the fact that, as mentioned, policy changes must be legislated and that takes time. Policy-making may therefore simply be a long-run decision, which naturally precludes the commitment problem.

More generally, the economists' current preoccupation with commitment, which insists on some form of credibility as a way of avoiding commitment, may simply be too extreme. Just like behavioral economics has taught us that individuals often do not behave selfishly, maybe keeping one's promise is a social norm or a character trait that is sufficiently strong to lead individuals and politicians to fulfill their promises. Of course, political promises cannot cover every contingency, especially if factors determining the effects of policy are not fully verifiable: they are like incomplete contracts in that regard. If unexpected events occur, it might be perfectly reasonable, and accepted to be so to the voters, for politicians to renege on their promises. The issue of commitment or promise-keeping is something on which future experimental research might shed some light.

Given the potential problems with commitment, the question arises as to how useful optimal tax theories that rely on the revelation principle actually are. The question is especially relevant given that, as we have mentioned, it is the binding incentive constraints that account for some of the specific features of optimal marginal tax schedules. One answer is that normative policy analysis is not meant to replicate the real-world policy problem. It is meant to provide normative policy prescriptions that can serve as a benchmark indicating the best outcomes that policy makers can achieve. More than that, since normative second-best analysis is based on highly abstract models, the policy advice it offers is more of a conceptual or intuitive nature in the sense that it helps us understand the nature of the policy problem at a fairly deep level. How relevant commitment issues are for the choice of an optimal income tax in practice is a matter for ongoing research.

5.3   Heterogeneous Preferences and Utility

The standard Mirrlees approach to optimal nonlinear income taxation assumes that all individuals have not only the same preference orderings over commodities but also the same utility functions. This, of course, simplifies the analysis considerably, and also reduces the value judgment required to aggregate utilities into a social welfare function to one dimension: the aversion to inequality in utilities. Indeed a reasonable specification of the social welfare function in this case leads to a one-parameter measure of aversion to inequality, the so-called coefficient of aversion to inequality.[7] If individuals can differ in both their preferences and their utility function, matters become both more complicated and more controversial. It is useful to consider differences in preferences and differences in utility functions separately.

Suppose first that individuals share the same preference orderings but differ in their utility functions. This case was considered long ago by Sen (1973) and again more recently by Kaplow (2008). If two persons differ in their utility functions, the presumption is that they differ in their ability to obtain welfare from the same commodity bundles. Given that we are in no position to measure utility scientifically, this presumption must be based on some judgment about the utility-generating capacity of different individuals. One might suppose, for example, following Kaplow, that children might need systematically smaller commodity bundles to achieve a given level of well-being than adults. Perhaps similar distinctions can be made for persons of different physical sizes, physiological makeups, and so on. However, these judgments are by no means obvious. One could argue that given their experience

---

7. In particular, (5.2) is a social welfare function where all individuals have the same utility function and the coefficient of aversion to inequality is ρ. For a recent application of this social welfare function for policy analysis, see Stern (2007).

and knowledge, adults actually need fewer resources to achieve a given level of utility than children. Similar arguments can be made for, say, smart people versus slow people, or people whose life experiences are different, such as males versus females. The comparison is fraught with difficulty, and apparently requires a significant value judgment on behalf of the normative planner.

For better or worse, there is much at stake in such utility comparisons. The manner in which different utility functions are aggregated into a social welfare function can have fairly dramatic consequences for policy prescriptions. If one takes a strict utilitarian perspective (i.e., a zero aversion to inequality), so is concerned with aggregate utility and not its distribution, policy should redistribute toward those who are better able to generate utility from resources and away from those less able. This might not be palatable on ethical grounds. At the other extreme, if one puts very high weight on the distribution of utilities, as in the maximin or leximin cases with infinite aversion to inequality, redistribution would go in the other direction. Those less efficient at generating utility would have to be favored in order to bring their utility levels as close as possible to the others.

A full analysis of the consequences of different utility functions for optimal policy has yet to be conducted. To the extent that the ability to generate utility is based on some observable characteristic, the technical problems would be minimal. However, the conceptual problems and the value judgments remain daunting.

Suppose next that individuals differ in their preference orderings. This is almost certainly the case, as casual observation suggests. Individuals buy different bundles of goods, save different amounts, take different risks, choose different occupations, and so on. Indeed, most actual tax policies discriminate among persons of different preferences, and this constitutes a significant challenge for normative policy analysis. There is no apparent general principle that suggests itself for comparing utilities of households who make different economic choices. Analysts who have studied optimal taxation in situations with heterogeneous preferences have tended to be somewhat agnostic about the social welfare weights given to persons of different preferences. The typical approach is simply to posit arbitrary weights and then study the policy consequences of different patterns of weights (e.g., Boadway, et al 2000; Saez 2002a; Choné and Laroque 2009). Unfortunately, the choice of weights matters for policy prescriptions, so once again much is at stake. Alternatively, the second-best policy problem might be posed as one of Pareto optimization, as in Blackorby and Donaldson (1988). Here too the policy prescription depends on the point on the second-best Pareto frontier that is chosen. Below, we will consider one approach that has been taken to deal with the issue of different preferences. First, it is worth considering some specific instances where the issue of heterogeneous preferences has been addressed in the literature.

5.3.1 Needs

One way of dealing with seemingly heterogeneous utilities while avoiding some of the problems above is to assume that individuals vary in their needs for particular commodities, a case I discussed briefly earlier. Following Rowe and Woolley (1999) and Boadway and Pestieau (2003, 2006), suppose that the utility function for household j can be written $u(x^j - r^j)$, where x^j is the vector of commodity demands and r^j is the vector of exogenous needs. (Needs could enter in other forms, such as multiplicative, without changing the nature of our argument.) This corresponds with the Stone–Geary utility function, where the needs correspond with nondiscretionary requirements. Alternatively, following Cremer, Pestieau, and Rochet (2001), the elements of r^j could also be interpreted as initial endowments. In this formulation a common utility function $u(\cdot)$ can be assumed to apply to all persons, while they can differ in their given needs. Given the common utility function, issues of comparability and measurability are finessed as in the standard optimal income tax problem.

Of course, allowing for needs differences complicates the optimal tax problem considerably. For example, if needs are observable, the second-best optimal nonlinear tax system would involve applying different income tax structures to different needs groups, and redistributing between needs groups to take account both of systematic differences in needs and differences in the skill distribution of different needs groups. However, if the government is constrained to applying a common income tax schedule economywide—for example, to satisfy horizontal equity—offering tax credits for needs becomes a useful redistributive device. It turns out to be optimal to overcompensate low-wage persons for needs and undercompensate high-wage persons (Boadway and Pestieau 2006). If needs are not observable, but the distribution of needs across commodities and skill groups is known, it becomes optimal to tax commodities differentially alongside a nonlinear income tax. For example, a differential commodity tax would be imposed on commodities for which needs by low-skilled persons are on average lowest (or endowments highest, as in Cremer, Pestieau, and Rochet 2001).

5.3.2 Disutility of Work

It is common in the redistribution literature to suppose that persons differ in the disutility of work. Such differences sometimes reflect the fact that the target of redistribution includes those with disabilities. Examples include Diamond and Sheshinski (1995) and Parsons (1996), who study the use of tagging to facilitate identifying the disabled, Boadway and Cuff (1999), who investigate how ex post monitoring of job search can assist in separating types, and Boadway, Marceau, and Sato (1999), who analyze how agency problems between the government and social workers can undermine the tagging of the disabled. Models of optimal nonlinear taxation when labor supply is on the extensive margin also assume differences in the disutility of work as the factor determining participation (Diamond 1980; Saez 2002b; Brewer, Saez, and Shephard 2010; Jacquet, Lehmann, and Van der Linden 2010). These studies often adopt either a strict utilitarian objective function or solve a Pareto-optimizing problem. In the former case utility is often taken to be additively separable in consumption and leisure, with the utility of consumption function common to all households. Problems of comparability and measurability of utility arising from differences in preferences are then essentially suppressed since the utilitarian objective implies that the planner is only interested in equalizing consumption to the extent that that is possible given the information constraints.

Cuff (2000) observes that a distaste for work can have alternative interpretations. It can reflect a disability, as in the above discussion, or it can reflect a taste for leisure (or "laziness"). Which interpretation applies can have an effect on policy prescriptions. She considers a simple example in which the high-skilled have a low distaste for work, while the low-skilled include both those with a high distaste and a low distaste for work. She compares two mutually exclusive alternatives: either a high distaste for work represents a disability or it represents laziness. In both cases income will be lowest for those with low skills and high distaste for labor, and highest for those with high skills. In the case where high distaste for work reflects a disability, the government is assumed to want to redistribute toward the disabled from the other two types, and the standard properties of the optimal nonlinear tax apply, with incentive constraints downward binding by income level. In the other case, redistribution is toward the low-skilled nonlazy types and away from the other two. The incentive constraints are now binding downward for the high-skilled workers and upward for the lazy low-skilled workers, implying a zero marginal tax rate at both the bottom and the top.

Cuff shows further, and this is the main point of the paper as mentioned earlier, that nonproductive workfare would not be used in the case where high distaste for work reflects disability but might be used where it is judged to reflect laziness. In the former case, workfare is more costly for the disabled types so would not be imposed on them. In the latter case, workfare weakens the incentive constraint on both the high-skilled type and on the lazy type: each would find it more costly to pretend to be the low-skilled type with a low distaste for labor.

A somewhat more complicated setting is one in which those with high distaste for work can include both the disabled and the lazy. Marchand, Pestieau, and Racionero (2003) adopt the model of Cuff to examine some consequences of this issue. If the disabled and the lazy are observationally equivalent—as they assume—the government can redistribute from the high-skilled to the low-skilled as a group but cannot favor the disabled among the latter. They argue that differential commodity taxes can indirectly achieve some preferential treatment of the disabled if the bundle of goods consumed differs between the disabled and the lazy. Whether that is the case depends on the preference orderings of the two types, which is an open question.

The interpersonal utility comparisons in the above approaches seem at first glance to be innocuous, at least for the case where those with a high distaste for work are disabled. However, on reflection, the case in which the distaste for work is simply a matter of individual preference poses more difficult normative problems. Assuming as we must that utility levels for persons with different preferences cannot be measured scientifically, either conceptually or because the scientific techniques—for example, those of neuroeconomics (Lohrenz and Montague 2008)—have not been perfected, some value judgment must be involved in comparing utilities of persons with different tastes for labor. Simply adding utilities together might give a misleading interpretation. For example, if the utility functions for persons differ only in the disutility of labor, those with a high distaste for labor will be given arbitrarily less weight in the social welfare function. Recognizing this, various authors have adopted an agnostic approach and simply either studied Pareto-optimizing problems or imposed arbitrary weights on persons of different preferences as mentioned above. Unfortunately, as mentioned, the pattern of weights matters, not only for determining which incentive constraints are binding but also for the form of the optimal income tax function.

No natural way has yet been found for aggregating the utilities of persons with different preferences. One potentially promising way out of the problem is discussed below, but it requires some further assumptions that are far from innocuous. As such, much remains to be accomplished to address the normative problems associated with devising policy when preferences are heterogeneous.

5.3.3   Other Dimensions of Taste Differences

There are other particular instances in which differences in preferences can have important potential effects on the form of the optimal policy prescription. One that we discussed concerned differences in utility discount rates. As Saez (2002a), Diamond (2007), and Diamond and Spinnewijn (forthcoming) argue, if utility discount rates fall with individual skills, a positive tax on capital income is warranted. Both Saez and Diamond assume that the correlation between skills and discount rate is perfect so that problems of multi-dimensional screening do not arise. Diamond and Spinnewijn allow the correlation to be imperfect, but they avoid problems of multi-dimensional screening by assuming that jobs have fixed earnings and are specific to skill-types in equilibrium. High-skilled workers can mimic low-skilled workers by taking their jobs, but will only be interested in mimicking low-skilled persons with the same preferences.

Multi-dimensional redistribution problems are relatively uncommon, perhaps because of the complexity involved. It is worth sidetracking briefly to consider some examples. One example concerns the risk of ill health. Suppose that individuals are endowed with two characteristics—skills and health risk. If the risk of ill health is higher for low-skilled persons than for the high-skilled, some form of social insurance is warranted, such as public provision or subsidization of health insurance (Rochet 1991; Cremer and Pestieau 1996). Moreover this can apply when moral hazard is present, either in an ex post form (where individual action affects the size of the damage in the event of ill health) or in an ex ante form (where individual action affects the probability of ill health) (Boadway et al. 2003). It can also apply when there is adverse selection in health insurance markets (Boadway et al. 2006).

Other examples have been touched on in the literature. They include cases where households differ in their risk aversion (Kihlstrom and Laffont 1979; Kanbur 1981; Boadway, Marchand, and Pestieau 1991), where they differ in the value of time in both the market and nonmarket sectors (Beaudry, Blackorby, and Szalay 2009), or where they differ in choices of family circumstances (Brett 2007; Apps and Rees 2007). Individuals may also differ in the regard they have for others, to which we now turn.

5.3.4   Interdependent Utilities

Another important dimension of heterogeneity that is particularly vexing from a normative point of view concerns interdependent utilities. These interdependencies can take different forms. One person's well-being may enter another's utility function either positively (the case of altruism) or negatively (avarice or envy). Altruism may be nonpaternalistic, so that the interdependent utility function respects the preferences of the person who is the object of the altruism. Alternatively, it may be paternalistic in the sense that the altruist puts particular weight on some aspects of others' well-being, such as their consumption of goods as opposed to their leisure. Altruism may motivate voluntary transfers from one person to another, and these can take the form of income transfers, in-kind transfers or provision of personal services. It may also motivate public provision of transfers in cases where free-riding precludes an optimal amount of voluntary transfers. However, altruism (or avarice) may be more passive and may not be consummated with actual transfers. One's welfare or "happiness" may be affected by relative status of one form or another: one's income relative to the average, one's relative wealth, or one's relative consumption of visible durables. Such status effects, or negative altruism more generally, may be reciprocal. Utility interdependency may take more indirect forms. Instead of obtaining utility from the well-being of others, one may obtain utility from the act of giving, the so-called joy-of-giving motive or what Andreoni (1990) has referred to as a "warm glow" effect. Altruism and the joy of giving can, in principle, be distinguished by revealed-preference implications, at least to the extent that they give rise to actual transfers. The extent of altruistic giving should be affected by the well-being of recipients, while that is not the case for the joy of giving.

The fundamental normative issue that must be resolved in studying the policy implications of interdependent utilities concerns their social welfare standing. Those who abide by strict welfarism, such as Kaplow (2008), insist that all sources of utility ought to have social welfare standing regardless of their type. Others, including Hammond (1987) and Harsanyi (1995), argue in favor of leaving them out of social preferences. The point is that including such things as altruistic or joy-of-giving utility in the social welfare function implies a form of double counting: the utility of those who are the object of altruism or the beneficiaries of joy of giving is counted both as a component of their utility and of the utility of the altruists or donors.

There is much at stake in the social welfare treatment of interdependent utilities. For expositional purposes, let us focus on altruism, although similar arguments apply to the joy of giving as well as to avarice or envy (although these will obviously not lead to voluntary transfers: indeed they may lead to property crime, which is another matter). Consider first the case where the altruism generates wealth transfers, whether voluntary by individuals or mandated by the government.

If the altruistic component of utility counts from a social welfare perspective, there will be an externality generated by voluntary transfers. The donor obtains altruistic utility and the recipient enjoys the benefit of the transfer. That is, the voluntary transfer is Pareto improving in the sense of Hochman and Rodgers (1969). However, in choosing the amount of the transfer, the donor takes into account only his or her own altruistic utility and neglects the utility obtained by the recipient. Kaplow (2008) argues that this justifies a Pigouvian subsidy on voluntary transfers so as to internalize the externality. The size of the Pigouvian subsidy should reflect the size of the externality, which might be relatively large, given that the benefit of the transfer to the recipient might substantially outweigh the altruistic benefit to the donor. Of course, it is the social utilities of the donor and recipient that should count in determining the benefit, so the size of the subsidy depends on how well off both are to begin with.

Contrast this with the case where the altruistic utility does not count. In that case the government counts only the benefit of the voluntary transfer to the recipient: the transfer is taken to make the donor worse off. The case for a subsidy on transfers remains, but the determination of its size become problematic. The transfer simultaneously increases the social utility of the recipient, but lowers that of the donor.

Apparently, the latter negative effect reduces the size of the optimal transfer.

An interesting extension of this argument concerning the externality of voluntary transfers anticipates our later discussion on behavioral public economics. If, following Fudenberg and Levine (2006), one makes a distinction between one's current and future selves, saving can be thought of as giving an altruistic-type benefit to one's current self while at the same time yielding a benefit to one's future self. Given that, there would be no distinction, in principle, between a bequest left for one's heir and an act of saving for one's own future use. The same externality argument would apply and the same justification for a subsidy, although no doubt this sort of argument would have little traction as a real-world policy rationale.

The logic of this simple story of a transfer from an altruistic donor to a recipient becomes more complicated when other factors are taken into account. For one thing, the altruism might be reciprocal so that the recipient also cares about the donor's utility. There is then a negative externality alongside the positive one to the extent that the donor does not take account of the negative effect the transfer has on the recipient's utility. More generally, there may be third parties who benefit from altruistic transfers. In the most general case, altruistic transfers are like pure public goods and therefore suffer from a significant free-rider problem. The implication of this is that the size of the externality is much larger since it now includes the altruistic benefits accruing to third (or nth) parties. This effect has been prominent in the literature on saving for future generations, especially the implications of inter-generational altruism for the social discount rate (Marglin 1963; Sen 1967).

More important, if altruism is to count in social welfare evaluation, logically it should count whether there is a voluntary transfer or not. Any feeling of altruism, avarice, envy, and so on, should count if altruism from actual transfers counts. Obviously it would be virtually impossible to take account of such utility externalities in formulating policies. The implications would be particularly stark for the family since one presumes that utility interdependencies are especially important there. Among other things, this would imply differentially high taxes on families on equity grounds.

It is interesting to note that the reciprocal nature of utility interdependencies might itself temper the case for intervention. Archibald and Donaldson (1976) show in a simple two-person example with no third-party effects that if voluntary transfers are not operational, reciprocal altruism does not lead to inefficiency as long as the altruism is nonpaternalistic, so that one person's altruism respects the preferences of the other. Yet some forms of reciprocity might enhance the case for intervention. If persons are motivated by improving their economic status relative to others, each person's effort imposes a negative externality on all others, justifying policies that discourage effort, such as more progressive income taxes (Boskin and Sheshinski 1978; Oswald 1983).

The implications of altruism for redistribution policy are also important. Suppose that altruism gives rise to voluntary transfers. Whether or not one counts the altruistic utility for social welfare purposes, there is an argument in principle for subsidizing transfers as long as the social benefit of the transfer to the recipient is large enough, and especially if third-party benefits are also large. Subsidizing voluntary transfers constitutes an alternative to the government undertaking the transfers itself. There are two arguments in favor of relying on subsidies to private transfers for redistributive purposes. One is that if the government must rely on distortionary taxes, the social cost of subsidizing a given level of transfers is less than the direct cost of transfers made by the government (which crowd out private transfers).

To see this, consider an economy with n identical individuals with quasilinear preferences in consumption x, labor ℓ and a public good G: $u(x, \ell, G) = x - h(\ell) + b(G)$. The wage rate is w and the price of consumption is unity. Voluntary contributions to the public good are g, those of other individuals are g_-, and that of the government is $\overline{G}$. Let $G_- = g_- + \overline{G}$. There is a linear labor income tax at the per unit rate t and a subsidy on voluntary contributions of σ. Assuming $g > 0$, the representative individual maximizes $(w-t)\ell - (1-\sigma)g - h(\ell) + b(g + G_-)$. The first-order condition on g, $b'(g + G_-) = 1 - \sigma$, yields $g(\sigma, G_-)$, where $g_\sigma = -1/b''$ and $g_{G_-} = -1$. In a symmetric Nash equilibrium with positive contributions, g is the same for all n households so the first-order condition in equilibrium is $b'(ng + \overline{G}) = 1 - \sigma$. This gives $g(\sigma, \overline{G})$, and comparative static analysis yields $\partial g/\partial \sigma = -1/nb''$ and $\partial g/\partial \overline{G} = -1/n$. Consider now the effect on the Nash equilibrium of a revenue-neutral shift from $\overline{G}$ to σ, assuming an interior solution for g. The government budget constraint is $nt\ell(w-t) - \overline{G} - n\sigma g(\sigma, \overline{G}) = 0$. Differentiating for given t and using the expressions for $\partial g/\partial \sigma$ and $\partial g/\partial \overline{G}$, we obtain

$$\left.\frac{d\overline{G}}{d\sigma}\right|_t = -\frac{ng - \sigma/b''}{1-\sigma} < 0.$$

The overall effect on household donations in the Nash equilibrium, $g(\sigma, \overline{G})$, is

$$\left. \frac{dg}{d\sigma} \right|_t = \frac{\partial g}{\partial \sigma} + \frac{\partial g}{\partial \overline{G}} \left. \frac{\partial \overline{G}}{\partial \sigma} \right|_t = \frac{1}{1-\sigma} \left(g - \frac{1}{nb''} \right).$$

Therefore the effect on the level of G is

$$\left. \frac{dG}{d\sigma} \right|_t = \left. \frac{d\overline{G}}{d\sigma} \right|_t + n \left. \frac{dg}{d\sigma} \right|_t = -\frac{ng - \sigma/b''}{1-\sigma} + \frac{n}{1-\sigma} \left(g - \frac{1}{nb''} \right) = -\frac{1}{b''} > 0.$$

Thus a revenue-neutral shift from $\overline{G}$ to σ increases total public goods supply G. That implies that a shift from $\overline{G}$ to σ accompanied by a tax rate reduction can keep public goods supply constant but reduce the labor tax distortion, and therefore will be welfare improving. That suggests that subsidizing voluntary contributions in second-best world should be superior to providing them publicly.

The second argument favoring subsidies to private donations is that private donors may have some advantage in terms of targeting the transfers to those most in need. Against this, relying on private donors to select transfer recipients can lead to preferential treatment of some classes of recipients relative to others (family members, members of one's own cultural or religious group, transfers that enforce paternalistic preferences, etc.). Government transfers will then be needed to achieve broader social welfare objectives.

More generally, the government will undoubtedly face informational problems in implementing policies based on utility interdependencies. The motive for wealth transfers will not always be apparent. For example, some transfers might be unintended, such as accidental bequests. Others might be based on implicit quid pro quos, an example being strategic bequests. Transfers might also be motivated by social or religious duty rather than altruism, and might even be done for reasons of prestige or status. These factors all affect how donors ought to be treated for tax purposes: it is presumably generally agreed that transfers enhance the well-being of recipients. To complicate matters further, individuals are bound to have different degrees of altruistic preferences. Moreover persons who have social preferences in favor of the government redistributing more to the less well off may well choose not to donate themselves but to rely on the government to do it for them. That is, increased government provision of public goods, redistribution, or, more generally, regulation of externalities might crowd out private socially motivated behavior (Frey 1994; Ostrom 2000).

However, Baron (2010) argues that the opposite may apply. The more do morally motivated persons voluntarily provide for the social good (i.e., the more they self-regulate to use Baron's terminology), the less will be the demand for government to provide publicly.

Tax systems typically provide some incentive for charitable donations, though only to registered charities and nonprofit organizations. It is less common to subsidize purely private donations or tax recipients. One exception is an area where the issue of altruism and its tax treatment are particularly important, that is, in dealing with bequests and inheritances, where voluntary private transfers are obviously relevant. Cremer and Pestieau (2006) have provided a thorough survey of this issue. See also Boadway, Chamberlain, and Emmerson (2010), on which some of the following is based.

Suppose first that altruistic (or joy-of-giving) utility counts as social welfare. In the case of voluntary bequests there are three considerations. First, inheritances should be treated as sources of income and taxed as such in the hands of recipients, either as a component of income or separately under an inheritance tax. Second, bequests represent the use of income by a donor analogous to any other form of consumption so should be taxed as such. Thus no deduction should be awarded for inter vivos bequests, and bequests at death should be taxed. Moreover, as acts of consumption, bequests should also bear any indirect consumption taxes, such as the VAT. Third, there is the externality argument, which, recall, notes that there is an externality associated with voluntary transfers since donors do not take full account of the benefits of their transfers. That is, they base their donations on the altruistic benefits they obtain for themselves but take no account of the additional benefit that accrues to the recipients. The force of this argument is obviously strongest in the case where the main source of redistribution affecting recipients of transfers are the transfers themselves. However, in the real world the government is engaging in redistribution as well. To the extent that the government redistribution adequately takes account of the well-being of recipients relative to others in the population, the force of the externality argument is reduced. Put differently, the force of the externality argument is stronger the more does the government prefer to rely on voluntary transfers rather than government transfers to achieve redistributive goals. To the extent that that is the case, some preferential treatment of bequests relative to other uses of one's income would be justified. In practice, preferential treatment of bequests and inheritances seems to be the norm. They are typically not taxed on a par with other income.

There are other considerations in the tax treatment of bequests. If bequests are accidental, they presumably give no benefit to the donor other than the risk-reduction benefit associated with holding wealth for precautionary purposes until one's uncertain death. Unfortunately, one cannot distinguish accidental from intended bequests. However, since accidental bequests more likely occur on death, while inter vivos bequests more likely entail intention, it might be argued that bequests on death should be treated more harshly for tax purposes than inter vivos transfers. After all, there are no efficiency costs associated with taxing accidental bequests.

However, a significant source of inter vivos transfers takes the form of in-kind transfers. These include not just the provision of food, shelter, clothing, and the like, but also the contribution to the human capital of children by various avenues. It is practically impossible to take direct account of this in an actual tax-transfer system, although to the extent that human capital acquisition leads to higher earnings, it will at least be indirectly accounted for.

If altruistic utility is deemed not to count, bequests are treated effectively as a transfer of purchasing power from donors to recipients. Donors' taxable income should fall on that account, while recipients' taxable income rises. In other words, inheritances should be taxable, while bequests should be tax deductible. Such a system is somewhat unwieldy since it is practically impossible to give tax relief to donors who have passed away. The alternative is simply neither to tax inheritances nor to give a deduction for bequests. This is a system that some countries deploy. Of course, the argument only applies for voluntary bequests. It does not apply for accidental bequests or for bequests in exchange for services from the recipients (strategic bequests). These should still be fully taxable, something that is difficult to achieve in a system that has no inheritance tax.

Note also that the relative treatment of altruists who leave bequests and the non-altruists who do not varies depending on whether the utility of bequests counts. In particular, if altruistic utility is deemed to count, altruistic donors will be treated more harshly than non-altruistic persons who choose not to donate (or less altruistic donors who choose to donate less).

There are apparently many challenging normative issues that arise for optimal policy analysis as a consequence of individuals having different preferences. One potentially interesting and important way to deal with preference heterogeneity has emerged in recent years, and we turn to that next.

5.3.5 Dealing with Differences in Preferences: One Proposed Approach

The presumption in the standard Mirrleesian optimal nonlinear income tax approach and its applications is that redistribution ought to undo the consequences of the fact that persons can achieve different levels of well-being because of being endowed with different amounts of relevant types of characteristics. Mirrlees focused on a single characteristic of individuals for simplicity, that is, their ability as reflected in the wage rate they could command. But this was mainly for expositional and analytical ease. Other characteristics could be, and have been, added, such as disability, health status, needs, initial endowments, and so on, all of which we have referred to. What is important about all these characteristics is that individuals have no control over them: they are simply endowed with them. It is true that they can enhance their skill by human capital investment as, for example, in Bovenberg and Jacobs (2005), Jacobs (2005), and Anderberg (2009). However, their ability to acquire human capital is itself likely correlated with their endowed skills.

How do differences in preferences compare with differences in endowed characteristics as sources of differences in well-being? To the extent that one views preference differences as endowments that individuals take as given, all the problems as outlined above apply. To do normative second-best analysis, we need to have a way of aggregating individual utilities, that is, measuring and comparing utilities of persons with different preferences. There seems no natural way to do that.

An alternative approach that has some promise in circumventing these difficulties has been proposed for the case in which preferences are considered a matter of choice. The approach is based on the notion that individuals ought to be compensated for those circumstances affecting their well-being over which they have no control, but they should be held responsible for those over which they do have control. The former is referred to as the Principle of Compensation and the latter the Principle of Responsibility, as briefly discussed earlier. These principles and some of their consequences are discussed in Roemer (1998), Fleurbaey (1994, 2008), Kolm (1996, 1998, 2004), and Fleurbaey and Maniquet (2010). We can do no more than highlight the approach here since the literature is quite technical and to do full justice to it would require considerable space.

The principles can be illustrated using a case that is often appealed to and that makes clear the distinction between compensation and responsibility. The case involves individuals who differ in two ways, their wage rates reflecting their skills and their distastes for work (or taste for leisure). This case is treated, for example, by Roemer (1998); Bossert, Fleurbaey, and Van de gaer (1999); Schokkaert et al. (2004); Fleurbaey and Maniquet (2006, 2007); and Jacquet and Van de gaer (2009). To make matters simple, the distaste for work can be parameterized by assuming the utility function takes the simple form $u(x) - \gamma g(y/w)$, where x is consumption, $y = w\ell$ is labor income and γ is a parameter reflecting the distaste for work or taste for leisure. Suppose one assumes that individuals are responsible for their own preferences (i.e., the choice of γ) while their wage rates are based on their endowed abilities and are beyond their control. This dichotomy is itself controversial since one may not freely choose their preferences for leisure: they may be conditioned by their physiological makeup or by their environment. Similarly, converting one's inherent skills into productivity may involve some effort that the person may control. Nonetheless, for purposes of exposition, assume that wage rates are exogenously given, while preferences are within one's control.[8]

When one is held responsible for their preference for leisure but not for their wage rate, the Principles of Responsibility and Compensation are assumed to call for the following desired outcomes (Fleurbaey 2004). Consider two persons with the same wage rate but different preference parameters. The Principle of Responsibility is taken to imply that they should receive the same transfers or pay the same taxes (i.e., equal transfers for equal wages). Alternatively, consider two persons who have the same preferences, but different wage rates. The Principle of Compensation is taken to imply that these two persons should obtain the same utility (i.e., equal welfare for equal preferences).

Although these principles seem eminently reasonable, there are a number of pitfalls with them. The first is that they are generally

---

8. Roemer (1998) takes an intermediate position with respect to the taste for leisure by assuming that it is partly affected by one's socioeconomic group. Within each socioeconomic group, there is some variability in preferences for leisure, and that variability is an individual's own responsibility. However, one has no responsibility for the average preference for leisure in the group to which one is attached.

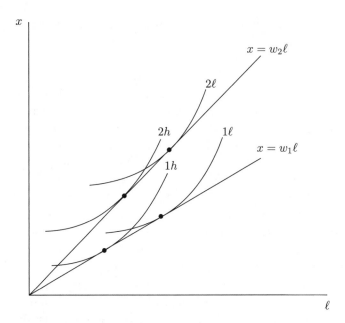

Figure 5.1
Principles of Compensation and Responsibility

mutually incompatible (Fleurbaey 1994; Bossert 1995). To see this, consider the case where there are two wage-types, $w_2 > w_1$, and two preference types, $\gamma_h > \gamma_\ell$, with the same number of each type for simplicity. Figure 5.1 shows the laissez-faire allocation, with $2h$ referring to the high-wage, high-distaste-for-work person, and so on. Suppose that the government knows who is who and is contemplating making lump-sum transfers to satisfy the Principles of Responsibility and Compensation. According to the Principle of Responsibility, taxes on the high-wage types $2h$ and 2ℓ must be the same for both, and similarly for the low-wage types $1h$ and 1ℓ. Lump-sum income redistributions between wage types must therefore involve parallel shifts in the two budget lines shown. If redistribution between wage types is such as to satisfy the Principle of Compensation for the high-distaste-for-work persons, the indifference curves for $1h$ and $2h$ must coincide, and this will imply a particular set of lump-sum transfers between wage types. However, given this much redistribution between wage types, the Principle of Compensation will not be satisfied for the low-distaste-for-work types 1ℓ and 2ℓ. It is apparent that it is not possible to satisfy the Principle of Compensation for the two preference types at the same time, while maintaining the Principle of Responsibility. Thus it is not possible to satisfy these two principles even in this simple case, and by extension more complicated cases.

Apparently some compromise between the two principles must be made. One might, for example, treat the Principle of Responsibility as sacrosanct but allow the Principle of Compensation to be violated. Thus, given wage-types would face the same tax or transfer, but these would not be sufficient to equalize utilities for persons with the same preferences. Some way of trading off inequality between the high-γ and low-γ types would have to be found, and that would seem to require interpersonal utility comparisons between persons with different tastes. Moreover one cannot appeal to a principle like maximin since that would require comparing levels of utility between preference types. Similar problems would arise if the Principle of Compensation were given priority, but the Principle of Responsibility violated. The utility of persons of given preference would be equalized, but some judgment would have to be made about the optimal relative levels of utility for persons of different preferences. Again, some interpersonal utility comparisons between persons of different preferences would have to be made.

These problems are compounded if type-specific lump-sum transfers are not available because the government cannot identify types. Satisfying the Principle of Compensation would violate incentive compatibility as in the standard case where there is only one preference type. Otherwise, the problems of requiring interpersonal utility comparisons across preference types would remain, as in the full-information case.

A further problem with applying the Principles of Compensation and Responsibility for prescriptive purposes is that the manner in which they should be operationalized is itself rather arbitrary. The literature has presumed, as we have mentioned, that the Principle of Compensation requires *equal* utilities for persons of equal preferences but different skills, while the Principle of Responsibility requires *equal* transfers or taxes for persons of the same skills but different preferences. Neither of these can be considered as unique ways of implementing the principles.

In the case of the Principle of Compensation, equal welfare for equal preferences is equivalent to a maximin criterion. Thus it would be satisfied in a world where preferences are identical and a normative policy maker used a maximin social welfare function. However, if the planner used any social welfare function with a finite nonnegative aversion to inequality, higher skilled persons would end up with lower welfare, following the well-known arguments of Mirrlees (1974). By extension, equal welfare for equal preference is not the appropriate criterion for the Principle of Compensation from a social welfare point of view. Of course, the maximin criterion might still be the preferred choice if one wants to limit interpersonal comparability to utility level comparisons, but that involves a value judgment.

The requirement of equal transfers for equal skills as a criterion for achieving the Principle of Responsibility is even more arbitrary. One thinks of the Principle of Responsibility as reflecting the idea that persons should neither be penalized nor rewarded for different choices they make from a given opportunity set, hence the identification of the Principle of Responsibility with equality of opportunity (Roemer 1998). Why that common opportunity set should entail identical lump-sum taxes or transfers for a given wage type is not obvious (although it might seem reasonable on intuitive grounds). Moreover how one ranks deviations from equal transfers for equal skills in the event that it cannot be fully achieved is not at all obvious. At least in the case of the Principle of Compensation, the implied maximin criterion can be used to rank outcomes when the full information case is not possible.

There have been attempts to get around some of these problems arising from heterogeneous preferences. Schokkaert et al. (2004) have taken a paternalistic approach and defined a reference preference ordering that can be used to obtain social orderings using an otherwise standard social welfare function (see also Fleurbaey 1995b; Adler, forthcoming). While this approach yields a well-defined social ordering and avoids the impossibility of achieving both compensation and responsibility, it has a couple of drawbacks. For one, it is not obvious how the reference preferences should be chosen. For another, rankings obtained using reference preferences are liable to violate the Pareto principle using individuals' own preferences.

Another interesting way to reach a compromise between the Principles of Compensation and Responsibility has been used by Roemer (1998), who develops his own criterion. A cursory summary of it is as follows. Suppose that individuals vary, as above, in their wage rate and in their preference for leisure, and the utility function for a wage-type i and preference-type j is assumed to be $u(x_{ij}) - \gamma g(y_{ij} / w_i)$. Continue to assume that individuals are responsible for their preferences but not for their wage rates. Roemer's analysis applies to more general settings, including those with different given characteristics and those in which individuals are only partly responsible for their preferences for work. Nonetheless, the same basic criterion applies and is as follows. For individuals with the same preferences but different wage rates, the maximin criterion applies. This gives a social ordering over each preference group, which can be written for preference group γ_j as $\min_i\{u(x_{ij}) - \gamma_j g(y_{ij} / w_i)\}$. Then, to aggregate over preference groups, the minimum utility levels for the different preference groups are simply averaged (equivalent to using a utilitarian criterion). This gives a well-defined social welfare ordering for the economy as a whole, which can be written as $\sum_j \min_i\{u(x_{ij}) - \gamma_j g(y_{ij} / w_i)\}$, where we assume there are the same number of persons in each preference group for simplicity. The drawback of this criterion is the manner in which persons with different preferences are treated. The least well off of each type are simply added together. While this avoids the incompatibility of the Principles of Compensation and Responsibility, it does so in a rather arbitrary manner.[9]

Despite the difficulties in coming to grips with different preferences in normative analysis, the idea of not penalizing people because of their preferences has some appeal. Potentially it could lead to important policy conclusions. For example, it can affect the relative treatment of single and married persons with or without children, of those who make wealth transfers and those who do not, of those who save a lot and those who save a little, and so on. As it stands, the literature has not developed to the point where policy prescriptions can be based on sound normative foundations. But it is an important and challenging avenue for future research.

5.4   Behavioral Issues

The standard normative second-best analysis based on welfarism assumes that individual preferences that form the basis for social preferences are accurately reflected by the choices individuals actually

---

9. An alternative to the Roemer procedure has been proposed by Van de gaer (1993). He defines the opportunity set available to persons of a given wage rate as the utility levels they could achieve if they "chose" to have different preferences for leisure. The size of the opportunity set available to those of a given wage rate is the average utility level across preference types. Then the social welfare criterion is the minimum of those opportunity sets, which will be the value of the opportunity set for the lowest wage persons. This criterion, like Roemer's, also involves adding utilities across preference types.

make. This is the standard revealed-preference assumption. The growing literature on behavioral economics, supported variously by experimental economics and neuroeconomics, has called into question this premise on a variety of grounds. This poses enormous conceptual issues for normative public economics, most of which have yet to be resolved (McCaffery and Slemrod 2006; Bernheim and Rangel 2007).

Behavioral anomalies might usefully be classified into three types: bounded rationality, seemingly irrational choices, and non–self-interested choices. Each of these pose different problems for normative analysis, and we consider them in turn.

A related literature studies the sources and consequences of happiness. It too seeks in part to explain individual choices and their welfare effects by invoking deeper interpretations of what actions or states makes people happy. In some circumstances the pursuit of happiness can have some adverse consequences as a result of forms of externalities among individuals, particularly interdependent utilities or psychic externalities. We briefly discuss some of these consequences as well.

5.4.1 Bounded Rationality

Bounded rationality refers to situations in which individuals are not well-enough informed to be able to make rational decisions in their own self-interest. This can be either because they do not have the relevant information, even though it is in principle available, or because making the optimal choice is too complicated or takes too much time relative to the capabilities of the individual. Bounded rationality apparently seems to be a concern in purchasing complex goods and services that may have many relevant characteristics. Financial assets are a case in point, but so are many modern communications and electronic products. Other relevant examples include health, educational, legal and insurance services, as well as the quality of consumer durables. Policies that help inform the individual, that regulate product quality, and that even involve taking decisions on behalf of the individual seem warranted on normative grounds provided they improve individual well-being. Thus, governments regulate some forms of product quality (especially with respect to health and safety) as well as some of the terms of financial contracts (e.g., credit card interest rates). They also regulate educational services to varying degrees as well as health services. Governments sometimes make financial portfolio decisions on behalf of individuals such as in public pension schemes, at least those that are funded. To the extent that public policy can mitigate the bounded-rationality problem in a way that improves outcomes for individuals, that should presumably be viewed as a good thing on social welfare grounds.

The complexity of the tax system may also give rise to problems of bounded rationality, leading to excessive costs of tax collection and compliance, and errors in reporting. Liebman and Zeckhauser (2004) discuss what they call "schmeduling"—the act of behaving as if one were facing an inaccurately perceived schedule, or schmedule, rather than the true schedule. They suggest this arises when people do one of two things: ironing (when faced with a multipart schedule, they respond only to the average price at the point of consumption) and spotlighting (when a consumer responds only to immediate or local prices, rather than the full schedule). For example, people sometimes confuse the marginal tax rate with the average tax rate, since an average is easier to calculate. This could eliminate some of the deadweight loss of high marginal tax rates, but it also creates significant challenges for optimal tax design. They then show that there is a Pareto-superior scheme to the traditional optimal schedule given schmeduling. Congdon, Kling, and Mullainathan (2009) add to this that taxpayers who are not so good at addressing tax matters may avoid certain employment choices, such as self-employment, that require or reward understanding of the tax system, creating distortionary effects. As a result they suggest that the distribution of the tax burden could potentially depend on cognitive ability or ability to understand the tax system. Bounded rationality, in addition to leading individuals to make ill-informed choices, might also leave them misinformed about incentive constraints facing them. Sheshinski (2003) explores this in a model involving the choice between work and retirement. The same misperception might apply in optimal tax models.

Perhaps a more difficult case of bounded rationality is where the consumer overestimates the future benefits that will be obtained from purchases of discretionary products, like new consumer durables. This may lead to the overaccumulation of consumer goods whose benefits turn out to be disappointing. Should the policy maker take actions to discourage such purchases, including by regulating advertising that may be partly responsible for the purchase of goods that are likely to generate lower future benefits to warrant their cost? The answer is not obvious. More generally, individuals may overestimate the happiness they will obtain from earning more income so that they can purchase more goods (quite apart from the unhappiness they may bring on others who envy their increase in income). We return briefly to the happiness literature below.

5.4.2 Irrational Choices

More controversial is the case of seemingly irrational decisions that are made by households. There are many instances of this that have been reported in the literature, some of them based on experimental evidence and others on empirical observation. Many involve the making of decisions based on the immediate payoff they have without taking account of the longer term consequences of the decisions for individual well-being. Examples include saving too little for retirement; overeating foods that contain ingredients such as salt, fatty acids, and sugar that lead to future health problems; consuming products that lead to addiction or habitual future use, including illegal drugs, tobacco products, and gambling; doing too little exercise; procrastinating in various ways; and so on. Persons will typically come to regret the decisions they have made, and may often try to overcome these biases toward short-term gratification by resorting to some personal commitment devices, where possible. Thus they may save in illiquid assets to avoid the temptation to dissave later on. Or they may refrain from buying certain goods in volume to make it more costly to consume small amounts later on. Or they may choose to purchase memberships in exercise facilities rather than relying on pay-as-you-go consumption.

A relevant first question before considering whether there is a case for government intervention is whether these instances of apparent shortsightedness or myopia represent irrational decision-making. After all, it is possible that individuals undertake a fully rational calculation when deciding on, for example, whether to ingest addictive substances, as Becker and Murphy (1988) argued. Similarly some persons may simply have relatively high utility discount rates that lead them to save little.

However, there is some evidence that suggests that at least some forms of shortsightedness are not the result of fully rational calculations in the way in which economists normally think of rationality. Laboratory experiments suggest that subjects exhibit time-inconsistent preferences or choice reversals when confronted with intertemporal choices. For example, in the case of monetary rewards, if confronted with the choice between x euros now and $x + y$ euros next period, they may choose the former.[10] At the same time, if they are faced with the choice of x euros t periods hence and $x + y$ euros in period $t + 1$, they choose the latter. This kind of choice reversal is commonly observed and suggests that the standard expected utility model with geometric discounting does not apply. The experimental evidence seems to be more consistent with hyperbolic discounting, or its simplified analogue, quasi-hyperbolic discounting (Laibson 1997). Expected utility at time zero under quasi-hyperbolic discounting can be written as

$$u(y_0) + \frac{1}{1+\beta} \sum_{t=1}^{T} \frac{u(y_t)}{(1+\delta)^t},$$

where y_t is real income in period t. The utility discount rate between period zero and period one is $(1 + \beta)^{-1}(1 + \delta)^{-1}$, whereas that between any two periods t and $t + 1$ beyond that is simply $(1 + \delta)^{-1}$. As time moves on to period t, the discount rate between t and $t + 1$ then becomes $(1 + \beta)^{-1}(1 + \delta)^{-1}$, and so on. Laibson (1997) shows that this framework explains quite well why the standard life-cycle consumption-smoothing hypothesis obtained by geometric discounting (or the permanent-income hypothesis) does not fit the data. Indeed consumption tends to track income, which fits the quasi-hyperbolic discounting assumption. Moreover individuals might have a preference for precommitting by appropriate saving devices, which is an indication that they understand their tendency to be time inconsistent in their choices.

Further support for the quasi-hyperbolic discounting model comes from findings in neuroeconomics (Lohrenz and Montague 2008) as it applies to intertemporal decision-making. At the risk of oversimplification, the study of brain activity in decision-making situations using neural techniques (e.g., functional magnetic resonance imaging) indicates that there are two separate neural systems that might be involved. One, called the "hot system" located in the mesolimbic system of the brain, is stimulated only by immediate rewards, whereas the other, the "cold system" in the frontal and parietal lobes, is able to make longer term calculations and is stimulated equally by both immediate and

10. Other experiments involving nonmonetary decisions can also give choice reversals. An example is the study by Read and van Leeuwen (1998) involving the choice between healthy and unhealthy food. Subjects were offered a choice between a piece of fruit and a piece of chocolate. When the choice had to be made one week in advance, most chose fruit. When they were offered to change their choice one week later before having consummated their earlier choice, most chose chocolate.

longer term rewards. One's capacity to take account of the longer term consequences of one's actions can be affected if the cold system is busy with some other activity, such as a cognitive activity. This is consistent with the observation of choice reversals. This dichotomy of brain functioning provides some neurological underpinnings of the quasi-hyperbolic discounting model. Thus the δ discount factor can be seen as reflecting cold system considerations, while β represents the hot system.

Given the inadequacy of standard geometric discounting models of expected utility to predict behavior, attempts have been made to develop alternative decision models that rationalize the above findings, in particular, time-inconsistent preferences, choice reversals, and preference for precommitment devices. Gul and Pesendorfer (2001) develop a theoretical model where a person might be tempted by an inferior choice ex ante and where there exists a costly self-control device. They show that a preference for precommitment in the presence of costly self-control devices can be derived as a straightforward extension of the standard model. In Gul and Pesendorfer (2004), they extend their theory to an infinite-horizon decision problem involving a consumption-saving choice. In a sense they rationalize what appear to be time-inconsistent choices. Bénabou and Pycia (2002) show that the quasi-hyperbolic discounting model can be obtained using a framework where the conflict between temptation and self-control can be viewed as a costly conflict between "divided selves," a planner and a doer. The planner plans for all periods in a forward-looking manner, while the doer only considers the current period. The problem of time-inconsistent preferences is thereby defined, though not avoided. Fudenberg and Levine (2006) generalize these results in a so-called dual-self model that is consistent with the idea of the two competing neural systems. The model is consistent with the axioms of Gul and Pesendorfer, and is capable of generating a broader range of nonstandard economic behaviors, including choice reversals and preferences for precommitment.

The policy implications of these models are not at all obvious. To the extent that individual preferences are truly time inconsistent and that individuals are unable to precommit to undo the consequences, the question is whether the government should intervene. To do so would imply some form of paternalism that overrides the revealed preferences of individuals. Many would agree that this is justified if it can be guaranteed to improve the long-run welfare of individuals. However, there are undoubtedly information problems that the government must face in determining exactly when individuals are making short-run choices that are not in their own long-run self-interest.

Another source of evidence that individuals might act irrationally concerns framing effects (although these may be perceived as being forms of bounded rationality). It has been observed that in certain instances, individuals effectively may choose different outcomes depending on how a given choice situation is presented to them. This is so even if the options are the same. One important example—and one that can magnify the time-consistency problem—concerns saving for retirement. Individuals who must choose whether to enroll in retirement saving schemes are much more likely to do so if enrollment is automatic unless they opt out than if they have to opt in. Choi et al. (2004) report on an experiment conducted in a group of companies. Enrollment rates in so-called 401(k) plans in the United States, which are tax-sheltered retirement savings schemes, rise from 20 to 65 percent when an opt-out scheme is substituted for an opt-in one. Moreover they note that the rate of contribution also depends on the default option. If the saving rate is set high, individuals rarely ask to change it. As well, if individuals choose to subscribe to plans whose contribution rates rise automatically with earnings, they save more than if they must change their contribution rate with discretion. Beshears et al. (2007) show that similar framing effects also affect asset allocations and post-retirement savings distributions. The fact that choices depend on default options may reflect some measure of bounded rationality as well as time-inconsistent decisions leading to procrastination.

Another example of framing concerns the salience of taxes and other charges, that is, the extent to which they are noticed by individuals. Finkelstein (2009) estimates that the introduction of electronic tolls on roads, which reduces their salience, has contributed to increased tolls. Similarly Chetty, Looney, and Kroft (2009) contrast the effect of taxes on goods when the tax is included in the posted price and when it is not. They find, using sales in a grocery store, that quantities sold are significantly lower when the price included the tax. They also find, using data on alcohol sales, that consumers underreact to a change in the tax which is less salient (i.e., less visible). However, deadweight losses seem not to differ much between visible and less visible taxes. More generally, McCaffery and Baron (2004b) argue that what the government calls a revenue levy—a tax, a fee, or a payment—can also change how it is perceived.

Given the importance of salience of taxation, the question of whether policy makers can improve welfare outcomes by deliberately manipulating tax salience becomes relevant (Congdon, Kling, and Mullainathan 2009). If taxpayers treat identical taxes as being different if they are framed differently, then there is significant potential for alterations to policy. Blumkin, Ruffle, and Ganun (2008), for example, find that in an experimental setting, subjects reduce their labor supply significantly more in response to an income tax than they do in response to an equivalent consumption tax, and speculate that this occurs because subjects underestimate the present value of the taxes levied on future consumption. Similarly Saez (2010) finds that taxpayers do not bunch at kink points in the income tax schedule, as they might be expected to do if they fully perceived the implied discontinuity in their budget constraint. Congdon, Kling, and Mullainathan (2009) also suggest that when some taxes can be hidden from consumers, this will entail a low elasticity of demand, which is desirable on efficiency grounds. However, spending too much on the good with a hidden tax will leave less income for future purchases, thereby distorting consumption and decreasing welfare. McCaffery and Baron (2004b) then pose the question as to whether there is a wedge between utility and wealth or income maximization in public finance, since some of the taxes people do not mind are actually less efficient than those that they do mind. Studying the consequences of tax salience for normative policy analysis constitutes a substantial challenge for optimal taxation.

McCaffery and Baron (2004a, 2005) characterize a number of other different situations that exhibit framing effects, using the family context as an example. One is what they refer to as the Schelling effect, based on a finding from a classroom survey reported in Schelling (1981). Students preferred higher bonuses for the poor for having children than for the rich, a choice for which there was a childless default outcome. At the same time, viewing the default as one involving having children, students preferred higher penalties for the rich for being childless than for the poor. Both policies in fact are equivalent in their relative effects, so preferring both was inconsistent. McCafferty and Baron attribute this to penalty aversion—a preference for a bonus for performance rather than a penalty for nonperformance that has the same implicit effect—as well as progressivity illusion.

A second effect is called neutrality bias and refers to individuals' preference for neutrality in the treatment of married versus nonmarried couples. Such neutrality can take two incompatible forms: marriage neutrality where married couples pay the same tax as nonmarried couples with the same incomes, and couples neutrality where all households with the same joint income pay the same tax. Framing the choice of tax systems in a way that emphasizes one form of neutrality influences individual preferences for tax systems. For example, respondents prefer separate income tax filing for married couples (i.e., marriage neutral but not couples neutral) more when it is presented in a format that emphasizes the effect of marriage than in a format that emphasizes the effect of the number of earners, where one-income-earner couples pay more under separate filing.

As well, McCaffery and Baron find that persons prefer the status quo over any change: the status quo effect. In addition respondents prefer more progressivity in tax burdens when taxes are expressed in percentages than when they are expressed in dollars.

Framing effects are clearly important for whatever reason they arise. The challenge posed for policy is that revealed preference, which is the main source of information about individual preferences, is not reliable. If individuals make different choices when options are framed differently, and when the choices are policy relevant, the policy maker is left in a quandary. It may, in some circumstances, be possible to argue that the fickleness of revealed preference is due to inattentiveness or miscalculation such that the true interests of the individual are compromised under one form of framing than another. But this is not always possible. Consider the prominent example of saving for retirement, where opt-out schemes lead to much greater saving than opt-in ones. Apart from issues of time inconsistency, should we regard opt-out pension schemes as superior because they increase both participation and contribution rates? That seems to be taken for granted when policy advisors recommend public pension schemes with opt out as a solution to the observed decline in occupation pension coverage. Similarly nudging the consumer toward what we think are sensible choices implies that we know what is best for the consumer (Thaler and Sunstein 2008).

5.4.3   Nonselfish Choices

A final case where revealed preference may not reflect individual preferences is where choices are purposely made that are not in the individual's narrow self-interest. Such cases have been frequently found in experimental settings. Three common examples are the dictator game, the ultimatum game and the voluntary contribution game (Fehr and Schmidt 1999).

In the dictator game, a proposer unilaterally offers a share s of a fixed amount of wealth w to a responder and keeps the proportion $1 - s$ for himself. Rationality predicts that the offer will be $s = 0$: the proposer will keep all the wealth for himself. Experimental evidence, however, suggests that when such games are played among anonymous agents, a majority of the proposals will be for $s > 0$, and a significant number will propose equal sharing, $s = 0.5$.

In the ultimatum game, the proposer again proposes a share s for the responder. If the responder accepts the proposal, the division is consummated. If not, neither party gets anything. Under standard rationality assumptions, the proposer will offer close to $s = 0$, and the responder will accept. However, experimental findings are that most proposed offers are for s in the range 0.4 to 0.5. Moreover offers significantly less than that are often rejected. Thus the rationality of neither proposers nor responders is found.

Experimental results for the voluntary contribution game are more mixed. In this game each of n persons endowed with a given sum of funds simultaneously and noncooperatively decides how much to contribute to a public good that benefits all and how much to keep for private consumption. Given that the private benefit from a unit of donation is less than from private consumption, the rational thing to do is to free ride and make no contribution. Evidence suggests that a minority of persons do give a positive contribution, while the rest free ride. However, suppose that after the initial contribution stage, players are allowed to punish other players based on their observed contribution. The punishment is assumed to be costly, so under full rationality, no punishment would be imposed and free-riding should be maintained. Experimental evidence, however, shows than the mere existence of the possibility of punishment induces the majority of players to make positive contributions. Clearly, in these settings standard rational behavior fails.

One explanation for this is that certain decisions may be made largely based on social norms rather than rational self-calculation. This could include community volunteering, helping one's neighbors, effort in the workplace, law-abiding behavior, and so on. In these circumstances real income and consumption—which are the bases for equitable taxation—may not reflect individual well-being defined more narrowly. Perhaps more striking, individuals may make some decisions on the basis of moral or ethical considerations. Almost by definition, these decisions will make the person worse off. Examples of this might be charitable giving or environmental behavior. Fehr and Schmidt (1999) show how cooperative behavior can arise in equilibrium in the above and other experiments if a large enough proportion of the population cares about equity or fairness and behaves as such.

How government policies ought to respond to these kinds of behavior is not obvious. To the extent that persons make voluntary wealth transfers out of moral obligations, arguments about double counting no longer apply. Presumably one wants to give a tax benefit for such transfers of wealth, but it is practically impossible to distinguish between voluntary transfers for, say, altruistic reasons, and those for moral reasons. In the case of environmental behavior that is based on moral grounds, there is the danger that government attempts to introduce policies that reward environmentally friendly choices given that not everyone will behave morally may undermine the behavior of those they do: a form of behavioral crowding out. As mentioned, Baron (2010) has argued that the opposite applies as well: to the extent that individuals "self-regulate" environmental externalities, there will be less demand for government action. Another example of policy affecting nonselfish behavior comes from a study conducted at a number of day-care centers by Gneezy and Rustichini (2000). The study involved fees that were imposed on families who picked up their children late. The study found that fees actually increased the number of parents who were late, reflecting the possibility that the existence of a monetary penalty reduced the societal pressure to be on time.

More generally, the willingness of taxpayers to pay taxes voluntarily may be affected by the manner in which tax policy is designed and enforced. Taxpayers seem to prefer taxes that have good intentions behind them (McCaffery and Baron 2004b) and are less likely to evade them (Levi 1997; Torgler 2003; Slemrod 2003). In addition it appears that people value fairness in the tax code—the feeling that all contribute fairly. Given that the fairest code may not be the traditionally optimal one, however, this also poses potential problems for normative analysis (Congdon, Kling, and Mullainathan 2009). Finally, Frey and Oberholzer-Gee (1997) argue that increasing penalties or enforcement of tax regimes (what they call extrinsic motivation) can crowd out intrinsic motivation by making people feel they have to pay taxes, rather than want to.

5.4.4 Happiness

In one sense, learning what makes people happy using survey and other methods should not pose fundamental problems for normative tax analysis. As long as individual actions are those that maximize happiness, revealed preference can be relied on to faithfully reflect individual utility orderings and the welfaristic approach is satisfied. However, there are a number of aspects of the happiness literature that might be consequential.

The first one is that we might learn something about the form of the utility function that could inform redistributive norms. For example, it might be established that increments in happiness decrease rapidly as income or consumption rises. Then the more rapidly does the marginal utility of income fall, the more redistribution would be called for, given the degree of aversion to inequality. At the same time studies reveal that happiness might be related to more than income, and this might make the task of the normative analyst more complicated. For example, job satisfaction may make a larger difference to happiness than income (Helliwell 2006). This can make it difficult to compare different people's levels of utility purely on income: persons working at a job they dislike for higher income may not be substantially better off than those earning less income in a more agreeable job.

Second, persons might overestimate the extent to which future increments in income will increase happiness, leading to excessive work effort from a long-run welfare perspective. Studies suggest that as with addictive behavior more generally, a person's happiness adapts quite rapidly to higher levels of income (Layard 2006) and ends up increasing much less than anticipated. Since people cannot predict that they will be less happy in the long term, they tend to work too hard and consume too much in the short term because they assume their initially high level of happiness will continue at that level. Normative governments may feel justified in tempering this behavioral tendency to overwork by setting marginal tax rates higher than they would otherwise, or even by quantitative controls such as maximum working hours.

Related to this, people report themselves to be happier when employed than when unemployed, even after controlling for income, social contacts, and health (Knabe et al. 2010). This enhances the case for policies that reduce involuntary unemployment on redistributive grounds. It also suggests that the traditional incentive constraint used in second-best analysis is too restrictive, since there are nonfinancial penalties associated with unemployment. This could have a significant impact on the maximin outcome, for example: redistributing to the unemployed could be carried to the point where their income is higher than those employed. However, Knabe et al. suggest that the unemployed may be able to adapt to their situation by making more effective use of the greater time they have available. This would have the opposite effect on the incentive constraint.

Another potentially important consequence of the happiness literature for normative analysis concerns the nonpecuniary externalities associated with relative income differences. Individuals' happiness might be based on their income position relative to others, or to average income (Layard 2006). This viewpoint might also be suggested by prospect theory, the notion that utility depends on how an outcome deviates from a given reference point. In this case the reference point could be interpreted as the mean income outcome of other individuals (Kanbur, Pirttilä, and Tuomala 2008). As Layard (2006) points out, this suggests taxes should be more progressive than would otherwise be optimal to correct for the externality of making others less happy as you become wealthier. However, the question arises here, as in the case of altruism discussed earlier, as to whether these happiness effects arising from one's relative income status should have standing for social welfare purposes. Once one counts happiness as relevant for redistributive policy, one is almost compelled to include other utility interdependencies such as distaste for others' consumption habits or appearances. Apart from being able to measure these externalities with sufficient precision to be useful for policy purposes, there is the conceptual question of whether they should count as sources of welfare for normative policy purposes.

Finally, some authors have pointed out that people may get satisfaction not just from social outcomes but also from the process by which policies are chosen. Helliwell (2006) finds that individuals may value engagement in the policy-making process per se. As a consequence tax regimes that are responsive to the needs or wishes of the population, even if not optimal from an economic point of view, may actually improve the utility of the population (Frey and Stutzer 2000). This suggests one avenue whereby political economy considerations may be useful for normative analysis.

5.5   Political Economy

Normative second-best analysis recommends policy choices using as an objective function some presumed welfaristic social preference ordering and imposing two sorts of constraints. One sort recognizes resource constraints imposed by the economy's endowments combined with its technology. The second sort takes account of the information constraints faced by government. In the standard optimal nonlinear income tax framework, the government can observe individual incomes but not their wage rates or effort. In other frameworks, they may not be able to observe incomes perfectly (e.g., when taxes can be evaded) or the distaste for work (e.g., in extensive-margin models of labor supply). The analysis also typically imposes some institutional assumptions on the problem, notably the assumption of a decentralized competitive economy and the assumption that the government is not wasteful. Although the use of a welfaristic social welfare function can be controversial for reasons we have discussed, the spirit of the assumptions that are imposed is likely widely accepted. That is, while one may argue that different assumptions might be made about information asymmetries—both between the government and the private sector or within the private sector—or about the institutions of the market economy, there is general agreement that these sorts of assumptions must be made.

Much more controversial is the normative approach itself. Actual policy choices apparently bear only limited resemblance to normative prescriptions. Policies seem to be inefficient and inequitable, at least in some dimensions. Some industries and activities are treated preferentially relative to others; policies seem to be of limited effect in addressing inequality and poverty (OECD 2008); policies, once enacted, are seemingly difficult to change; future generations seem to be given relatively little weight in current policies; and the size of the public sector seems to be much larger than is needed to accomplish reasonable normative objectives. Many of these features of policies can be accounted for as resulting from political processes. The question naturally arises as to whether political economy considerations should be taken into account in prescriptive policy analysis. The arguments are carefully considered in Winer and Shibata (2002).

Three broad potential responses to this question come to mind. First, one could make a case for pursuing normative second-best analysis without taking political economy considerations into account. Second, one could add political economy constraints to the normative analysis alongside resource and informational constraints. Third, one could argue that normative analysis should be eschewed entirely in favor of political economy approaches, that is, approaches where policy choices are made through the political process rather than prescribed by some fictitious benevolent government invoking an equally fictitious social welfare function. The choice among these options obviously goes to the heart of normative second-best policy analysis and its role as a methodology for informing policy makers. The options in fact are not mutually exclusive, and some merit may be found in pursuing all three. In particular, both normative and political economy approaches are informative in their own right, and also informative for the policy process. To address the issue, it is useful to step back and recount some relevant features of the political economy literature. The intention is not to do justice to the literature, but to highlight factors that will be useful in our discussion.

Political economy models, like descriptive economic models, are abstractions from reality that are intended to emphasize particular relevant points. At the same time one might question whether using abstract models to characterize aspects of political decision-making can be as convincing as the comparable use of models in economic analysis. Objectives of decision makers are more clearly defined in economic models than in political ones, and economic markets provide a unifying principle for achieving outcomes—especially equilibrium ones—that does not exist in anywhere near as clear a form in the political sphere. Political decision-making is apparently much more complex and multidimensional than economic decision-making. The latter can often usefully be distilled down to unidimensional profit-maximization or utility-maximization, whereas the former inevitably involves historical, institutional, and leadership factors of the sort that economists often feel comfortable abstracting from. Not surprisingly, political scientists as a whole have been relatively slow to embrace political economy approaches to political decision-making favored by economists. With that caveat in mind, consider a simplistic caricature of political economy approaches.

In political economy models, decisions typically involve economic issues and focus on one of two dimensions. Some models, following Buchanan and Tullock (1962), emphasize collective decision-making as a means of internalizing the free-rider problem, such as deciding on the level of public goods. Other models focus mainly on redistribution, the extreme case being the division of a given pie of wealth among the population, as in simple probabilistic voting models like that of Lindbeck and Weibull (1987). More generally, issues of both efficiency and equity may be involved. In all cases a key issue, which remains surprisingly unresolved, concerns the existence of political equilibrium, the issue initially highlighted by Arrow (1951). Given the presumed extent of conflict among the preferences of persons in the economy, equilibria can generally only be obtained by making fairly strong assumptions, such as restricting the policy space or the form of individual preferences, constraining the timing of decisions, giving certain decision makers important influence, or introducing enough uncertainty about voter preferences to generate an equilibrium outcome. However, these assumptions are far from convincing, as recognized early and often by Downs (1957) in his seminal treatise. For example, even the celebrated probabilistic voting model is prone to vote-cycling unless fairly strong assumptions are made about the distribution of party preferences among voters (Usher 1994), assumptions that are hard to reconcile with reality. Yet these models are often used as if the problem did not exist.

Many modeling choices have to be made in constructing political economy models. One concerns behavioral assumptions. Voters might be assumed to vote purely in their self-interest, according to ideology or social preferences, or in some combination. Of course, voting according to self-interest runs into the conceptual problem that self-interest alone typically dictates not voting at all (Dhillon and Peralta 2002). Presumably one must appeal to social duty or responsibility to account for voting, which leaves as an open question how people make their voting choices. Similarly political decision makers may maximize votes or the chance of election, may act in their own self-interest, may act according to ideology, or some combination. Different assumptions can lead to very different outcomes. There may also be other actors in the political sphere, such as bureaucrats, advisors, lobbyists, and political activists, all of whom may have varying motives and varying degrees of influence.

The institutions in which political choices are made may also differ, albeit in often rudimentary ways. Political decisions may be made by direct democracy, by political parties that form a majority, or by voting and bargaining among representatives in the legislature. In the latter, agenda-setting becomes important (Baron and Ferejohn 1987). There may be a division of powers between the executive and legislative branches, and between levels of government.

An important element of political decision-making is the order in which choices and actions take place, or equivalently, the ability of political agents to commit. The standard approach, implicit in the classical treatises by Downs (1957) and Buchanan and Tullock (1962), is analogous to the standard approach in normative analysis. There are two decision makers—politicians and voters. Politicians or political parties announce policy platforms. Then voters vote, and finally policies are enacted in accordance with announced polices (whereupon private agents make economic choices).

The political announcement stage can be somewhat more complicated, given that more than one political party or decision maker is involved. Announcements of political platforms may be simultaneous and noncooperative, as in typical probabilistic voting models (Lindbeck and Weibull 1987; Dixit and Londregan 1998; Hettich and Winer 2005). Given that each party's expected votes depend on the platforms offered by the other party, the political equilibrium in platforms, assuming it exists, is a Nash equilibrium. Whether this is a plausible political outcome is not at all clear. Given that the political announcement stage is a one-shot game in which each party noncooperatively announces its platform, it is not obvious why the simultaneous announcements should be the Nash equilibrium values. After all, Nash equilibrium policies are not dominant strategies. That, however, is a quibble that applies to all one-shot Nash equilibrium games. Downs proposed sequential party announcements, with the incumbent party announcing its policies first, followed by the challenging party. In the case where there is no Condorcet winning platform, this is a useful way of pinning down the pattern of vote-cycling.

Quite apart from the questionable assumptions that political decision makers can commit to announced platforms, the supposition that once elected, they simply enact their announced policies might be viewed as unrealistic. If there is uncertainty about the future state of the world, it is not clear that policies announcements can be couched in a way that adequately takes such contingencies into account. In other words, like private contracts, political contracts are bound to be incomplete, so the exercise of discretion seems inevitable. In these circumstances the assumption of commitment seems strained.

When there is uncertainty about the future, another form of commitment is sometimes invoked, and that is commitment by the voters. In the classical model just discussed, the political cycle consists of a sequence of voting periods within which there is a policy announcement, a vote based on that announcement and policy enactment as promised. In this sequence, choices are forward-looking and history plays little role. It in fact seems reasonable to assume that voters base their votes at least partly on the past performance of parties, and this might be especially relevant if political platforms are necessarily incomplete as just discussed. Models of political decision-making where voters hold politicians accountable for their past decisions were originally proposed by Barro (1973) and Ferejohn (1986), and have recently become increasingly popular (e.g., Persson, Roland, and Tabellini 1997; Besley 2006; Besley and Smart 2007; Alesina, Campante, and Tabellini 2008; Acemoglu, Golosov, and Tsyvinski 2010, 2011).

In these models the order of decision-making is reversed so that political decisions are made and then voters vote. Moreover voting decisions are based on the performance of politicians, so the issue of commitment by politicians is now irrelevant. It is implicitly assumed instead, at least in the simplest political accountability models, that voters can commit to voting incumbents out of office when their performance is judged sufficiently wanting. Voters decide on a cut-off level of performance by politicians based on imperfect information about either the behavior of the latter or their quality, and politicians know that cutoff level. There is asymmetric information in the sense that politicians observe some shock to the economy that voters do not. In the Barro–Ferejohn version of the model, all potential politicians are identical, so if one is voted out of office for not meeting the voters' cutoff level of net benefits from public spending less taxes, an identical one is voted in. The implicit assumption is that voters are able to commit to voting such politicians out of office even though there is no real incentive to do so. Thus voter commitment replaces political party commitment in these simple political accountability models. Voter commitment is not such a critical issue where the quality of politicians differ, as in Besley and Smart (2007), discussed briefly below.

Alternatively, it may be assumed that no political decision makers can commit. Politicians cannot commit to policies that will maximize votes, and will only decide on their policies once they must be enacted, and after voters have voted. In the extreme case where politicians are selfish, they cannot help but enact policies that are in their own self-interest, and voters anticipate that before they vote. The starkest models reflecting the absence of commitment are the so-called citizen-candidate models of Osborne and Slivinski (1996) and Besley and Coate (1997). In these models generally only those potential political candidates for whom the chances of getting elected outweigh the net costs of running for office (taking account of the perks of office) will run for election. (It is, however, possible that a candidate who chooses to run for office will have no chance of being elected, but whose candidacy might influence who is elected.) Even in the simplest cases where there is only one person being elected, there can be multiple equilibria in which the number of persons running for office and their type are indeterminate. These models are suggestive of the consequences of the inability of political decision makers to commit, but they are also until now somewhat unsatisfactory as representations of actual political processes. Apart from the indeterminacy of political equilibria, they tend to focus on elections of a single representative who once elected has the authority to choose economic policies. Like party competition models, they also typically avoid voting instability issues by assumption.

There is much at stake in the issue of commitment. The type of politician attracted to run for office will be affected by the ability to commit. Equivalently the policies chosen will be affected. With full commitment there is no reason for inefficient policies, as argued by Downs (1957). Almost by definition, some efficient policy could defeat any inefficient policy by offering a Pareto-superior platform. The absence of commitment can result in inefficient policy choices and policy instruments, as in Coate and Morris (1995) and Acemoglu and Robinson (2001). And, of course, the inability of politicians to commit can lead to the same sort of inferior outcomes that are associated with the inability of benevolent governments to commit.

At the same time there may be political economy devices that can mitigate the problem of commitment by using precommitment types of mechanisms. One example of this in the context of the citizen-candidate model is the use of strategic voting. Persson and Tabellini (2002) consider the classical case of the inability of government to commit to multi-period tax policies that affect the level of capital accumulation. As we have seen, in a time-consistent policy equilibrium, the inability to commit leads to an excessive capital income tax rate as governments cannot avoid taxing previously accumulated capital at a high rate. Anticipating this, too little capital is accumulated and the equilibrium is inferior to a full-commitment second-best one. In a citizen-candidate context, Persson and Tabellini show that voters might be able to counter this problem by choosing to elect a candidate from the wealthier class since that candidate will be more reluctant to impose high taxes on capital income. This will succeed to the extent that such candidates will voluntarily run for office.

Another example, and one that we have already encountered above, where political economy devices have been proposed to overcome commitment problems involves the use of political accountability models. Acemoglu, Golosov, and Tsyvinski (2010) show how retrospective voting by voters that are farsighted and live indefinitely can lead politicians who are subject to periodic elections to choose optimal redistributive nonlinear income tax policies that mimic full-commitment policies (albeit ones that are not fully second-best because of the fact that politicians are able to divert some informational rents to themselves). In a follow-up paper (Acemoglu, Golosov, and Tsyvinski 2011), they show that a similar logic applies in a dynamic Ramsey-type model in which the government is restricted to linear taxes on labor and capital income. These models, however, require that voters can commit to retrospective voting, and they also involve the unattractive assumption that voters and politicians live forever. Nonetheless, they do suggest a political economy mechanism for overcoming the commitment problem that can be built on in future research.

A final important class of issues in political economy models concerns asymmetric information. This can take different forms. Politicians may be imperfectly informed about voters' preferences, as in probabilistic voting models mentioned above. Alternatively, voters may not observe either the actions or the characteristics of politicians. The original political accountability models of Barro (1973) and Ferejohn (1986) focused on the hidden actions of politicians who had knowledge of the true state of nature and could exploit that by diverting rents from tax revenues to themselves. In Ferejohn's model, voters are principals to the politicians as agents. Politicians pursue their own self-interest when in office, but the threat of being voted out of office constrains their policies to be those that are tolerable to the voters. The tolerance of voters is restricted by the fact that politicians have privileged information about the state of the economy, and the fact that if voted out, they will be replaced by some other self-interested politician. The problem is of the moral hazard sort, with voters unable to observe the costly effort of the politician. Retrospective voting by the electorate leads to a threshold level of political outcomes below which voters remove the incumbent from office. Incumbents know this and exercise restraint in taking political rents in order to stay in office. In the end, rents obtained reflect the informational advantage of the politician.

Besley (2006) and Besley and Smart (2007) extend the political accountability—or political agency—model to include both moral hazard and adverse selection. Thus politicians can be "good" or "bad," where bad politicians are self-interested and good ones act in the interest of the voters. The politicians—both incumbents and challengers—are drawn from a pool of these types, and the type of a given politician is private information. This information is imperfectly revealed to voters by the choices that politicians make, where those choices are influenced by voting. The model is a simple two-period model in which the quality of the incumbent is randomly chosen to begin with, and the incumbent decides on expenditures on public goods and rent diversion in the first period. Since the cost of providing the public good is private information to the politicians, voters cannot observe rent diversion. Retrospective voting occurs after the first period, and either the re-elected incumbent or the elected challenger then decides on second-period public goods and rents. Voting can serve two purposes in the Besley–Smart model. On the one hand, as in the Ferejohn model, it can restrain rent-seeking by bad politicians, the "discipline" effect. Bad politicians may have an incentive to pretend to be good politicians in the first period in order to be re-elected. This involves restraining rent-diversion to make themselves indistinguishable from good politicians. On the other hand, voting might displace bad politicians with good ones, the "selection" effect. The strength of these effects depends on the parameters of the model and the political institutions (e.g., whether there is yardstick competition).

Other configurations of asymmetric information are possible. Politicians may be imperfectly informed about the state of the world or about the effect of policies on outcomes, and may rely on bureaucrats for advice or decision-making (Alesina and Tabellini 2008). Decision-making may also be influenced by third parties, such as lobbyists for special interests (Grossman and Helpman 1994; Dixit 1996), party activists (Aldrich 1983), political contributions and advertising (Coate 2004), and the media (Bernhardt, Krasa, and Polborn 2008).

The point is that there is a wide array of political economy models that emphasize different elements of political decision-making. They emphasize quite different aspects of political decision-making, and many abstract from relevant key problems facing the literature. For example, problems of vote cycling are typically assumed away, even in contexts where they would naturally arise (e.g., Downsian party competition models). It would not be at all obvious what kind of political constraint should be imposed on normative analysis. Political economy models are better thought of as models of collective decision-making that, like normative models, yield deterministic outcomes. To impose a political economy constraint would be to render normative analysis somewhat pointless since the scope for normative choice would be removed.

It is perhaps not surprising that political economy constraints have not been imposed in normative analysis in the past. On the contrary, we would argue that there are sound reasons for conducting normative analysis free of political economy constraints. Normative analysis serves as a benchmark against which to judge political outcomes. Moreover the choice among political institutions can be informed by normative analysis. This includes the writing of constitutions, the assignment of powers in a federation, the division of powers among legislative, executive and judicial branches, representative versus parliamentary democracies, and so on. Furthermore political constraints are endogenous and depend on the consensus that societies might achieve on social values and objectives as well as on the persuasive role that political leaders play. Normative analysis serves both to inform voters and to influence the views of political decision makers. To constrain normative analysis by political considerations would, on those grounds, be self-defeating by ruling out options that are deemed to violate fleeting political constraints.

More generally, actual political decision-making can be thought to be in part a reflection of the normative judgment of voters to the extent that voters vote expressively according to their social values (Brennan and Hamlin 1998). The argument is that it is irrational to vote if one is simply pursuing one's self-interest. Those who take the trouble to vote do so from a sense of duty or civic obligation, and one might expect that since their self-interest is not at stake, they might be expressing their social preferences when they vote. To the extent that is true, one could interpret policy values exhibited in policies actually implemented as reflecting social values. This view can be supported by the observation that many policies that governments undertake, especially those that form the foundation of the welfare state, would not exist if persons voted purely according to self-interest. The literature on experimental and behavioral economics further supports this view that persons often act out of nonselfish motives in social situations. To the extent that this is true, normative analysis is complementary with political economy rather than competing.

The notion that collective decision-making embodies the extent of social consensus over social values suggests that normative analysis can look to political outcomes to recover at least some value judgments. These might include the aversion to inequality, the social discount rate to be used in giving weight to future generations, and the manner in which persons of different preferences for leisure are treated. This perspective has been taken by various authors, including Christiansen and Jansen (1978), Ahmad and Stern (1984), and Gordon and Cullen (forthcoming). The latter try to recover values about redistribution used by the government from observed income tax schedules in the United States.

In any case, these arguments reinforce the idea that normative second-best analysis is a fruitful enterprise alongside political economy analysis. Normative analysis is useful in its own right and serves as a useful benchmark for policy-making. To constrain it by political feasibility requirements would stifle its usefulness as an approach that informs the policy process rather than being restricted by it.

5.6   Concluding Comments

The broad purpose of these lectures has been to explore the symbiotic relationship that exists among ideas developed in the normative optimal tax literature, policies proposed by influential policy advisors and commissions, and ultimately reforms enacted by policy makers. I have argued that normative second-best analysis, far from being an end in itself, is an indispensable tool for informing the policy process. Optimal policy analysis is of necessity based on abstract manageable models that focus on particular aspects of problems to the exclusion of others. As such, the literature lends itself to a taxonomy of approaches, many of which turn out to be much less useful and insightful than others. No doubt this plethora of models, some differing in minute details or representing only minor extensions of the literature, contributes to what its detractors view as a bloated academic literature with little policy relevance. However, the core contributions and their refinements have been of considerable importance in framing the policy debates and the way of thinking about policy problems.

The manner in which ideas from the normative policy literature are infused in policy thinking takes diverse forms. Presumably policy makers do not read academic journals, and could not fully understand their content even if they did. The ideas do, however, permeate teaching in academia. They are learned by specialists in the bureaucracy, in think-tanks and in the media where public perceptions are formed. They form the background for commissioned studies and consultations by the public sector. Perhaps most overtly, they find their way into periodic reports that define tax policy thinking in given periods. Examples of the latter are many. The Royal Commission on the Taxation of Profits and Income (1955) in the United Kingdom and the Carter Report in Canada (Royal Commission on Taxation 1966) together proposed far-reaching templates for taxing comprehensive income according to the then-accepted Schanz–Haig–Simons comprehensive income base with a rate structure informed by classical utilitarianism (Schanz 1986; Haig 1921; Simons 1938). The US Treasury Blueprints (US Treasury 1977) and the Meade Report (1978), reflecting the thinking of Kaldor (1955) that originated in his minority report to the UK Royal Commission on the Taxation of Profits and Income, argued in favor of personal consumption or expenditure taxation rather than comprehensive income taxation. The corollary of this was a system of business taxation based on cash flows to avoid all taxation of capital income, rather than the corporation tax on equity income that is the hallmark of income tax systems. The generalization of cash-flow taxation that preserved its neutrality with respect to firms' investment decisions was the so-called allowance for corporate equity, which was forcefully advocated by the Institute for Fiscal Studies (1991) and more recently has found its way into proposals for resource taxation in the Henry Review in Australia (Australian Treasury 2010). Complementing this were government policy proposals for value-added taxation, such as the Green Paper (1971) in the United Kingdom. Comprehensive income and personal consumption taxation represent two extreme approaches to direct taxation. More recently dual-income tax systems in which capital income is treated preferentially and at a fixed rate have been introduced in the Nordic countries and proposed elsewhere. (Sørensen 1994 provides a comprehensive account of the principles and background of the Nordic dual income tax.) Proponents of a version of the dual-income tax include the President's Advisory Panel on Federal Tax Reform (2005) in the United States. Recent background studies for the Mirrlees Review (Banks and Diamond 2010) have also probed schedular tax systems in which earnings and capital income are subject to different rates. Recall from the discussion above that in the end the Mirrlees Review opted for a variant of the progressive consumption or expenditure tax system, albeit with a lifetime inheritance tax system as a backstop.

It is clear that ideas about the optimal tax-transfer system evolve. Normative analysis informs the policy process, and vice versa. Policy innovations like the VAT and dual-income taxation have been at the leading edge and have encouraged analytical investigation. Others like personal consumption taxation and cash-flow business taxation or its equivalent have largely originated in the theoretical literature. Similarly refundable tax credits for low-income workers were introduced and later vindicated by the theory.

The dialectic process by which ideas are put into practice and subject to analytical scrutiny is not limited to normative analysis. Empirical analysis is an important component of the formation of policy views. It can provide evidence on the orders of magnitude of key effects emphasized in the theory. For example, it can provide some indication of the relative importance of intensive and extensive labor responses to tax rates, which, as we have seen, are key determinants of the choice of marginal tax rates at various points in the income distribution (Brewer, Saez, and Shephard 2010). Similarly the political economy literature can also bring a useful perspective to the choice of tax policies. In the end, tax reforms in democratic countries must obtain electoral consent, and the values implicit in them must reflect the consensus of citizens. This consensus is no doubt informed by normative analysis, especially as it influences decision makers and opinion leaders. The political economy perspective can also be useful in designing institutions for policy-making. However, neither empirical analysis nor political economy are substitutes for normative analysis. They are complementary ways of approaching policy issues. By the same token, I insist that normative analysis should not be compromised by considerations of political feasibility. That would partly defeat the purpose of taking a normative perspective.

In earlier chapters we observed the importance of optimal second-best policy analysis on a selected number of policy-relevant results from the literature that have been influential in tax policy proposals. We started with the celebrated Corlett–Hague theorem, which was one of the earliest formalizations of second-best analysis and formed the basis for thinking about the appropriate way to impose differential taxes on different commodities, including future consumption. Despite being set in a very simple representative-person setting, the fundamental intuition of the Corlett–Hague theorem survived in the nonlinear tax setting of the Atkinson–Stiglitz theorem. The production efficiency theorem turned out to be of fundamental importance for both cost–benefit analysis and as an argument for value-added taxation. We studied various extensions to the optimal nonlinear tax literature, including especially its generalization to dynamic settings. That literature also provided several insights into the optimal rate structure, particularly the recent emphasis on labor variability along the extensive margin which results in arguments for refundable tax credits for low-income workers. The emphasis on incentive constraints in modern second-best analysis leads naturally to studying possible ways of relaxing such constraints either by the use of nonconventional policy instruments, including in-kind transfers, work requirements and price controls, or by seeking ways of improving the information available to the government through tagging and monitoring.

As the literature has evolved, new challenges have been uncovered. This final chapter has focused on a number of these. Some of them challenge the normative basis of much of optimal tax analysis. The fact that persons have different preferences requires additional and nonobvious value judgments to be made in order to compare welfare across households. The welfaristic basis for traditional normative analysis is challenged by recent findings of behavioral economics that question the rationality of individuals' decision-making, the feasibility of making informed decisions, and the possibility that self-interest is not always the sole objective of choices. As well, in a dynamic setting, problems of commitment either by the government or by individuals pose difficult normative problems. We reviewed some innovative ways at looking at some of these problems without pretending that they are close to being resolved. As has always been the case, there are challenges that normative analysis must face, some of which will change our way of looking at policy problems. However, what is clear is that we cannot dispense with normative analysis and substitute for it empirical or political economy approaches.

References

Acemoglu, Daren, Michael Golosov, and Aleh Tsyvinski. 2010. Dynamic Mirrlees taxation under political economy constraints. *Review of Economic Studies* 77: 841–81.

Acemoglu, Daren, Michael Golosov, and Aleh Tsyvinski. 2011. Political economy of Ramsey taxation. *Journal of Public Economics* 95: 467–75.

Acemoglu, Daren, and James A. Robinson. 2001. Inefficient redistribution. *American Political Science Review* 95: 649–62.

Adler, Matthew (forthcoming). *Well-Being and Fair Distribution: A Framework for Policy Analysis*. Oxford: Oxford University Press.

Ahmad, Ehtisham, and Nicholas Stern. 1984. The theory of reform and Indian indirect taxes. *Journal of Public Economics* 25: 259–98.

Ahmad, Ehtisham, and Nicholas Stern. 1991. *The Theory and Practice of Tax Reform in Developing Countries*. Cambridge: Cambridge University Press.

Aiyagari, S. Rao. 1995. Optimal capital income taxation with incomplete markets, borrowing constraints, and constant discounting. *Journal of Political Economy* 103: 1158–75.

Akerlof, George A. 1970. The market for lemons: Quality uncertainty and the market mechanism. *Quarterly Journal of Economics* 84: 488–500.

Akerlof, George A. 1978. The economics of "tagging" as applied to the optimal income tax, welfare programs, and manpower training. *American Economic Review* 68: 8–19.

Akerlof, George A. 1980. A theory of social custom, of which unemployment may be one consequence. *Quarterly Journal of Economics* 94: 749–75.

Albouy, David. 2009. Evaluating the efficiency and equity of federal fiscal equalization. Mimeo. University of Michigan.

Aldrich, John H. 1983. A Downsian spatial model with party activism. *American Political Science Review* 77: 974–90.

Alesina, Alberto, Filipe R. Campante, and Guido Tabellini. 2008. Why is fiscal policy often procyclical? *Journal of the European Economic Association* 6: 1006–36.

Alesina, Alberto, and Eliana La Ferrara. 2005. Preferences for redistribution in the land of opportunities. *Journal of Public Economics* 89: 897–931.

Alesina, Alberta, and Edward Glaeser. 2004. *Fighting Poverty in the US and Europe: A World of Difference*. Oxford: Oxford University Press.

Alesina, Alberto, Edward Glaeser, and Bruce Sacerdote. 2001. Why doesn't the United States have a European-style welfare state? *Brookings Papers on Economic Activity*.

Alesina, Alberto, and Guido Tabellini. 2008. Bureaucrats or politicians? Part II: Multiple policy tasks. *Journal of Public Economics* 92: 426–47.

Allen, Stephen. 1987. Taxes, redistribution, and the minimum wage: A theoretical analysis. *Quarterly Journal of Economics* 102: 477–90.

Allingham, Michael G., and Agnar Sandmo. 1972. Income tax evasion: A theoretical analysis. *Journal of Public Economics* 1: 323–38.

Alvarez, Yvette, John Burbidge, Ted Farrell, and Leigh Palmer. 1992. Optimal taxation in a life-cycle model. *Canadian Journal of Economics. Revue Canadienne d'Economique* 25: 111–22.

Anderberg, Dan. 2009. Optimal policy and the risk properties of human capital reconsidered. *Journal of Public Economics* 93: 1017–26.

Andreoni, James. 1990. Impure altruism and donations to public goods: A theory of warm glow giving. *Economic Journal* 100: 464–77.

Andreoni, James. 2001. The economics of philanthropy. In N. Smeltser and P. Baltes, eds., *International Encyclopedia of Social and Behavioral Sciences*. Oxford: Elsevier, 11369–76.

Apps, Patricia, and Ray Rees. 1988. Taxation and the household. *Journal of Public Economics* 35: 355–69.

Apps, Patricia, and Ray Rees. 2006. Repeated optimal nonlinear income taxation. Mimeo.

Apps, Patricia, and Ray Rees. 2007. The taxation of couples. CEPR discussion paper 559, IZA discussion paper 2910.

Apps, Patricia, and Ray Rees. 2009. *Public Economics and the Household*. Cambridge: Cambridge University Press.

Archibald, Christopher, and David Donaldson. 1976. Non-paternalism and externalities. *Canadian Journal of Economics. Revue Canadienne d'Economique* 9: 492–507.

Arozamena, Leandro, Martin Besfamille, and Pablo Sanguinetti. 2008. Optimal taxes and penalties when the government cannot commit to its audit policy. Mimeo. Universidad Torcuato Di Tella.

Arrow, Kenneth J. 1951. *Social Choice and Individual Values*. New York: Wiley.

Arrow, Kenneth. 1971. A utilitarian approach to the concept of equality in public expenditures. *Quarterly Journal of Economics* 85: 409–415.

Atkinson, Anthony B. 1973. How progressive should income tax be? In Michael Parkin and A. Robert Nobay, eds., *Essays in Modern Economics*. London: Longman, 90–109.

Atkinson, Anthony B. 1977. Optimal taxation and the direct versus indirect tax controversy. *Canadian Journal of Economics. Revue Canadienne d'Economique* 10: 590–606.

Atkinson, Anthony B. 1996. *Public Economics in Action: The Basic Income/Flat Tax Proposal, The Lindahl Lectures*. Oxford: Clarendon Press.

Atkinson, Anthony B. 1999. *The Economic Consequences of Rolling Back the Welfare State*. Cambridge: MIT Press.

Atkinson, Anthony B., and Agnar Sandmo. 1980. Welfare implications of the taxation of savings. *Economic Journal* 90: 529–49.

Atkinson, Anthony B., and Nicholas Stern. 1974. Pigou, taxation and public goods. *Review of Economic Studies* 41: 119–28.

Atkinson, Anthony B., and Joseph E. Stiglitz. 1976. The design of tax structure: Direct vs. indirect taxation. *Journal of Public Economics* 6: 55–75.

Atkinson, Anthony B., and Joseph E. Stiglitz. 1980. *Lectures on Public Economics*. New York: McGraw-Hill.

Auerbach, Alan, Michael Devereux, and Helen Simpson. 2010. Taxing corporate income. In James Mirrlees, Stuart Adam, Timothy Besley, Richard Blundell, Stephen Bond, Robert Chote, Malcolm Gammie, Paul Johnson, Gareth Myles, and James Poterba, eds., *Dimensions of Tax Design: The Mirrlees Review*. Oxford: Oxford University Press, 837–93.

Auerbach, Alan J., and James R. Hines Jr. 2002. Taxation and economic efficiency. In Alan J. Auerbach and Martin Feldstein, eds., *Handbook of Public Economics*, vol. 3. Amsterdam: North Holland, 1347–421.

Australian Treasury. 2010. *Australia's Future Tax System (The Henry Review)*. Canberra: Commonwealth of Australia.

Banks, James, and Peter Diamond. 2010. The base for direct taxation. In James Mirrlees, Stuart Adam, Timothy Besley, Richard Blundell, Stephen Bond, Robert Chote, Malcolm Gammie, Paul Johnson, Gareth Myles, and James Poterba, eds., *Dimensions of Tax Design: The Mirrlees Review*. Oxford: Oxford University Press, 548–648.

Baron, David B. 2010. Morally-motivated self-regulation. *American Economic Review* 100: 1299–1329.

Baron, David B., and John Ferejohn. 1987. Bargaining and agenda formation in legislatures. *American Economic Review* 77: 303–309.

Barro, Robert J. 1973. The control of politicians: An economic model. *Public Choice* 14: 19–42.

Barro, Robert J. 1974. Are government bonds net wealth? *Journal of Political Economy* 82: 1095–1117.

Baumol, William J., and David F. Bradford. 1970. Optimal departures from marginal cost pricing. *American Economic Review* 60: 265–83.

Beaudry, Paul, Charles Blackorby, and Dezsö Szalay. 2009. Taxes and employment subsidies in optimal redistribution programs. *American Economic Review* 99: 216–42.

Becker, Gary S. 1965. A theory of the allocation of time. *Economic Journal* 75: 493–517.

Becker, Gary S., and Kevin M. Murphy. 1988. A theory of rational addiction. *Journal of Political Economy* 96: 675–700.

Belan, Pascal, Stéphane Gauthier, and Guy Laroque. 2008. Optimal grouping of commodities for indirect taxation. *Journal of Public Economics* 92: 1738–50.

Bénabou, Roland, and Marek Pycia. 2002. Dynamic inconsistency and self-control: A planner-doer interpretation. *Economics Letters* 77: 419–24.

Bénabou, Roland, and Jean Tirole. 2006. Belief in a just world and redistributive politics. *Quarterly Journal of Economics* 121: 699–746.

Bentham, Jeremy. 1791. *Principles of Morals and Legislation*. London: Doubleday.

Berliant, Marcus, and John Ledyard. 2005. Optimal dynamic nonlinear income taxes with no commitment. Mimeo.

Bernhardt, Dan, Stefan Krasa, and Mattias Polborn. 2008. Political polarization and the electoral effects of media bias. *Journal of Public Economics* 92: 1092–1104.

Bernheim, B. Douglas. 2002. Taxation and Saving. In Alan J. Auerbach and Martin Feldstein, eds., *Handbook of Public Economics*, vol. 3. Amsterdam: North Holland, 1173–249.

Bernheim, B. Douglas, and Kyle Bagwell. 1988. Is everything neutral? *Journal of Political Economy* 96: 308–38.

Bernheim, B. Douglas, and Antonio Rangel. 2007. Behavioral public economics: Welfare and policy analysis with non-standard decision-makers. In Peter A. Diamond and Hannu Vartiainen, eds., *Behavioral Economics and Its Applications*. Princeton: Princeton University Press, 7–77.

Beshears, John, James J. Choi, David Laibson, and Brigitte C. Madrian. 2007. The importance of default options for retirement saving outcomes: Evidence from the United States. In Stephen J. Kay and Tapen Sinha, eds., *Lessons from Pension Reform in the Americas*. Oxford: Oxford University Press, 59–87.

Besley, Timothy. 2006. *Principled Agents? The Political Economy of Good Government, The Lindahl Lectures*. Oxford: Oxford University Press.

Besley, Timothy, and Stephen Coate. 1992. Workfare versus welfare: Incentive arguments for work requirements in poverty-alleviation programs. *American Economic Review* 82: 249–61.

Besley, Timothy, and Stephen Coate. 1995. The design of income maintenance programmes. *Review of Economic Studies* 62: 187–221.

Besley, Timothy, and Stephen Coate. 1997. An economic model of representative democracy. *Quarterly Journal of Economics* 112: 85–114.

Besley, Timothy, and Ian Jewitt. 1991. Decentralising public good supply. *Econometrica* 59: 1769–78.

Besley, Timothy, and Richard Layard, eds. 2008. Special Issue: Happiness and Public Economics. *Journal of Public Economics* 92: 1773–1862.

Besley, Timothy, and Michael Smart. 2007. Fiscal restraints and voter welfare. *Journal of Public Economics* 91: 755–73.

Blackorby, Charles, Walter Bossert, and David Donaldson. 2002. Utilitarianism and the theory of justice. In K. J. Arrow, A. K. Sen, and K. Suzumura, eds., *Handbook of Social Choice and Welfare*, vol. 1. Amsterdam: North Holland, 543–96.

Blackorby, Charles, and Craig Brett. 2004. Production efficiency and the direct–indirect tax mix. *Journal of Public Economic Theory* 6: 165–80.

Blackorby, Charles, and David Donaldson. 1988. Cash versus kind, self selection and efficient transfers. *American Economic Review* 78: 691–700.

Blackorby, Charles, and David Donaldson. 1990. A review article: The case against the use of the sum of compensating variations in cost–benefit analysis. *Canadian Journal of Economics. Revue Canadienne d'Economique* 23: 471–94.

Blackorby, Charles, and David Donaldson. 1994. Information and intergroup transfers. *American Economic Review Papers and Proceedings* 84: 440–47.

Blackorby, Charles, Russell Davidson, and William Schworm. 1991a. Implicit separability: Characterisation and implications for consumer demands. *Journal of Economic Theory* 55: 364–99.

Blackorby, Charles, Russell Davidson, and William Schworm. 1991b. The validity of piecemeal second-best policy. *Journal of Public Economics* 46: 267–90.

Blackorby, Charles, and Sushama Murty. 2009. Constraints on income distribution and production efficiency in economies with Ramsey taxation. Mimeo.

Blomquist, Sören, and Vidar Christiansen. 1995. Public provision of private goods as a redistributive device in an optimum income tax model. *Scandinavian Journal of Economics* 97: 547–67.

Blomquist, Sören, and Vidar Christiansen. 1998a. Topping up or opting out? The optimal design of public provision schemes. *International Economic Review* 39: 399–411.

Blomquist, Sören, and Vidar Christiansen. 1998b. Price subsidies versus public provision. *International Tax and Public Finance* 5: 283–306.

Blomquist, Sören, and Vidar Christiansen. 2008. Taxation and heterogeneous preferences. *Finanz Archiv* 64: 218–44.

Blumkin, Tomer, Bradley J. Ruffle, and Yosef Ganun. 2008. Are income and consumption taxes ever really equivalent? Evidence from a real-effort experiment with real goods. CESifo working paper 2194.

Boadway, Robin. 1974. The welfare foundations of cost–benefit analysis. *Economic Journal* 84: 926–39.

Boadway, Robin. 1975. Cost–benefit rules in general equilibrium. *Review of Economic Studies* 42: 361–73.

Boadway, Robin W. 1976. Integrating equity and efficiency in applied welfare economics. *Quarterly Journal of Economics* 90: 541–56.

Boadway, Robin. 2002. The role of public choice considerations in normative public economics. In Stanley L. Winer and Hirofumi Shibata, eds., *The Role of Political Economy in the Theory and Practice of Public Finance*. Cheltenham, UK: Edward Elgar, 47–68.

Boadway, Robin. 2004b. The dual income tax system — An overview. *CESifo DICE Report. Journal for Institutional Comparisons* 2: 3–8.

Boadway, Robin. 2010. Efficiency and redistribution: An evaluative review of Louis Kaplow's *The Theory of Taxation and Public Economics*. *Journal of Economic Literature* 48: 964–79.

Boadway, Robin, and Neil Bruce. 1984a. *Welfare Economics*. Oxford: Blackwell.

Boadway, Robin, and Neil Bruce. 1984b. A general proposition on the design of a neutral business tax. *Journal of Public Economics* 24: 231–39.

Boadway, Robin, Emma Chamberlain, and Carl Emmerson. (2010). Taxation of wealth and wealth transfers. In James Mirrlees, Stuart Adam, Timothy Besley, Richard Blundell, Stephen Bond, Robert Chote, Malcolm Gammie, Paul Johnson, Gareth Myles, and James Poterba, eds., *Dimensions of Tax Design: The Mirrlees Review*. Oxford: Oxford University Press, 737–814.

Boadway, Robin, and Katherine Cuff. 1999. Monitoring job search as an instrument for targeting transfers. *International Tax and Public Finance* 6: 317–37.

Boadway, Robin, and Katherine Cuff. 2001. A minimum wage can be welfare-improving and employment-enhancing. *European Economic Review* 45: 553–76.

Boadway, Robin, Katherine Cuff, and Nicolas Marceau. 2003. Redistribution and employment policies with endogenous unemployment. *Journal of Public Economics* 87: 2407–30.

Boadway, Robin, Katherine Cuff, and Maurice Marchand. 2000. Optimal income taxation with quasi-linear preferences revisited. *Journal of Public Economic Theory* 2: 435–60.

Boadway, Robin, and Firouz Gahvari. 2006. Optimal taxation with consumption time as a leisure or labor substitute. *Journal of Public Economics* 90: 1851–78.

Boadway, Robin, and Richard G. Harris. 1977. A characterization of piecemeal second best policy. *Journal of Public Economics* 8: 169–90.

Boadway, Robin, and Laurence Jacquet. 2008. Optimal marginal and average income taxation under maximin. *Journal of Economic Theory* 143: 425–41.

Boadway, Robin W., and Michael Keen. 1993. Public goods, self-selection and optimal income taxation. *International Economic Review* 34: 463–78.

Boadway, Robin W., and Michael Keen. 1998. Evasion and time consistency in the taxation of capital income. *International Economic Review* 39: 461–76.

Boadway, Robin, and Michael Keen. 2000. Redistribution. In Anthony B. Atkinson and Francois Bourguignon, eds., *Handbook of Income Distribution*, vol. 1. Amsterdam: North-Holland, 677–789.

Boadway, Robin, and Michael Keen. 2003. Theoretical perspectives on the taxation of capital income and financial services. In Patrick Honohan, ed., *Taxation of Financial Intermediation: Theory and Practice for Emerging Economies*. New York: World Bank and Oxford University Press, 31–80.

Boadway, Robin, and Michael Keen. 2006. Financing and taxing new firms under asymmetric information. *Finanz-Archiv* 62: 471–502.

Boadway, Robin, and Michael Keen. 2010. Theoretical perspectives on resource tax design. In Philip Daniel, Michael Keen, and Charles McPherson, eds., *The Taxation of Petroleum and Minerals: Principles, Problems and Practice*. London: Routledge, 13–74.

Boadway, Robin, Manuel Leite-Monteiro, Maurice Marchand, and Pierre Pestieau. 2003. Social insurance and redistribution. In Sijbren Cnossen and Hans-Werner Sinn, eds., *Public Finance and Public Policy in the New Century* in celebration of Richard A. Musgrave's 90th birthday and the tenth anniversary of CES. Cambridge: MIT Press, 333–58.

Boadway, Robin, Manuel Leite-Monteiro, Maurice Marchand, and Pierre Pestieau. 2006. Social insurance and redistribution with moral hazard and adverse selection. *Scandinavian Journal of Economics* 108: 279–98.

Boadway, Robin, and Nicolas Marceau. 1994. Time inconsistency as a rationale for public unemployment insurance. *International Tax and Public Finance* 1: 107–26.

Boadway, Robin, Nicolas Marceau, and Maurice Marchand. 1996. Investment in education and the time inconsistency of redistributive tax policy. *Economica* 63: 171–89.

Boadway, Robin, Nicolas Marceau, Maurice Marchand, and Marianne Vigneault. 1998. Entrepreneurship, asymmetric information, and unemployment. *International Tax and Public Finance* 5: 307–27.

Boadway, Robin, Nicolas Marceau, and Steeve Mongrain. 2007. Redistributive taxation under ethical behaviour. *Scandinavian Journal of Economics* 109: 505–29.

Boadway, Robin, Nicolas Marceau, and Motohiro Sato. 1999. Agency and the design of welfare systems. *Journal of Public Economics* 73: 1–30.

Boadway, Robin, and Maurice Marchand. 1995. The use of public expenditures for redistributive purposes. *Oxford Economic Papers* 47: 45–59.

Boadway, Robin, Maurice Marchand, and Pierre Pestieau. 1991. Optimal linear income taxation in models with occupational choice. *Journal of Public Economics* 46: 133–62.

Boadway, Robin, Maurice Marchand, and Pierre Pestieau. 1994. Towards a theory of the direct-indirect tax mix. *Journal of Public Economics* 55: 71–88.

Boadway, Robin, Maurice Marchand, and Pierre Pestieau. 2000. Redistribution with unobservable bequests: A case for taxing capital income. *Scandinavian Journal of Economics* 102: 253–67.

Boadway, Robin, Maurice Marchand, Pierre Pestieau, and Maria del Mar Racionero. 2000. Optimal redistribution with heterogeneous preferences for leisure. *Journal of Public Economic Theory* 4: 475–98.

Boadway, Robin, Maurice Marchand, and Motohiro Sato. 1998. Subsidies versus public provision of private goods as instruments for redistribution. *Scandinavian Journal of Economics* 100: 545–64.

Boadway, Robin, and Pierre Pestieau. 2003. Indirect taxation and redistribution: The scope of the Atkinson–Stiglitz theorem. In Richard Arnott, Bruce Greenwald, Ravi Kanbur, and Barry Nalebuff, eds., *Economics for an Imperfect World: Essays in Honor of Joseph E. Stiglitz.* Cambridge: MIT Press, 387–403.

Boadway, Robin, and Pierre Pestieau. 2006. Tagging and redistributive taxation. *Annales d'Economie et de Statistique* 83–84: 123–47.

Boadway, Robin, and Pierre Pestieau. 2011. The use of indirect taxes for redistribution. Mimeo. Queen's University.

Boadway, Robin, and Motohiro Sato. 1999. Information acquisition and government intervention in credit markets. *Journal of Public Economic Theory* 1: 283–308.

Boadway, Robin, and Motohiro Sato. 2000. The optimality of punishing only the innocent: The case of tax evasion. *International Tax and Public Finance* 7: 641–64.

Boadway, Robin, and Motohiro Sato. 2011. Entrepreneurship and asymmetric information in input markets. *International Tax and Public Finance* 18: 166–92.

Boadway, Robin, and Motohiro Sato. 2009. Optimal tax design and enforcement with an informal sector. *American Economic Journal, Economic Policy*, 1: 1–27.

Boadway, Robin, and Jean-François Tremblay. 2006. A theory of fiscal imbalance. *Finanz-Archiv* 62: 1–27.

Boadway, Robin, and Jean-François Tremblay. 2008. Pigouvian taxation in a Ramsey world. *Asia–Pacific Journal of Accounting & Economics* 15: 183–204.

Boadway, Robin, and David Wildasin. 1994. Taxation and savings: A survey. *Fiscal Studies* 15: 19–63.

Boiteux, Marcel. 1956. Sur la gestion des monopoles publics astreints a l'equilibre budgetaire. *Econometrica* 24: 22–40; trans. as Boiteux, Marcel. 1971. On the management of public monopolies subject to budgetary constraints. *Journal of Economic Theory* 3: 219–40.

Bond, Stephen R., and Michael P. Devereux. 1995. On the design of a neutral business tax under uncertainty. *Journal of Public Economics* 58: 57–71.

Boone, Jan, and Lans Bovenberg. 2002. Optimal labour taxation and search. *Journal of Public Economics* 85: 53–97.

Bordignon, Massimo. 1990. Was Kant right? Voluntary provision of public goods under the principle of unconditional commitment. *Economic Notes* 3: 342–72.

Bordignon, Massimo. 1993. A fairness approach to income tax evasion. *Journal of Public Economics* 52: 345–62.

Bös, Dieter. 1985. Public sector pricing. In Alan J. Auerbach and Martin Feldstein, eds., *Handbook of Public Economics*, vol. 2. Amsterdam: North Holland, 129–211.

Boskin, Michael J., and Eytan Sheshinski. 1978. Optimal redistributive taxation when individual welfare depends on relative income. *Quarterly Journal of Economics* 43: 589–601.

Bossert, Walter. 1995. Redistribution mechanisms based on individual characteristics. *Mathematical Social Sciences* 29: 1–17.

Bossert, Walter, Marc Fleurbaey, and Dirk Van de gaer. 1999. Responsibility, talent and compensation: Second-best analysis. *Review of Economic Design* 4: 33–55.

Bovenberg, A. Lans, and Bas Jacobs. 2005. Redistribution and education subsidies are Siamese twins. *Journal of Public Economics* 89: 2005–35.

Bovenberg, A. Lans, Martin Hansen, and Peter Birch Sørensen. 2008. Individual savings accounts for social insurance: Rationale and alternative designs. *International Tax and Public Finance* 15: 67–86.

Bovenberg, A. Lans, and Ruud A. de Mooij. 1994. Environmental levies and distortionary taxation. *American Economic Review* 94: 1085–89.

Bovenberg, A. Lans, and Peter Birch Sørensen. 2004. Improving the equity–efficiency trade-off: Mandatory savings accounts for social insurance. *International Tax and Public Finance* 11: 507–29.

Bovenberg, A. Lans, and Peter Birch Sørensen. 2006. Optimal taxation and social insurance in a lifetime perspective. CESifo working paper 1690.

Brennan, Geoffrey, and Alan Hamlin. 1998. Expressive voting and electoral equilibrium. *Public Choice* 95: 149–75.

Brett, Craig. 1998. Who should be on workfare? The use of work requirements as part of the optimal tax mix. *Oxford Economic Papers* 50: 607–22.

Brett, Craig. 2007. Optimal nonlinear taxes for families. *International Tax and Public Finance* 14: 225–61.

Brett, Craig, and John Weymark. 2003. Financing education using optimal redistributive taxation. *Journal of Public Economics* 87: 2549–69.

Brett, Craig, and John Weymark. 2008a. The impact of changing skill levels on optimal nonlinear income taxes. *Journal of Public Economics* 92: 1765–71.

Brett, Craig, and John Weymark. 2008b. Optimal nonlinear taxation of income and savings without commitment. Working paper 08–W05. Vanderbilt University.

Brewer, Mike, Emmanuel Saez, and Andrew Shephard. 2010. Means-testing and tax rates on earninigs. In James Mirrlees, Stuart Adam, Timothy Besley, Richard Blundell, Stephen Bond, Robert Chote, Malcolm Gammie, Paul Johnson, Gareth Myles, and James Poterba, eds., *Dimensions of Tax Design: The Mirrlees Review*. Oxford: Oxford University Press, 90–173.

Brito, Dagobert L., Jonathan H. Hamilton, Steven M. Slutsky, and Joseph E. Stiglitz. 1991. Dynamic optimal income taxation with government commitment. *Journal of Public Economics* 44: 15–35.

Brown, E. Cary. 1948. Business-income taxation and investment incentives. In *Income, Employment and Public Policy: Essays in Honor of Alvin H. Hansen*. New York: Norton.

Browning, Edgar K. 1976. The marginal cost of public funds. *Journal of Political Economy* 84: 283–98.

Bruce, Neil, and Michael Waldman. 1991. Transfers in kind: Why they can be efficient and nonpaternalistic. *American Economic Review* 81: 1345–51.

Bruno, Michael. 1976. Equality, complementarity and the incidence of public expenditures. *Journal of Public Economics* 6: 395–407.

Buchanan, James M., and Charles Goetz. 1972. Efficiency limits of fiscal mobility: As assessment of the Tiebout model. *Journal of Public Economics* 1: 25–43.

Buchanan, James M., and Gordon Tullock. 1962. *The Calculus of Consent*. Ann Arbor: University of Michigan Press.

Calvo, Guillermo A., and Maurice Obstfeld. 1988. Optimal time-consistent fiscal policy with finite lifetimes. *Econometrica* 56: 411–32.

Chamley, Christophe. 1986. Optimal taxation of capital income in general equilibrium with infinite lives. *Econometrica* 54: 607–22.

Chander, Parkash, and Louis L. Wilde. 1998. A general characterization of optimal income tax enforcement. *Review of Economic Studies* 65: 165–83.

Chetty, Raj. 2009. Is the taxable income elasticity sufficient to calculate deadweight loss? The implications of evasion and avoidance. *American Economic Journal, Economic Policy*, 1: 31–52.

Chetty, Raj, and Adam Looney. 2006. Consumption smoothing and the welfare conse-quences of social insurance in developing economies. *Journal of Public Economics* 90: 2351–56.

Chetty, Raj, Adam Looney, and Kory Kroft. 2009. Salience and taxation: Theory and evidence. *American Economic Review* 99: 1145–77.

Choi, James J., David Laibson, Brigitte C. Madrian, and Andrew Metrick. 2004. For better or worse: Default effects in 401(k) savings behavior. In David A. Wise, ed., *In Perspectives in the Economics of Aging.* Chicago: University of Chicago Press, 81–121.

Choné, Philippe, and Guy Laroque. 2009. Negative marginal tax rates and heterogeneity. Working paper W09/12. Institute for Fiscal Studies, London.

Christiansen, Vidar, and Eilev S. Jansen. 1978. Implicit social preferences in the Norwe-gian system of indirect taxation. *Journal of Public Economics* 10: 217–45.

Christiansen, Vidar. 1981. Evaluation of public projects under optimal taxation. *Review of Economic Studies* 48: 447–57.

Christiansen, Vidar. 1984. Which commodity taxes should supplement the income tax? *Journal of Public Economics* 24: 195–220.

Christiansen, Vidar. 2007. Two approaches to determine public good provision under distortionary taxation. *National Tax Journal* 60: 25–43.

Coate, Stephen. 1995. Altruism, the Samaritan's dilemma, and government transfer policy. *American Economic Review* 85: 46–57.

Coate, Stephen. 2000. An efficiency approach to the evaluation of policy changes. *Economic Journal* 110: 437–55.

Coate, Stephen. 2004. Political competition with campaign contributions and informative advertising. *Journal of the European Economic Association* 2: 772–804.

Coate, Stephen, and Stephen Morris. 1995. On the form of transfers in special interests. *Journal of Political Economy* 103: 1210–35.

Conesa, Juan Carlos, Sagiri Kitao, and Dirk Krueger. 2009. Taxing capital? Not a bad idea after all. *American Economic Review* 99: 25–48.

Congdon, William J., Jeffrey R. Kling, and Sendhil Mullainathan. 2009. Behavioral eco-nomics and tax policy. NBER working paper w15328.

Conrad, Robert, Zmarak Shalizi, and Janet Syme. 1990. Issues in evaluating tax and payments arrangements for publicly owned minerals. Working paper WPS 496. Public Economics Department, World Bank, Washington, DC.

Corlett, W. J., and D. C. Hague. 1953. Complementarity and the excess burden of taxation. *Review of Economic Studies* 21: 21–30.

Courchene, Thomas J., and John R. Allan. 2008. Climate change: The case for a carbon tariff/tax. *Policy Options* 29: 59–64.

Cremer, Helmuth, and Firouz Gahvari. 1995. Uncertainty, optimal taxation and the direct versus indirect tax controversy. *Economic Journal* 105: 1165–79.

Cremer, Helmuth, and Firouz Gahvari. 1996. Tax evasion and the optimum general income tax. *Journal of Public Economics* 60: 235–49.

Cremer, Helmuth, and Firouz Gahvari. 1997. In-kind transfers, self-selection and optimal tax policy. *European Economic Review* 41: 97–114.

Cremer, Helmuth, Firouz Gahvari, and Norbert Ladoux. 1998. Externalities and optimal taxation. *Journal of Public Economics* 70: 343–64.

Cremer, Helmuth, Firouz Gahvari, and Norbert Ladoux. 2001. Second-best pollution taxes and the structure of preferences. *Southern Economic Journal* 68: 258–80.

Cremer, Helmuth, Jean-Marie Lozachmeur, and Pierre Pestieau. 2010. collective annuities and redistribution. *Journal of Public Economic Theory* 12: 23–43.

Cremer, Helmuth, and Pierre Pestieau. 2006a. Redistributive taxation and social insurance. *International Tax and Public Finance* 3: 281–95.

Cremer, Helmuth, and Pierre Pestieau. 2006b. Wealth transfer taxation: A survey of the theoretical literature. In Louis-André Gérard-Varet, Serge-Christophe Kolm, and Jean Mercier Ythier, eds., *Handbook of the Economics of Giving, Reciprocity and Altruism*, vol. 2. Amsterdam: North Holland, 1107–34.

Cremer, Helmuth, Pierre Pestieau, and Maria del Mar Racionero. 2008. Unequal wages for equal utilities. Working paper.

Cremer, Helmuth, Pierre Pestieau, and Jean-Charles Rochet. 2001. Direct versus indirect taxation: The design of the tax structure revisited. *International Economic Review* 42: 781–99.

Cuff, Katherine. 2000. Optimality of workfare with heterogeneous preferences. *Canadian Journal of Economics. Revue Canadienne d'Economique* 33: 149–74.

Cuff, Katherine, and Nicolas Marceau. 2009. Equilibrium excess demand in the rental housing market for the poor. Paper presented at Challenges in Public Economics, a conference in honor of Pierre Pestieau, June 2–3, 2009, CORE, Belgium.

Currie, Janet, and Firouz Gahvari. 2008. Transfers in cash and in-kind: Theory meets the data. *Journal of Economic Literature* 46: 333–83.

Dahlby, Bev. 1981. Adverse selection and Pareto improvements through compulsory insurance. *Public Choice* 37: 547–58.

Dahlby, Bev. 2008. *The Marginal Cost of Public Funds: Theory and Applications*. Cambridge: MIT Press.

Dasgupta, Partha. 1972. A comparative analysis of the UNIDO guidelines and the OECD manual. *Bulletin of the Oxford University Institute of Economics and Statistics* 34: 33–51.

Dasgupta, Partha, Stephen A. Margin, and Amartya Sen. 1972. *Guidelines for Project Evaluation*. New York: UNIDO.

Dasgupta, Partha, and Joseph E. Stiglitz. 1972. On optimal taxation and public production. *Review of Economic Studies* 39: 87–103.

de Van Graaff, Jan. 1957. *Theoretical Welfare Economics*. London: Cambridge University Press.

Deaton, Angus. 1979. Optimally uniform commodity taxes. *Economics Letters* 2: 357–61.

Della Vigna, Stefano. 2009. Psychology and economics: Evidence from the field. *Journal of Economic Literature* 47: 315–72.

de Meza, David, and David C. Webb. 1987. Too much investment: A problem of asymmetric information. *Quarterly Journal of Economics* 102: 281–92.

Department of Finance. 2010. *Tax Expenditures and Evaluations 2010.* Ottawa: Department of Finance.

Deschamps, R., and Louis Gevers. 1978. Leximin and utilitarian rules: A joint characterization. *Journal of Economic Theory* 17: 143–63.

Dhillon, Amrita, and Susana Peralta. 2002. Economic theories of voter turnout. *Economic Journal* 112: 332–52.

Diamond, Peter A. 1980. Income taxation with fixed hours of work. *Journal of Public Economics* 13: 101–10.

Diamond, Peter A. 1982. Aggregate demand management in search equilibrium. *Journal of Political Economy* 90: 881–94.

Diamond, Peter A. 1998. Optimal income taxation: An example with a U–shaped pattern of optimal marginal tax rates. *American Economic Review* 88: 83–95.

Diamond, Peter A. 2007. Comment on Golosov et al. *NBER Macroeconomics Annual* 2006: 365–79.

Diamond, Peter A. 2008. Behavioral economics. *Journal of Public Economics* 92: 1858–62.

Diamond, Peter A., and Botond Köszegi. 2003. Quasi-hyperbolic discounting and retirement. *Journal of Public Economics* 87: 1839–72.

Diamond, Peter A., and James A. Mirrlees. 1971. Optimal taxation and public production I: Production efficiency and II: Tax rules. *American Economic Review* 61: 8–27 and 261–78.

Diamond, Peter A., and Eytan Sheshinski. 1995. Economic aspects of optimal disability benefits. *Journal of Public Economics* 57: 1–23.

Diamond, Peter A., and Johannes Spinnewijn. (forthcoming). Capital income taxes with heterogeneous discount rates. *American Economic Journal: Economic Policy.*

Diamond, Peter A., and Hannu Vartiainen. 2007. *Behavioral Economics and Its Applications.* Princeton: Princeton University Press.

Dixit, Avinash K. 1996. Special-interest lobbying and endogenous commodity taxation. *Eastern Economic Journal* 22: 375–88.

Dixit, Avinash K., and John Londregan. 1998. Ideology, tactics, and efficiency in redistributive politics. *Quarterly Journal of Economics* 113: 497–529.

Dixit, Avinash K., and Thomas Romer. 2006. Political explanations of inefficient economic policies—An overview of some theoretical and empirical literature. Presentation at the IIPF conference Public Finance: Fifty Years of the Second Best—and Beyond. Paphos, Cyprus, August 2006.

Downs, Anthony. 1957. *An Economic Theory of Democracy.* New York: Harper.

Drèze, Jean, and Nicholas Stern. 1987. The theory of cost–benefit analysis. In Alan J. Auerbach and Martin Feldstein, eds., *Handbook of Public Economics,* vol. 2. Amsterdam: North Holland, 909–89.

Dupuit, A. Jules E. J. 1844. De la mesure de l'utilité des travaux publics. *Annales des Ponts et Chaussées*, 2nd series, 8; reprinted as Dupuit, A. Jules E. J. 1969. On the measurement of the utility of public works. In Kenneth J. Arrow and Tibor Scitovsky, eds., *Readings in Welfare Economics* (Homewood, IL: Richard D. Irwin) 255–83.

Eaton, Jonathan, and Harvey S. Rosen. 1980. Optimal redistributive taxation and uncertainty. *Quarterly Journal of Economics* 95: 357–64.

Ebert, Udo. 1992. A reexamination of the optimal nonlinear income tax. *Journal of Public Economics* 49: 47–73.

Edwards, Jeremy, Michael Keen, and Matti Tuomala. 1994. Income tax, commodity taxes and public good provision: A brief guide. *FinanzArchiv* 51: 472–97.

Emran, Shahe M., and Joseph E. Stiglitz. 2005. On selective indirect tax reform in developing countries. *Journal of Public Economics* 89: 599–623.

Erosa, Andrés, and Martin Gervais. 2001. Optimal taxation in infinitely-lived agent and overlapping generations models: A review. *Federal Reserve Bank of Richmond Economic Quarterly* 87: 23–44.

Erosa, Andrés, and Martin Gervais. 2002. Optimal taxation in life-cycle economies. *Journal of Economic Theory* 105: 338–69.

Falk, Armin, Ernst Fehr, and Christian Zehnder. 2006. Fairness perceptions and reservation wages—The behavioral effects of minimum wage laws. *Quarterly Journal of Economics* 121: 1347–81.

Fehr, Ernst. 2001. Why social preferences matter—The impact of non-selfish motives on competition, cooperation and incentives. *Economic Journal* 112: C1–C33.

Fehr, Ernst, and Klaus M. Schmidt. 1999. A theory of fairness, competition, and cooperation. *Quarterly Journal of Economics* 114: 817–68.

Fehr, Ernst, and Klaus M. Schmidt. 2002. Theories of fairness and reciprocity—Evidence and economic epplications. In Matthias Dewatripont, Lars Hansen, and Steven Turnovsky, eds., *Advances in Economics and Econometrics—8th World Congress*, Econometric Society Monographs, Cambridge: Cambridge University Press.

Feldstein, Martin S. 1972. Distributional equity and the optimal structure of public sector prices. *American Economic Review* 62: 32–36.

Feldstein, Martin S. 1999. Tax avoidance and the deadweight loss of the income tax. *Review of Economics and Statistics* 81: 674–80.

Feldstein, Martin S. 2005. Rethinking social insurance. *American Economic Review* 95: 1–24.

Ferejohn, John. 1986. Incumbent performance and electoral control. *Public Choice* 50: 5–25.

Finkelstein, Amy. 2009. E-ZTAX: Tax salience and tax rates. *Quarterly Journal of Economics* 124: 969–1010.

Fischer, Stanley. 1980. Dynamic inconsistency, cooperation and the benevolent dissembling government. *Journal of Economic Dynamics & Control* 2: 93–107.

Fisher, Irving. 1937. Income in theory and income taxation in practice. *Econometrica* 5: 1–55.

Fisher, Irving. 1938. The double taxation of savings. *American Economic Review* 28: 16–33.

Flatters, Frank, Vernon Henderson, and Peter Mieszkowski. 1974. Public goods, efficiency, and regional fiscal equalization. *Journal of Public Economics* 3: 99–112.

Fleurbaey, Marc. 1994. On fair compensation. *Theory and Decision* 36: 277–307.

Fleurbaey, Marc. 1995a. Equality and responsibility. *European Economic Review* 39: 683–89.

Fleurbaey, Marc. 1995b. Three solutions for the compensation problem. *Journal of Economic Theory* 65: 505–21.

Fleurbaey, Marc. 2008. *Fairness, Responsibility, and Welfare.* Oxford: Oxford University Press.

Marc, Fleurbaey, Robert J. Gary-Bobo, and Denis Maguain. 2002. Education, distributive justice, and adverse selection. *Journal of Public Economics* 84: 113–50.

Fleurbaey, Marc, and François Maniquet. 2006. Fair income tax. *Review of Economic Studies* 73: 55–83.

Fleurbaey, Marc, and François Maniquet. 2007. Help the low skilled or let the hardworking thrive? A study of fairness in optimal income taxation. *Journal of Public Economic Theory* 9: 467–500.

Fleurbaey, Marc, and François Maniquet. 2010. Compensation and responsibility. In K. J. Arrow, A. K. Sen and K. Suzumura, eds., *Handbook of Social Choice and Welfare*, vol. 2. (Amsterdam: North Holland), ch. 22.

Foster, Edward, and Hugo Sonnschein. 1970. Price distortion and economic welfare. *Econometrica* 38: 281–97.

Frederick, Shane, George Loewenstein, and Ted O'Donoghue. 2002. Time discounting and time preference: A critical review. *Journal of Economic Literature* 40: 351–401.

Frey, Bruno S. 1994. How intrinsic motivation is crowded out and in. *Rationality and Society* 6: 334–52.

Frey, Bruno, and Felix Oberholzer-Gee. 1997. The cost of price incentives: An empirical analysis of motivation crowding-out. *American Economic Review* 87: 746–755.

Frey, Bruno S., and Alois Stutzer. 2000. Happiness, economy and institutions. *Economic Journal* 110: 918–38.

Friedman, Milton. 1952. The "welfare" effects of an income tax and an excise tax. *Journal of Political Economy* 60: 25–33.

Fudenberg, Drew, and David K. Levine. 2006. A dual-self model of impulse control. *American Economic Review* 96: 1449–76.

Garnaut, Ross, and Anthony Clunies Ross. 1975. Uncertainty, risk aversion and the taxing of natural resource projects. *Economic Journal* 85: 272–87.

Gahvari, Firouz. 1995. In-kind versus cash transfers in the presence of distortionary taxes. *Economic Inquiry* 33: 45–53.

Gahvari, Firouz. 2006. On the marginal cost of public funds and the optimal provision of public goods. *Journal of Public Economics* 90: 1251–62.

Gahvari, Firouz, and C. C. Yang. 1993. Optimal commodity taxation and household consumption activities. *Public Finance Quarterly* 21: 479–87.

Gauthier, Stéphane, and Guy Laroque. 2009. Separability and public finance. *Journal of Public Economics* 93: 1168–74.

Gneezy, Uri, and Aldo Rustichini. 2000. A fine is a price. *Journal of Legal Studies* 29: 1–17.

Golosov, Mikhael, Narayana Kocherlakota, and Aleh Tsyvinski. 2003. Optimal indirect and capital taxation. *Review of Economic Studies* 70: 569–97.

Golosov, Mikhael, Aleh Tsyvinski, and Iván Werning. 2007. New dynamic public finance: A user's guide. *NBER. Macroeconomics Annual* 2006: 317–63.

Goodspeed, Timothy J. 2002. Bailouts in a federation. *International Tax and Public Finance* 9: 409–21.

Gordon, Roger, and Julie Cullen. (forthcoming). Income redistribution in a federal system of governments. *Journal of Public Economics*.

Gorman, William M. 1961. On a class of preference fields. *Metroeconomica* 13: 53–56.

Green Paper. 1971. *Value Added Tax, Cmnd. 4621*. London: Her Majesty's Stationery Office.

Grossman, Gene, and Elhanan Helpman. 1994. Protection for sale. *American Economic Review* 85: 667–90.

Gruber, Jonathan, and Botond Köszegi. 2004. Tax incidence when individuals are time-inconsistent: The case of cigarette excise taxes. *Journal of Public Economics* 88: 1959–87.

Gruber, Jonathan, and Emmanuel Saez. 2002. The elasticity of taxable income: Evidence and implications. *Journal of Public Economics* 84: 1–32.

Guesnerie, Roger. 1995. *A Contribution to the Pure Theory of Taxation*. Cambridge: Cambridge University Press.

Guesnerie, Roger, and Kevin Roberts. 1984. Effective policy tools and quantity controls. *Econometrica* 52: 59–82.

Guesnerie, Roger, and Kevin Roberts. 1987. Minimum wage legislation as a second best policy. *European Economic Review* 31: 490–98.

Guesnerie, Roger, and Jesus Seade. 1982. Nonlinear pricing in a finite economy. *Journal of Public Economics* 17: 157–79.

Gul, Faruk, and Wolfgang Pesendorfer. 2001. Temptation and self-control. *Econometrica* 69: 1403–35.

Gul, Faruk, and Wolfgang Pesendorfer. 2004. Self-control and the theory of consumption. *Econometrica* 72: 119–58.

Frank, Hahn. 1973. On optimum taxation. *Journal of Economic Theory* 6: 96–106.

Haig, Robert M. 1921. *The Federal Income Tax*. New York: Columbia University Press.

Hamilton, John, and Pierre Pestieau. 2005. Optimal income taxation and the ability distribution: Implications for migration equilibria. *International Tax and Public Finance* 12: 29–45.

Hammond, Peter. 1987. Altruism. In J. Eatwell, M. Milgate, and Peter Newman, eds., *The New Palgrave: A Dictionary of Economics*. London: Macmillan, 165–67.

Harberger, Arnold C. 1964. Taxation, resource allocation and welfare. In John Due, ed., *The Role of Direct and Indirect Taxes in the Federal Revenue System*. Princeton: Princeton University Press, 25–80.

Harberger, Arnold C. 1971. Three basic postulates for applied welfare economics. *Journal of Economic Literature* 9: 785–97.

Hare, Paul G., and David T. Ulph. 1979. On education and redistribution. *Journal of Political Economy* 87: S193–S212.

Harris, Richard G. 1977. Non-convexities and the optimal tax problem. Paper presented to the Public Choice Society Meeting, New Orleans.

Harris, Richard G., and James G. MacKinnon. 1979. Computing optimal tax equilibria. *Journal of Public Economics* 11: 197–212.

Harsanyi, John C. 1955. Cardinal welfare, individualist ethics, and interpersonal comparisons of utility. *Journal of Political Economy* 63: 309–21.

Harsanyi, John C. 1977. *Rational Behavior and Bargaining Equilibrium in Games and Social Situations*. Cambridge: Cambridge University Press.

Harsanyi, John. 1995. A theory of social values and a rule utilitarian theory of morality. *Social Choice and Welfare* 12: 319–44.

Helliwell, John. 2006. Well-being, social capital and public policy: What's new? *Economic Journal* 116: C34–C45.

Hellmann, Thomas, and Joseph Stiglitz. 2000. Credit and equity rationing in markets with adverse selection. *European Economic Review* 44: 281–304.

Hettich, Walter, and Stanley L. Winer. 2005. *Democratic Choice and Taxation: A Theoretical and Empirical Analysis*. Cambridge: Cambridge University Press.

Hicks, John. 1939. The foundations of welfare economics. *Economic Journal* 49: 696–712.

Hicks, John R. 1946. *Value and Capital*, 2nd ed. Oxford: Clarendon Press.

Hillier, Brian, and James M. Malcomson. 1984. Dynamic inconsistency, rational expectations, and optimal government policy. *Econometrica* 52: 1437–51.

Hochman, Harold M., and James D. Rodgers. 1969. Pareto optimal redistribution. *American Economic Review* 59: 542–57.

Hotelling, Harold. 1932. Edgeworth's taxation paradox and the nature of supply and demand functions. *Journal of Political Economy* 40: 577–616.

Hubbard, R. Glenn, and Kenneth L. Judd. 1987. Social security and individuals welfare: Precautionary saving, liquidity constraints, and the payroll tax. *American Economic Review* 77: 630–46.

Hungerbühler, Mathias, Etienne Lehmann, Alexis Parmentier, and Bruno Van der Linden. 2006. Optimal redistributive taxation in a search equilibrium model. *Review of Economic Studies* 73: 743–67.

Immonen, Ritva, Ravi Kanbur, Michael Keen, and Matti Tuomala. 1998. Tagging and taxing: The optimal use of categorical and income information in designing tax/transfer schemes. *Economica* 65: 179–92.

Institute for Fiscal Studies. 1991. Equity for companies: A corporation tax for the 1990s. Commentary. Institute for Fiscal Studies, London. http://www.ifs.orguk/publications/1914.

Jacobs, Bas. 2005. Optimal income taxation with endogenous human capital. *Journal of Public Economic Theory* 7: 295–315.

Jacobs, Bas, and A. Lans Bovenberg. 2010. Human capital and optimal positive taxation of capital income. *International Tax and Public Finance* 17: 451–78.

Jacobsen Kleven, Henrik, and Wojciech Kopczuk. 2011. Transfer program complexity and the take up of social benefits. *American Economic Journal. Economic Policy* 3: 54–90.

Jacquet, Laurence, Etienne Lehmann, and Bruno Van der Linden. 2010. Optimal redistributive taxation with both extensive and intensive responses. Mimeo. Université catholique de Louvain, Belgium.

Jacquet, Laurence, and Dirk Van de gaer. 2009. A comparison of optimal tax policies when compensation or responsibility matter. Discussion paper 12/09. Norwegian School of Economics and Business Administration, Bergen.

Jacquet, Laurence, and Bruno Van der Linden. 2006. The normative analysis of tagging revisited: Dealing with stigmatization. *FinanzArchiv* 62: 168–98.

Jewitt, Ian. 1981. Preference structure and piecemeal second best policy. *Journal of Public Economics* 16: 215–31.

Judd, Kenneth L. 1985. Redistributive taxation in a simple perfect foresight model. *Journal of Public Economics* 28: 59–83.

Kaldor, Nicholas. 1939. Welfare propositions in economics and interpersonal comparisons of utility. *Economic Journal* 49: 549–52.

Kaldor, Nicholas. 1955. *An Expenditure Tax*. London: Allen and Unwin.

Kanbur, S. M. 1981. Risk taking and taxation: An alternative perspective. *Journal of Public Economics* 15: 163–84.

Kanbur, Ravi, Jukka Pirttilä, and Matti Tuomala. 2008. Moral hazard, income taxation and prospect theory. *Scandinavian Journal of Economics* 110: 321–37.

Kaplow, Louis. 2006. On the desirability of commodity taxation even when income taxation is not optimal. *Journal of Public Economics* 90: 1235–50.

Kaplow, Louis. 2008. *The Theory of Taxation and Public Economics*. Princeton: Princeton University Press.

Kaplow, Louis. 2010. Concavity of utility, concavity of welfare, and redistribution of income. *International Tax and Public Finance* 17: 25–42.

Keen, Michael. 1992. Needs and targeting. *Economic Journal* 102: 67–79.

Keen, Michael. 1997. Peculiar institutions: A British perspective on tax policy in the United States. *National Tax Journal* 50: 779–802.

Keen, Michael. 2008. VAT, tariffs, and withholding: Border taxes and informality in developing countries. *Journal of Public Economics* 92: 1892–1906.

Keen, Michael, and David Wildasin. 2008. Pareto-efficient international taxation. *American Economic Review* 94: 259–75.

Keuschnigg, Christian, and Søren Bo Nielsen. 2003. Tax policy, venture capital, and entrepreneurship. *Journal of Public Economics* 87: 175–203.

Keuschnigg, Christian, and Søren Bo Nielsen. 2004. Start-ups, venture capitalists, and the capital gains tax. *Journal of Public Economics* 88: 1011–42.

Kihlstrom, Richard E., and Jean-Jacques Laffont. 1979. A general equilibrium theory of firm formation based on risk aversion. *Journal of Political Economy* 87: 719–48.

King, Mervyn A. 1980. Savings and taxation. In Gordon A. Hughes and Geoffrey M. Heal, eds., *Public Policy and the Tax System*. London: Allen and Unwin, 1–35.

King, Mervyn A. 1986. A Pigovian rule for optimal provision of public goods. *Journal of Public Economics* 30: 273–91.

Klemm, Alexander. 2007. Allowances for corporate equity in practice. *CESifo Economic Studies* 53: 229–62.

Kleven, Henrik J. 2004. Optimum taxation and the allocation of time. *Journal of Public Economics* 88: 545–57.

Knabe, Andreas, Steffen Rätzel, Ronnie Schöb, and Joachim Weimann. 2010. Dissatisfied with life but having a good day: Time-use and well-being of the unemployed. *Economic Journal* 120: 867–89.

Kolm, Serge-Christophe. 1996. *Modern Theories of Justice*. Cambridge: MIT Press.

Kolm, Serge-Christophe. 1998. *Justice and Equity*. Cambridge: MIT Press.

Kolm, Serge-Christophe. 2004. *Macrojustice: The Political Economy of Fairness*. Cambridge: Cambridge University Press.

Konishi, Hideo. 1995. A Pareto-improving commodity tax reform under a smooth nonlinear income tax. *Journal of Public Economics* 56: 413–46.

Konrad, Kai A. 2001. Privacy and time-consistent optimal labor income taxation. *Journal of Public Economics* 79: 503–19.

Kocherlakota, Narayana R. 2004. Wedges and taxes. *American Economic Review* 94: 109–13.

Kocherlakota, Narayana R. 2005. Zero expected wealth taxes: A Mirrlees approach to dynamic optimal taxation. *Econometrica* 73: 1587–1621.

Krause, Alan. 2006. Redistributive taxation and public education. *Journal of Public Economic Theory* 8: 807–19.

Krause, Alan. 2009. Optimal nonlinear income taxation with learning-by-doing. *Journal of Public Economics* 93: 1098–10.

Kydland, Finn E., and Edward C. Prescott. 1977. Rules rather than discretion: The inconsistency of optimal plans. *Journal of Political Economy* 3: 473–92.

Laffont, Jean-Jacques. 2005. *Regulation and Development*. Cambridge: Cambridge University Press.

Laffont, Jean-Jacques, and Jean Tirole. 1993. *A Theory of Incentives in Regulation and Procurement*. Cambridge: MIT Press.

Laibson, David. 1997. Golden eggs and hyperbolic discounting. *Quarterly Journal of Economics* 112: 443–77.

Laroque, Guy. 2005. Indirect taxation is superfluous under separability and taste homogeneity: A simple proof. *Economics Letters* 87: 141–44.

Lau, Lawrence J., Eytan Sheshinski, and Joseph E. Stiglitz. 1978. Efficiency in the optimum supply of public goods. *Econometrica* 46: 269–84.

Layard, Richard. 2005. *Happiness: Lessons from a New Science*. London: Penguin.

Richard, Layard. 2006. Happiness and public policy: A challenge to the profession. *Economic Journal* 116: C24–C33.

Lee, David, and Emmanuel Saez. 2009. Optimal minimum wage policy in competitive labor markets. Mimeo. University of California at Berkeley.

Levi, Margaret. 1997. *Consent, Dissent, and Patriotism*. New York: Cambridge University Press.

Liebman, Jeffrey B., and Richard J. Zeckhauser. 2004. Schmeduling. Mimeo. Harvard University.

Lindbeck, Assar, and Joergen Weibull. 1987. Balanced-budget redistribution as the outcome of political competition. *Public Choice* 52: 273–97.

Lipsey, Richard G., and Kelvin Lancaster. 1956–57. The general theory of second best. *Review of Economic Studies* 24: 11–32.

Little, Ian M. D. 1951. Direct versus indirect taxes. *Economic Journal* 61: 577–84.

Little, Ian M. D. 1957. *A Critique of Welfare Economics*, 2nd ed. Oxford: Clarendon Press.

Little, Ian M. D., and James A. Mirrlees. 1974. *Project Appraisal and Planning for Developing Countries*. London: Heinemann.

Lohrenz, Terry, and P. Read Montague. 2008. Neuroeconomics: What neuroscience can learn from economics. In Alan Lewis, ed., *The Cambridge Handbook of Psychology and Economic Behaviour*. Cambridge: Cambridge University Press, 457–92.

Low, Hamish, and Daniel Maldoom. 2004. Optimal taxation, prudence and risk-sharing. *Journal of Public Economics* 88: 443–64.

Mankiw, N. Gregory. 1986. The allocation of credit and financial collapse. *Quarterly Journal of Economics* 101: 455–70.

Manski, Charles F. 2000. Economic analysis of social interactions. *Journal of Economic Perspectives* 14: 115–36.

Marceau, Nicolas, and Robin Boadway. 1994. Minimum wage legislation and unemployment insurance as instruments for redistribution. *Scandinavian Journal of Economics* 96: 67–81.

Marchand, Maurice, Pierre Pestieau, and Maria Racionero. 2003. Optimal redistribution when different workers are indistinguishable. *Canadian Journal of Economics, Revue Canadienne d'Economique*, 36: 911–22.

Marglin, Stephen A. 1963. The social discount rate and the optimal rate of investment. *Quarterly Journal of Economics* 77: 95–111.

Marhuenda, Francisco, and Ignacio Ortuño-Ortin. 1997. Tax enforcement problems. *Scandinavian Journal of Economics* 99: 61–72.

McCaffery, Edward J., and Jonathan Baron. 2004a. Framing and taxation: Evaluation of tax policies involving household composition. *Journal of Economic Psychology* 25: 679–705.

McCaffery, Edward J., and Jonathan Baron. 2004b. Thinking about tax. Olin research paper 04–13. USC Law School.

McCaffery, Edward J., and Jonathan Baron. 2005. The political psychology of redistribution. *UCLA Law Review, University of California, Los Angeles, School of Law,* 52: 1745–92.

McCaffery, Edward J., and Joel Slemrod. 2006. Toward an agenda for behavioral public finance. In Edward J. McCaffery and Joel Slemrod, eds., *Behavioral Public Finance.* New York: Russell Sage Foundation, 3–31.

Meade Report. 1978. *The Structure and Reform of Direct Taxation, Report of a Committee chaired by Professor J. E. Meade.* London: Allen and Unwin.

Meghir, Costas, and David Phillips. 2010. Labour supply and taxes. In James Mirrlees, Stuart Adam, Timothy Besley, Richard Blundell, Stephen Bond, Robert Chote, Malcolm Gammie, Paul Johnson, Gareth Myles, and James Poterba, eds., *Dimensions of Tax Design: The Mirrlees Review.* Oxford, Oxford University Press, 202–74.

Mill, John Stuart. 1848. *Principles of Political Economy, with Some of their Applications to Social Philosophy.* London: J.W. Parker.

Mirrlees, James A. 1971. An exploration in the theory of optimum income taxation. *Review of Economic Studies* 38: 175–208.

Mirrlees, James A. 1972a. The optimum town. *Swedish Journal of Economics* 74: 114–35.

Mirrlees, James A. 1972b. On producer taxation. *Review of Economic Studies* 39: 105–11.

Mirrlees, James A. 1974. Notes on welfare economics, information and uncertainty. In M. Balch, D. McFadden, and S. Wu, eds., *Essays in Equilibrium Behavior under Uncertainty.* Amsterdam: North Holland, 243–58.

Mirrlees, James A. 1986. The theory of optimal taxation. In K. J. Arrow and M. D. Intriligator, eds., *Handbook of Mathematical Economics,* vol. 3. Amsterdam: North Holland, 1197–249.

Mirrlees, James, Stuart Adam, Timothy Besley, Richard Blundell, Stephen Bond, Robert Chote, Malcolm Gammie, Paul Johnson, Gareth Myles, and James Poterba, eds. 2010. *Dimensions of Tax Design: The Mirrlees Review.* Oxford: Oxford University Press.

Mirrlees, James, Stuart Adam, Timothy Besley, Richard Blundell, Stephen Bond, Robert Chote, Malcolm Gammie, Paul Johnson, Gareth Myles, and James Poterba, eds. 2011. *Tax by Design: The Mirrlees Review*. Oxford: Oxford University Press.

Mitsui, Kiyoshi, and Motohiro Sato. 2001. Ex ante free mobility, ex post immobility, and time-consistent policy in a federal system. *Journal of Public Economics* 82: 445–60.

Mullainathan, Sendhil, and Richard H. Thaler. 2001. Behavioral economics. In *International Encyclopedia of Social Sciences*. Oxford: Pergamon Press, 1094–1100.

Munro, Alistair. 1991. The optimal public provision of private goods. *Journal of Public Economics* 44: 239–61.

Musgrave, Richard A. 1967. In defense of an income concept. *Harvard Law Review* 81: 44–62.

Myers, Stewart C., and Nicholas S. Majluf. 1984. Corporate financing and investment decisions when firms have information that investors do not have. *Journal of Financial Economics* 13: 187–221.

Myles, Gareth D. 1995. *Public Economics*. Cambridge: Cambridge University Press.

Naito, Hisahiro. 1999. Re-examination of uniform commodity taxes under a non-linear income tax system and its implication for production efficiency. *Journal of Public Economics* 71: 165–88.

Nava, Mario, Fred Schroyen, and Maurice Marchand. 1996. Optimal fiscal and public expenditure policy in a two-class economy. *Journal of Public Economics* 61: 119–37.

Neumann, John von, and Oskar Morgenstern. 1944. *Theory of Games and Economic Behavior*. Princeton: Princeton University Press.

Newbery, David M. 1986. On the desirability of input taxes. *Economics Letters* 20: 267–70.

Nichols, Albert L., and Richard J. Zeckhauser. 1982. Targetting transfers through restrictions on recipients. *American Economic Review* 72: 372–77.

Nyborg, Karine, Richard B. Howarth, and Kjell Arne Brekke. 2006. Green consumers and public policy: On socially contingent moral motivation. *Resource and Energy Economics* 28: 351–66.

O'Donoghue, Ted, and Matthew Rabin. 2006. Optimal sin taxes. *Journal of Public Economics* 90: 1825–49.

Organisation for Economic Co-operation and Development. 2007. *Fundamental Reform of Corporate Income Tax, Policy Studies 16*. Paris: OECD.

Organisation for Economic Co-operation and Development. 2008. *Growing Unequal: Income Distribution and Poverty in OECD Countries*. Paris: OECD.

Osborne, Martin J., and Al Slivinski. 1996. A model of political competition with citizen-candidates. *Quarterly Journal of Economics* 111: 65–96.

Osmundsen, Petter. 2010. Time consistency in petroleum taxation: Lessons from Norway. In Philip Daniel, Michael Keen, and Charles McPherson, eds., *The Taxation of Petroleum and Minerals: Principles, Problems and Practice*. London: Routledge, 425–44.

Ostrom, Elinor. 2000. Collective action and the evolution of collective norms. *Journal of Economic Perspectives* 14: 137–58.

Oswald, Andrew. 1983. Altruism, jealousy and the theory of optimal non-linear taxation. *Journal of Public Economics* 20: 77–87.

Parsons, Donald O. 1996. Imperfect "tagging" in social insurance programs. *Journal of Public Economics* 62: 183–207.

Pereira, Joana. 2009a. Essays on time-consistent fiscal policy with unbalanced budgets: The role of public debt. PhD thesis. European University Institute, Florence, Italy.

Pereira, Joana. 2009b. Optimal education subsidies: Comparing the second best with a time-consistent redistribution policy. Paper presented at the CESifo Area Conference on Public Economics, Munich, April 24–26, 2009.

Persson, Torsten, Gérard Roland, and Guido Tabellini. 1997. Separation of powers and political accountability. *Quarterly Journal of Economics* 112: 1163–1202.

Persson, Torsten, and Guido Tabellini. 2002. Political economics and public finance. In Alan J. Auerbach and Martin Feldstein, eds., *Handbook of Public Economics*, vol. 3. Amsterdam: North Holland, 1549–659.

Pestieau, Pierre M. 1974. Optimal taxation and discount rate for public investment in a growth setting. *Journal of Public Economics* 3: 217–35.

Pigou, Arthur C. 1928. *A Study in Public Finance*. London: Macmillan.

Piketty, Thomas. 1996. Mobilité économique et attitudes politiques face à la redistribution. CEPREMAP working paper 9603.

Pirttilä, Jukka, and Matti Tuomala. 1997. Income tax, commodity tax and environmental policy. *International Tax and Public Finance* 4: 37–54.

Prendergast, Canice. 2007. The motivation and bias of bureaucrats. *American Economic Review* 97: 180–96.

President's Advisory Panel on Federal Tax Reform. 2005. *Simple, Fair, and Pro-Growth: Proposals to Fix America's Tax System*. Washington, DC: US Treasury.

Rabin, Matthew. 1993. Incorporating fairness into game theory and economics. *American Economic Review* 83: 1281–1302.

Rabin, Matthew. 1998. Psychology and economics. *Journal of Economic Literature* 36: 11–46.

Ramsey, Frank P. 1927. A contribution to the theory of taxation. *Economic Journal* 37: 47–61.

Ramsey, Frank P. 1928. A mathematical theory of saving. *Economic Journal* 38: 543–59.

Ray, Anandarup. 1984. *Cost–Benefit Analysis: Issues and Methodologies*. Baltimore: Johns Hopkins Press for the World Bank.

Read, Daniel, and Barbara van Leeuven. 1998. Predicting hunger: The effects of appetite and delay on choice. *Organizational Behavior and Human Decision Processes* 76: 189–205.

Rees, Ray. 1984. *Public Enterprise Economics*. London: Weiderfeld and Nicolson.

Roberts, Kevin. 1984. Theoretical limits to redistribution. *Review of Economic Studies* 51: 177–95.

Roberts, Marc J., and Michael Spence. 1976. Effluent charges and licenses under uncertainty. *Journal of Public Economics* 5: 193–208.

Rochet, Jean-Charles. 1991. Incentives, redistribution and social insurance. *Geneva Papers of Risk and Insurance* 16: 143–65.

Rodden, Jonathan, Gunnar Eskeland, and Jennie Litvack, eds. 2002. *Fiscal Decentralization and the Challenge of the Hard Budget Constraints*. Cambridge: MIT Press.

Roemer, John E. 1998. *Equality of Opportunity*. Cambridge: Harvard University Press.

Rogers, Carolyn. 1987. Expenditure taxes, income taxes and time-inconsistency. *Journal of Public Economics* 32: 215–30.

Rothschild, Michael, and Joseph E. Stiglitz. 1976. Equilibrium in competitive insurance markets. *Quarterly Journal of Economics* 90: 629–50.

Rowe, Nicholas, and Frances Woolley. 1999. The efficiency case for universality. *Canadian Journal of Economics. Revue Canadienne d'Economique* 32: 613–29.

Royal Commission on Taxation (Carter Commission). 1966. *Report*. Ottawa: Queen's Printer.

Royal Commission on the Taxation of Profits and Income. 1955. *Final Report*. London: HMSO.

Sadka, Efraim. 1976. On progressive income taxation. *American Economic Review* 66: 931–35.

Saez, Emmanuel. 2001. Using elasticities to derive optimal income tax rates. *Review of Economic Studies* 68: 205–29.

Saez, Emmanuel. 2002a. The desirability of commodity taxation under non-linear income taxation and heterogeneous tastes. *Journal of Public Economics* 83: 217–30.

Saez, Emmanuel. 2002b. Optimal income transfer programs: Intensive vs. extensive labor supply responses. *Quarterly Journal of Economics* 117: 1039–73.

Saez, Emmanuel. 2004. Direct or indirect tax instruments for redistribution: Short-run versus long-run. *Journal of Public Economics* 88: 503–18.

Saez, Emmanuel. 2010. Do taxpayers bunch at kink points? *American Economic Journal: Economic Policy* 2: 180–212.

Salanié, Bernard. 2002. Optimal demogrants with imperfect tagging. *Economics Letters* 75: 319–24.

Samuelson, Paul A. 1950. The evaluation of real national income. *Oxford Economic Papers* 2: 1–29.

Samuelson, Paul A. 1964. Tax deductibility of economic depreciation to insure invariant valuations. *Journal of Political Economy* 72: 604–606.

Samuelson, Paul A. 1986. Theory of optimal taxation. *Journal of Public Economics* 30: 137–43.

Sandmo, Agnar. 1975. Optimal taxation in the presence of externalities. *Swedish Journal of Economics* 77: 86–98.

Sandmo, Agnar. 1976. Optimal taxation: An introduction to the literature. *Journal of Public Economics* 6: 37–54.

Sandmo, Agnar. 1998. Redistribution and the marginal cost of public funds. *Journal of Public Economics* 70: 365–82.

Sandmo, Agnar. 2005. The theory of tax evasion: A retrospective view. *National Tax Journal* 58: 643–63.

Sandmo, Agnar. 2006. Global public economics: Public goods and externalities. Discussion paper 32/06. Norwegian School of Economics and Business Administration, Bergen.

Sato, Motohiro. 2000. Fiscal externalities and efficient transfers in a federation. *International Tax and Public Finance* 7: 119–39.

Schall, Lawrence D. 1972. Interdependent utilities and Pareto optimality. *Quarterly Journal of Economics* 86: 19–24.

Schanz, George von. 1896. Der Einkommensbegriff und die Einkommensteuergesetze. *Finanz Archiv* 13: 1–87.

Schokkaert, Erik, Dirk Van de gaer, Frank Vandenbroucke and Roland I. Luttens. 2004. Responsibility sensitive egalitarianism and optimal linear income taxation. *Mathematical Social Sciences* 48: 151–82.

Scitovsky, Tibor. 1941. A note on welfare propositions in economics. *Review of Economic Studies* 9: 77–88.

Seade, Jesus K. 1977. On the shape of optimal tax schedules. *Journal of Public Economics* 7: 203–35.

Sen, Amartya K. 1967. Isolation, assurance and the social discount rate. *Quarterly Journal of Economics* 81: 112–24.

Sen, Amartya K. 1970. The impossibility of a Paretian liberal. *Journal of Political Economy* 78: 152–57.

Sen, Amartya K. 1973. *On Economic Inequality*. Oxford: Clarendon Press.

Sen, Amartya K. 1977. Social choice theory: A re-examination. *Econometrica* 45: 53–89.

Shapiro, Carl, and Joseph E. Stiglitz. 1984. Equilibrium unemployment as a worker discipline device. *American Economic Review* 74: 433–44.

Sheshinski, Eytan. 2003. Bounded rationality and socially optimal limits on choice in a self-selection model. CESifo working paper 868.

Shoven, John B., and John Whalley. 2005. Irving Fisher's spendings (consumption) tax in retrospect. *American Journal of Economics and Sociology* 64: 215–35.

Simons, Henry C. 1938. *Personal Income Taxation*. Chicago: University of Chicago Press.

Sinn, Hans-Werner. 1996. Social insurance, incentives and risk-taking. *International Tax and Public Finance* 3: 259–80.

Sinn, Hans-Werner. 2008. *The Green Paradox—An Argument for Illusion-Free Climate Policies*. Berlin: Econ Verlag.

Slemrod, Joel. 2003. Trust in public finance. In Sijbren Cnossen and Hans-Werner Sinn, eds., *Public Finance and Public Policy in the New Century*. Cambridge: MIT Press, 49–88.

Slemrod, Joel, and Shlomo Yitzhaki. 2002. Tax avoidance, evasion, and administration. In Alan J. Auerbach and Martin Feldstein, eds., *Handbook of Public Economics*, vol. 3. Amsterdam: North Holland, 1423–70.

Sørensen, Peter Birch. 1994. From the global income tax to the dual income tax: Recent tax reforms in the Nordic countries. *International Tax and Public Finance* 1: 57–80.

Sørensen, Peter Birch. 2009. The theory of optimal taxation: New developments and policy relevance. Lecture given at the 20th Scientific Meeting of the Società italiana di economia pubblica, Pavia.

Spence, A. Michael. 1973. Job market signaling. *Quarterly Journal of Economics* 87: 355–74.

Stern, Nicholas. 1982. Optimum taxation with errors in administration. *Journal of Public Economics* 17: 131–33.

Stern, Nicholas. 2007. *The Economics of Climate Change (The Stern Review)*. Cambridge: Cambridge University Press.

Stephens, Eric. 2009. Constraints and public policy. PhD thesis. Queen's University, Canada.

Stiglitz, Joseph E. 1982. Self-selection and Pareto efficient taxation. *Journal of Public Economics* 17: 213–40.

Stiglitz, Joseph E. 1987. Pareto efficient and optimal taxation and the new new welfare economics. In Alan J. Auerbach and Martin Feldstein, eds., *Handbook of Public Economics*, vol. 2. Amsterdam: North Holland, 991–1042.

Stiglitz, Joseph E., and Andrew Weiss. 1981. Credit rationing in markets with imperfect information. *American Economic Review* 71: 393–410.

Strotz, Robert H. 1955. Myopia and inconsistency in dynamic utility maximization. *Review of Economic Studies* 23: 165–80.

Stuart, Charles. 1984. Welfare costs per dollar of additional tax revenue in the United States. *American Economic Review* 74: 352–62.

Summers, Lawrence H. 1981. Capital taxation and accumulation in a life-cycle growth model. *American Economic Review* 71: 533–44.

Tanzi, Vito. 2008. *People, Places and Policies: China, Japan and Southeast Asia*. New York: Jorge Pinto Books.

Targetti, Ferdinando. 1992. *Nicolas Kaldor*. Oxford: Oxford University Press.

Technical Committee on Business Taxation. 1997. *Report*. Ottawa: Department of Finance.

Thaler, Richard H., and Cass R. Sunstein. 2008. *Nudge: Improving Decisions about Health, Wealth, and Happiness*. New Haven: Yale University Press.

Torgler, Benno. 2003. Tax morale, rule-governed behaviour and trust. *Constitutional Political Economy* 14: 119–40.

Tuomala, Matti. 1984. Optimal degree of progressivity under income uncertainty. *Scandinavian Journal of Economics* 86: 184–93.

Tuomala, Matti. 1990. *Optimal Income Tax and Redistribution*. Oxford: Clarendon Press.

Ulph, David T. 1977. On the optimal distribution of income and educational expenditure. *Journal of Public Economics* 8: 341–56.

United States Treasury. 1977. *Blueprints for Basic Tax Reform*. Washington, DC: Government Printing Office.

Usher, Dan. 1986. Tax evasion and the marginal cost of public funds. *Economic Inquiry* 24: 563–86.

Usher, Dan. 1994. The significance of the probabilistic voting theorem. *Canadian Journal of Economics, Revue Canadienne d'Economique*, 27: 433–45.

Van de gaer, Dirk. 1993. Equality of opportunity and investment in human capital. PhD thesis. Katholieke Universiteit Leuven, Belgium.

Van Parijs, Philippe. 1995. *Real Freedom for All, What (If Anything) Can Justify Capitalism*. Oxford: Clarendon Press.

Varian, Hal. 1980. Redistributive taxation as social insurance. *Journal of Public Economics* 14: 49–68.

Viard, Alan D. 2001. Optimal categorical transfer payments: The welfare economics of limited lump-sum redistribution. *Journal of Public Economic Theory* 3: 483–500.

Vickrey, William. 1945. Measuring marginal utility by reactions to risk. *Econometrica* 13: 215–36.

Vigneault, Marianne. 1996. Commitment and the time structure of taxation of foreign direct investment. *International Tax and Public Finance* 3: 479–94.

Vigneault, Marianne. 2007. Grants and soft budget constraint. In Robin Boadway and Anwar Shah, eds., *Intergovernmental Fiscal Transfers*. Washington, DC: World Bank, 133–71.

Weiss, Andrew. 1980. Job queues and layoffs in labor markets with flexible wages. *Journal of Political Economy* 88: 526–38.

Wen, Jean-François. 1997. Tax holidays and the international capital market. *International Tax and Public Finance* 4: 129–48.

Wildasin, David E. 1984. On public good provision with distortionary taxation. *Economic Inquiry* 22: 227–43.

Wildasin, David E. 1990. R. M. Haig: Pioneer advocate of expenditure taxation? *Journal of Economic Literature* 28: 649–60.

Wildasin, David E. 2004. The institutions of federalism. *National Tax Journal* 57: 247–72.

Williamson, Stephen. 1987. Costly monitoring, loan contracts, and equilibrium credit rationing. *Quarterly Journal of Economics* 101: 135–45.

Winer, Stanley L., and Hirofumi Shibata, eds. 2002. *The Role of Political Economy in the Theory and Practice of Public Finance*. Cheltenham, UK: Edward Elgar.

Yitzhaki, Shlomo. 1974. A note on "Income tax evasion: A theoretical analysis." *Journal of Public Economics* 3: 201–202.

Index